A Model
Development Plan

A Model Development Plan

New Strategies and Perspectives

DAVID H. LEMPERT
KIM McCARTY
CRAIG MITCHELL

Westport, Connecticut
London

HD
82
L357
1995

Library of Congress Cataloging-in-Publication Data

Lempert, David H.
  A model development plan : new strategies and perspectives / David
H. Lempert, Kim McCarty, Craig Mitchell.
    p.   cm.
  Includes bibliographical references and index.
  ISBN 0–275–95068–9 (alk. paper)
  1. Economic development.   I. McCarty, Kim.   II. Mitchell, Craig.
III. Title.
  HD82.L357   1995
  338.9—dc20   95–2225

British Library Cataloguing in Publication Data is available.

Library of Congress Catalog Card Number: 95–2225
ISBN: 0–275–95068–9

First published in 1995

Praeger Publishers, 88 Post Road West, Westport, CT 06881
An imprint of Greenwood Publishing Group, Inc.

Printed in the United States of America

The paper used in this book complies with the
Permanent Paper Standard issued by the National
Information Standards Organization (Z39.48–1984).

10 9 8 7 6 5 4 3 2 1

Contents

Illustrations

FIGURES

Preface

Although the decade of the 1980s was marked by the end of military or one-party rule in countries across the globe and by the rise of market systems, there was another side to the picture of economic and political transformation. The 1980s was also a decade of continued impoverishment in the Third World, degradation of world resources, diminishing accountability of large "private" (and increasingly global) institutions, and continued assimilation and disintegration of the world's remaining indigenous cultures.

In Latin America, as in much of the developing world, the 1980s have been labeled the "lost decade" in development. Despite political changes and structural reforms, development planners view the decade as one of lost opportunities and, in many cases, misguided policies. Many of the mistakes were the results of decisions made at the request, or under the direction, of the governments of the major industrialized countries and of the planning and development agencies they support.

The 1980s was more, however, than just a decade of lost opportunities and mistaken policies. It was also a decade of lost approaches to development. A number of non-governmental and private voluntary organizations experimented during the past several years with creative projects on a small scale at the community level. Many of these projects remain virtually unrecognized and lack the funding that would enable them to make a real difference in the lives of millions of the world's peoples. Among those development programs that were "lost" in the 1980s were creative and fresh perspectives on development planning itself.

This work represents one of those perspectives.

In 1988, a group of five young and idealistic development planners — from Harvard, Brown, and the University of California — set out to write a model development plan with implications for much of the developing world. We chose Ecuador as a microcosm for issues in development because of its size and the diversity of its peoples, geography, and economic needs. Moreover, we believed it presented a range of problems found throughout the developing world and that it would be a place where five dedicated individuals could make a difference.

Through fieldwork and the combination of disciplinary specialties, we sought to create a singular document as a first step in a new approach to development and to test a project that would also serve as a new model for development education. Our goal was to incorporate state-of-the-art knowledge in our various disciplines and integrate them into a single, innovative framework for development planning. We present that work here, in English, for the first time.

The original version of this work was written in Spanish and completed under the title, *Ecuador y El Desarollo: Nuevas Ideas, Nuevas Estrategías, Nuevas Perspectivas* (Ecuador and development: new ideas, new strategies, new perspectives). We presented it, personally, to Ecuador's newly inaugurated President, Rodrigo Borja Cevallos, as well as to organizational leaders, scholars, former Ecuadorian Presidents, and the Ecuadorian media. Articles about this work appeared on the front pages of the Ecuador's major daily paper, *El Comercio*, in Quito, and we defended the work in a press conference carried on national Ecuadorian television.

While this work was little noted in the major media in the United States, the project was presented with a national award by the Giraffe Project and we were featured in a picture with President Borja as individuals who "stick their necks out" at personal risk for the common good.

Seven years have now elapsed since this work was completed. While its ideas have been put to the test of time, they retain their freshness and timeliness. As a model of development planning, many of the specific proposals that we made for the country of Ecuador remain valid for Ecuador's new president. Beyond Ecuador, the approach we have taken in this work is applicable elsewhere, not only in Latin America and other countries of the Third World, but also in the countries of the First and Second Worlds — including countries in transition to the market: the Newly Independent States of the former Soviet Union, the countries of Eastern Europe, Vietnam, and Mongolia — and countries with diverse populations undergoing political and economic transformations, like South Africa. In areas where community development and economic and political changes have become part of a new strategy in the United States for economic revitalization, demanding new and fresh solutions, the approach taken in this work might even serve as a model of development and growth in this country.

WHAT THIS WORK OFFERS THAT SETS IT APART FROM OTHER DEVELOPMENT PLANS

This model development plan is unlike any other by virtue of its most basic assumption. It is a development plan that was written in the belief that people and cultures matter as much as their present and future contribution to the global economy.

The typical development plan is written by bankers and economists or by Western-educated technicians from developed countries and the most privileged sectors of developing countries; these are specialists whose particular skills have been perfected but whose overall view of development has often been limited. Often, the plans they present are a series of measures that reduce a developing country to the level of a business enterprise rather than recognizing it as an amalgam of peoples, interests, and traditions.

The standard development plan, as prepared by the World Bank or a bilateral agency like the U.S. Agency for International Development or funded by the government of an industrialized nation or the host government, begins with a particular worldview that drives its conclusions and, in many cases, the mistakes that have been made in the name of development.

Institutions that have set the agenda for development planning often begin and end with their own assumptions of what constitutes quality of life and who is most entitled to it. While many of the measures are universal — life expectancy, health, and, increasingly, concerns about equity — a number of them are appropriate to development planners and their circles but not to most of the peoples of the world. Often, particular aspirations for real political autonomy, accountability, meaningful participation, control over the use of resources, and concerns about human dignity and individual identity never even enter into the development equation. In the grossest example, dollar measurements of average income or indicators measuring numbers of television sets or washing machines per household provide planners with standards of comparison that may have meaning for foreign bankers and investors hoping to sell products or extract resources but have little value in terms of improvements in the quality of life and the real measures of "development" for many of the peoples whose lives are changed by their policies.

A development model that starts with an understanding of, and an empathy for, the aspirations of the peoples and cultures to be "developed" measures progress less in terms of simple accounts, but incorporates concerns about the strength of communities and sense of rootedness of members of society, of autonomy and participation, and of self-image and emotional well being.

Many of these concerns have been neglected not only because of who does the planning — or who hires and trains the planners — but because few alternative models were available. Many economists and development planners have well-meaningly argued that "other," less tangible measures are too difficult to address, too fuzzy to measure, or only peripheral to economic progress. They have claimed that while it was easy to criticize what was available, there were few alternative models.

In answer to this challenge and in order to test these arguments on a real problem, we went out to measure these qualitative factors, draw from the full wealth of the social sciences and broaden the theoretical base of development plans, test and challenge the assumptions that development planners have used in the past, and structure and incorporate measurement and theory into a model development plan.

Recent scholarly work has provided justification for such alternative approaches even within the confines of economics itself. Economists and their colleagues in related fields have begun to measure those factors that previously were considered immeasurable or less worthy of attention — the long-term social costs of policies, the future losses associated with the current gains of depleting resources (Brown 1993), the value of diversity (while current measures are of ecological diversity — see Weitzman, 1992 — the same techniques can be used to value cultural diversity), and the value of female household labor and other noninstitutional and nontraditional forms of production and exchange. Other social indicators — such as crime, addiction, and underemployment — and the understanding of the causes underlying them have long been available but have yet to be integrated into a full development model that considers the net economic losses that social pathologies create and the effective means for minimizing them.

This work incorporates a number of these different types of measures and integrates them into a single picture and strategy of development. At the same time, the model plan presented here does not shy away from a discussion of national accounts, tax policies, monetary and fiscal policies, or sectorial strategies. Instead of focusing on these topics, however, it puts these standard measures and concerns in context of larger issues that are also a part of development planning.

In our view, a development plan must not only be feasible, it must also be consistent with basic human aspirations — with respect for human needs. The true measure of our work is not in its immediate use by the powers that be but in its ability to change minds and build coalitions over time, to articulate an approach that is more than just a more efficient allocation of existing power between the institutional actors (at the national and international levels) who currently propose plans.

We believe that if the International Monetary Fund (IMF) and World Bank can pressure countries to cut their government expenditures on health or education in order to balance their budgets, they could just as well choose to pressure those governments to increase taxes on imported alcohol, luxury automobiles, and tobacco; to restructure their political or legal institutions, militaries, and national police; or to create greater oversight of foreign and domestic economic institutions.

The model development plan presented here is one in which strengthening communities, maintaining cultural identity, protecting the rights and security of women, safeguarding resources, privatizing economies to enable individuals to be owners of their means of production (rather than victims of the organizations to which ownership has been reassigned), and promoting equity and citizen participation all take priority over the availability of markets and resources to outsiders and the conformity of different cultures within industrial societies, while still promoting economic growth and, more important, sustainable growth.

STRUCTURE OF THE WORK

This work is structured to make it accessible to the needs of several different audiences. Readers will note that it is not presented as either a series of theoretical arguments, as one might find in an academic work, nor as a series of stories about development that one might find in a book for general readers. Rather, it is presented as a development plan.

The goal of this work is to present an action-oriented model for use by development planners in several countries, students of development, scholars wishing to see how different development theories apply in an actual setting, and volunteers wishing to see the larger picture of the process of development in which they are playing a role.

The particular plan presented within this work has been retained almost entirely in its original form, as it was presented to President Borja and various Ecuadorian and development agencies in 1988. Despite the passage of time, very little of the plan required change to make it current either for Ecuadorians or for those who read this book as a model development plan that can be applied elsewhere. Although there has been some editing to make the draft of the plan itself more readable and accessible to a large American audience, it retains not only its structure and content, but its original flavor in translation as well.

For readers who are interested in the basic model and the theory behind it for application in a variety of countries at different stages of development, the introductory sections of each chapter and of each section within the chapters describes how the model and the concepts underlying it can be adapted applied in a variety of circumstances.

Readers who have a specific interest in Ecuador and wish to read the plan in its entirety and the evidence on which it is based (gathered in the field, without the theoretical explanations), can start with the model plan itself in the first section of the book, with a summary of its major recommendations, and then turn to the subsections within the major chapters of the book, beginning with the parts marked, "Recommendations" and "Report."

The work begins with an immersion into the model plan, using Ecuador as a case study. The initial section of the book presents the introduction to the original report. The plan begins with a quick summary of the most serious problems facing Ecuador in 1988 (and now), which are of top priority. These are problems similar to those faced in many developing countries. This list of priorities is followed by a quick summary of the solutions we propose to meet these specific problems head on. The rest of the overview presents our strategy in somewhat more detail, with commentary explaining how each part of the strategy fits into a whole and how the recommendations complement each other. The summary has been modestly annotated to show how all of the various chapters relate to each other and comprise a single strategy and unified approach.

The body of the work provides detailed explanations of the problems facing Ecuador and complete descriptions of our proposals. Each of the chapters is in several sections. An overview in each chapter presents a short theoretical overview and discussion. Each chapter also describes how assumptions of previous development planners have been in error or incomplete and explains how we reconsider and restructure the theory. Here, we describe the strategies and solutions that we propose for developing (and, in many cases, developed) countries and how they can be applied in different contexts. This is followed in each section by an application of the theory in Ecuador, with a short section of recommendations from the Ecuador plan, followed by data collected in the field and detailed descriptions of the recommendations and how they address particular problems.

While the chapters are presented in order of the urgency of problems facing developing countries and the priorities we place on different recommendations, readers should envision the process of development planning as part of an interrelated web of policy recommendations rather than a linear sequence of actions to be taken.

Overall, we structure our plan into seven chapters representing a set of priorities but also a coherent and interlinking strategy.

1. _Slowing Population Growth and Community Development_: We begin with the most urgent problem facing all societies: that of balancing population with resources. Unlike other planners, our approach is to look at population not as a problem resulting from lack of contraceptive technology or information or from slow urbanization and transition to patterns of population growth in industrial societies. It focuses, instead, on the underlying reasons why societies seek to expand their population and on the psychological regions for child bearing and places population growth in the context of other population issues such as rural-urban migration and the explosion of urban areas. We present alternatives that focus on building communities and on changing social roles of men and women, as well as providing social security to the aged, as a means of changing overall incentives while promoting economic growth.

2. _Governmental Reform and Community Development_: We expand a strategy of community development by turning next to issues of governmental reform, culture, and the protection of indigenous peoples. While these reforms are often viewed as only secondary concerns in current development-planning efforts, we see political and social reforms as inextricably linked to economic development, while viewing current systems that centralize authority and seek to homogenize and rapidly urbanize national cultures as one of the greatest impediments to economic growth.

3. _Using the Full Potential of Human Resources_: At the basis of a plan to develop economic resources and community is the need to strengthen any country's most important and critical asset: its human resources. We focus on education and health reforms that inspire, encourage, and fortify the minds and bodies of a country's population.

4. _Macroeconomic Financial Strategy_: While many development plans make macroeconomic and financial strategies their centerpiece

and a prelude to development — often as viewed in terms of the ability to attract foreign investment and promote rapid industrialization — we view it, instead, as a way to fund commitment to communities and human resources, without the pressure to commit to foreign borrowing, foreign investors, or factory models of production. While we agree with many of the intermediate goals of other development planners — for balanced budgets and stable exchange rates — we achieve these goals for other, overall purposes and through different ends, reflecting larger implications for development.

5. _Macro-Economic Production Strategy with Sectorial Focus_: In looking at means of improving economic productivity, we focus on sectors of the economy and how they might be made more efficient, but in doing so we add several new criteria that include, but go beyond, short-term measures of efficiency in output and profitability. We look at the sustainability of particular industries — their influence on environment, resources, and social and political relations, as well as qualitative issues of cultural and individual pride and dignity in the forms of production.

6. _The Appropriate Role of the Major Institutional Actors in Development_: Too often, development planners are afraid or unable to turn the lens back on themselves, as well as on the larger picture of the institutional and social context in which development takes place. A number of institutions, from within and outside particular countries, play direct roles in development and indirect roles in influencing cultural change. We pay specific attention to national armed forces and police, to organized religion and missionaries, and to the arms of foreign governments as actors in the development process, suggesting ways in which they can make a greater contribution or either restrict or open to scrutiny activities that are of questionable economic benefit.

7. _Changing the State of Mind_: One of the most intangible aspects of development and social change is influencing attitudes and reorienting national and individual outlooks in order to make the most out of particular circumstances. In our final chapter, we present ideas for overcoming attitudes of dependency and fatalism and for changing a country's symbols and environment in order to generate pride and inspire initiative.

In a short, photographic essay, we highlight several different development concerns as they can be seen in the context of Ecuador; illustrating the people and concerns behind the statistics.

•

For those readers who are interested in this project, not only as a model of development planning, but also as a model and experiment in development education, this work is also a starting point for a discussion of educational reform at the university level. Readers should refer to *Escape from the Ivory Tower: Student Adventures in Experiential and Democratic Education* (Lempert 1995). "The Ecuador Development Project" — a university-level educational workshop through which this book was researched and developed — is described in detail in one of the chapters of that work, with an outline of the tasks required to run such a project, its logistics, curriculum, accreditation, and responsibilities; and even guidelines on processes of selecting students. That work describes how the project fits into a larger sequence of experiential university courses that have been developed and taught at both Stanford University and the University of California, and how these courses and projects fit into a unique philosophy of education that can contribute to improving the American economy as well as spurring global development.

DEVELOPMENT PLANNING IN ECUADOR SEVEN YEARS LATER

Recent Scholarly Developments

Since this work was written, new scholarly works have appeared as models of development for Ecuador. As these have yet to incorporate novel assumptions for development, this work continues to provide a fresh alternative.

Among these other attempts to model Ecuadorian development are recent works by Alain de Janvry, Elisabeth Sadoulet and Andre Fargeix (1991) and by Joan B. Anderson (1990). While both these analyses are departures from traditional (institutional) development plans in that they pay much greater attention to issues of equity than do institutional plans, they still follow much of the approach of previous models. Both continue to place primary emphasis on standard economic measures — gross domestic product, balance of payments, monetary growth, income, and inflation — and mostly focus on the short term. Little in these models touches on the reality of implementation: the cultural and social environment, the importance of communities and cultures, or even the protection of individual choice (a concern that lies at the very basis of economics but too often neglected by economists). The models pay little attention to the long term: to investments in individuals and the long-term sustainability of Ecuadorian cultures. Like much other scholarly work by economists in development, they rely heavily on statistics gathered and processed in offices located far away from the people being affected by these computer models.

Also among the recent work on Ecuador is a scholarly essay by Francisco Thoumi (1990), former section chief at the Inter-American Development Bank, which confirms many of our conclusions from the perspective of someone who has a long-term association with Ecuadorian culture. In describing the failures of the World Bank's formula approach to development in Ecuador, Thoumi showed how the bank's recent recommendations — chiefly, reductions in domestic oil subsidies and changes in the earmarking of government revenues for specific outlays — had little relation to Ecuadorian reality. Not only did the bank's recommendations fail to adequately reflect local needs, they also failed to come to grips with the existing political structure in the country (the influence of business elites), which was destined to frustrate or distort the implementation of any of their recommendations.

These criticisms of other plans are not meant to imply that the model development plan that we developed is complete, nor even that it would be easy to implement. It has its own shortcomings; it is not a full model with every number falling into place and every step laid out for government officials and development organizations to follow. Given the realities of political power in Ecuador and in the global economy, perhaps it is also utopian. It is, however, an overview and a sketch; a first draft of a plan that could be expanded into a much more detailed agenda for implementation at all levels of the society, in Ecuador and elsewhere, given public or outside support.

Economists might claim that the changes proposed in the model plan are not feasible or not politically viable, and they might be justified. However, it is our contention that the plans submitted by scholars and development agencies are viable only because they have become self-fulfilling prophesies. They have left dissenting scholars, as well as the mass public in countries being "developed," without any comprehensive alternative for which to advocate. Our goal was to create such an alternative.

The Impact of the Plan on Development in Ecuador

While Ecuadorian President Borja assured us that he would implement those of our recommendations that he found useful ("*utiles*"), and while we would like to believe that writing and submitting this plan at least made a small difference in improving the lives of the Ecuadorian people, it is difficult to trace specific suggestions to particular policies put into effect by the Ecuadorian government, independent agencies, or the U.S. governmental agencies in Ecuador. Any adoption of policies we recommended (including those macroeconomic recommendations that were heralded in a masthead editorial and front page story in *El Comercio*, August 24, 1988 and August 25, 1988) are more likely to have been a result of a coincidence of interest than of our influence. As researchers, we had no clout in Ecuador other than our convictions and the strength of our arguments. At best, we expected to set a precedent for the incorporation of a number of previously neglected issues in macrodevelopment planning in Ecuador.

Aside from the particular merits of Borja's policies, even when they overlapped with our recommendations, many were driven by World Bank policy objectives and the interests of industry leaders who backed him. Among those changes that were not among our priorities, we were in agreement with the World Bank in its calls for reducing the government deficit and advocated that the Ecuadorian government seek to improve its tax collection, which it did. We were also in favor of promoting major exports and in restructuring export and import tariffs to force certain industries to be competitive. As President, Borja did cut government spending and decreased the size of government (cutting the deficit to 5.1 % of gross domestic product). He also changed the structure of export and import tariffs (which we supported), doubled domestic oil prices to 75 % of the world market price (about which we were uncertain), and devalued the Ecuadorian *sucre* against world currencies (World Bank 1991). While we did not advocate devaluation to increase exports, the Borja government's approach was consistent with our call for avoiding exchange rate controls.

In addressing the concerns of indigenous Ecuadorian peoples, President Borja arranged for legal title of more than 3 million acres (1.2 million hectares) of Amazon lands to rest with 148 indigenous groups. While this agreement did not go as far as we would have liked to preserve the homeland of 1,600 Huaoroni people from oil pipelines, it does protect the Huaoroni from commercial development on their land and provides them with 1 % of oil revenues from the region (*Economist* 1/4/92, p. 36). This marks at least a trend in the direction of policies that we promoted as part of a development strategy.

In short, while the majority of our recommendations for political and social development — those that go beyond the standard measures of economic policy — have yet to be adopted, the Borja government did begin to establish more objective criteria for transferring funds to local communities (something we recommended, although it caused local government revenues and expenditures to fall), while also increasing the coverage of social insurance (pensions).

Overall, seven years later, most of the problems we foresaw in 1988, seem only closer. Population growth, overuse and degradation of resources, migration, and the weakening of communities threaten to have severe consequences for Ecuador in this decade (Ecuador 1990). Perhaps as a sign of things to come, border disputes flared with Peru in 1991 and have intensified in early 1995, as we go to press, suggesting that our strongest prediction — that of increasing pressure for a full scale war with Peru as a result of Ecuador's inability to control population growth and better use its existing assets, and increasing militarization of the Peruvian government and weakening of its democracy — may, unfortunately, be coming true. If anything, the Borja government only kept the situation under temporary control and postponed the reckoning. The proposals we made in 1988 as our top priorities seem even more urgent now.

Even in terms of aggregate macromeasures, under President Borja the economy grew slowly — by .6 % in 1989, 2.4 % in 1990, 4.4 % in 1991 and 3.5 % in 1992 — with much of that due to the sale of oil. Inflation rose to about 50 % per year for most of Borja's term, which contributed to the drop in the value of the sucre from 500 per $1 U.S. to 1,500 per $1 U.S. (Economist Intelligence Unit 1993 I p. 3).

As perhaps another sign of things to come, early 1993 was marked by a number of strikes which continue, in different sectors, into 1995.

Recent Developments in Ecuador

More striking than what is new in Ecuador since this plan was written is how little things seem to have changed. While the presidency has changed hands from one party to another, with the incumbent Rodrigo Borja unable to seek another term by the limitations of the constitution, the issues, and even the political candidates, seem unchanged. Two of the three strongest candidates in 1992, current President Sixto Duran Ballán and Guayaquil populist Abdala Bucaram, were major figures in the 1988 presidential elections. Their positions were well known, and we met with many of their supporters and considered the solutions they proposed in writing the plan we prepared in 1988. As in 1988, Ecuadorian national politics seem to be little more than a seesaw between shifting coalitions of the country's controlling groups: the social democrats and the right-wing aristocrats, which are split between the two axes of the country, the Sierra and the coast.

President Borja, a social democrat from the Sierra, has been replaced by a conservative aristocrat who, like Borja, is also from Quito. Like other previous Ecuadorian Presidents, both men were members of the country's white (Spanish descended) elite, unlike most Ecuadorians. President Duran was born in Boston, graduated from Columbia University, and worked for the Inter-American Development Bank in Washington, D.C., before becoming mayor of Quito. The policies for which Duran called in his campaign were straight out of the standard World Bank structural adjustment model. Duran ran on a platform of "change" which included the privatization of state industries and cuts in government spending.

As of early 1993, unemployment in Ecuador remained at 15 %. Inflation continued at about 50 % per year. While 1992 growth in gross domestic product, at 3.5 %, was higher than the population growth rate (2.9 % in the late 1980s), the country continues to deplete the oil and land that account for much of this growth (Economist Intelligence Unit 1993 I).

Opposition to Duran continues to mount from within and outside of government, not only in the form of strikes but in parliamentary opposition to his policies and in calls for his impeachment (Economist

Intelligence Unit 1993). By paying no attention to alternative forms of development, Ecuador appears to be carrying the policies of the "lost decade" of the 1980s into the 1990s.

David Lempert

REFERENCES

Anderson, Joan B. *Economic Policy Alternatives for the Latin American Crisis* New York: Taylor and Francis, 1990.

Brown, Lester, ed. *The State of the World* Washington, D.C.: Worldwatch Institute, Washington, D.C., 1993.

Conaghan, Catherine M. "Ecuador Swings toward Social Democracy" *Current History* 88 (March 1989) 137.

Economist 316 (August 25, 1990): 36.

Economist 320 (July 6, 1991):44.

Economist 316 (January 4, 1992): 36.

Economist Intelligence Unit. *Economist Country Reports: Ecuador* No. 1. 1993.

Ecuador. Instituto Nacional de Estadísticos y Censos. *V Censo de Población y IV de Vivienda* Quito 1990.

Lempert, David. *Escape from the Ivory Tower: Student Adventures in Democratic Experiential Education.* San Francisco: Jossey-Bass Inc., Publishers 1995 (forthcoming).

Janvry, Alain de, Elisabeth Sadoulet and André Fargeix. *Adjustment and Equity in Ecuador* Paris: Organization for Economic Cooperation and Development, 1991.

Thoumi, Francisco E. "The Hidden Logic of 'Irrational' Economic Policies in Ecuador" *Journal of Interamerican Studies and World Affairs* 3 (Summer 1990): 43-68.

United States. *U.S. Department of State Dispatch* 3 (March 2, 1992): 174-175.

Weitzman, Martin L. "What to Preserve? An Application of Diversity Theory to Crane Conservation" *Quarterly Journal of Economics* Draft presented at Harvard University, John F. Kennedy School of Government seminar, March 1, 1992.

World Bank. *Ecuador: Public Sector Reforms for Growth in the Era of Declining Oil Output* Washington, D.C.: 1991.

Acknowledgments

While we thanked those who offered their time and help in the introduction and bibliography of our initial report, there are additional people and institutions who ought to be acknowledged in the English version of this work.

First, former Ecuadorian President Galo Plaza Lassos (now deceased), offered his encouragement and humor in getting this project off the ground in Quito in 1987. In addition, Luis Lopez Silva of the Centro Andino De Estudios Económicos, Sociales y Tecnológicos in Quito, good-naturedly stood by this project even when an agreement with the Universidad Católica did not survive departmental reshuffling there. Working with us in Ecuador as part of the original project team were researchers Thomas A. Lewis III and Shannon Wright, then students at Brown University, without whose help the original model plan would never have been written.

While neither Harvard nor Brown universities have yet institutionalized programs like this one, the placement offices of both schools, as well as those of Princeton, Wellesley and Yale, were gracious in publicizing the project to their students, without which this project team would never have come together. Now, months later, Harvard has begun to increase ties and educational exchanges with Ecuador in connection with the Latin American Scholarship Program of American Universities (LASPAU), possibly opening the way for more opportunities like this one.

Finally, special congratulations are due from this book's main author to the coauthors and fellow researchers of this work who were undergraduates when this project was undertaken, but who performed as professionals and bore much of the hardship of any who take the risk in br   'ing something new. They are not only a new generation of development specialists and scholars, rising in the ranks of the profession, but also trail blazers of opportunities for future students, who owe them a debt of gratitude.

THE MODEL PLAN

Original Introduction: Presented to the President of Ecuador

This development plan is the culmination of 11 weeks of research by five researchers from the United States of America. We arrived in Ecuador during the month of June, with few preconceptions and few contacts except for Dr. Luis Lopez Silva, Dean of the Centro Andino de Estudios Económicos, Sociales y Tecnológicos, with the goals of understanding the problems that Ecuador faces, considering new solutions to those problems, and presenting a few proposals that could provoke debate. We hope at least that this plan will contribute one or two new or helpful ideas.

Our conclusions are our own and do not represent the opinions of the Centro Andino, of our universities, nor of our government. We do not work for any organization and have not received funds from any institution.

We tried several times to establish contacts with Ecuadorian students at our educational level to work with us, as students, in our research. Unfortunately, we were not successful. We decided to come to Ecuador anyway, in order to learn and to test a new type of field education. As students in the United States, we are accustomed to study development in books and through lectures. We wanted to see the reality of underdevelopment directly, to test our ideas in the field, and to share our opinions in the native language of the country.

METHODS

During our 11 week stay, we visited 19 of the 20 provinces of the country (all except the Galápagos islands).

• We traveled by bus, motorboat, plane, truck, jeep, train, and on foot.

• We attended a Shuar wedding in the Amazon region and a Catholic first communion in the north of Quito.

• We danced and wore costumes with the Otavalenians and accompanied a funeral procession in San Lorenzo.

• We ate guinea pig and larvae and drank *chicha* (chewed, fermented yuca) in rural areas; we also dined in the best restaurants in Quito, Guayaquil, and Cuenca.

• We spoke with smugglers and governors, prisoners and deputies of Congress, executives of multinational corporations and shoeless peasants, mayors and beggars.

• We travelled 16 hours in order to meet with Texaco corporation employees in the Amazon region and the same distance to arrive at a Chachi Indian community on the Cayapas river.

• We listened to the views of the U.S. and Soviet Embassies; of Peace Corps Volunteers and Evangelical missionaries.

• We visited ports and construction sites, museums and parks, fields of sugar cane and fish farms, ecological reserves and oil wells.

In all, we met with hundreds of Ecuadorians (too many to name) in all walks of life. The majority spoke to us in confidence and we have decided to protect them by not citing them by name. We are in debt to all of them for their time and patience.

Our experiences here in Ecuador have affected each one of us. We arrived with different perspectives, but we all agree on our love and respect for Ecuador.

At times it was difficult to look beyond the faces of peasants dressed in dazzling color to see the reality and sadness of their prematurely aged bodies and deformed bones, and to see beyond the appearance of smiling children, their malnutrition and lives of labor in place of the liberty of youth.

At times, the poverty did not affect us directly. For example, there are more homeless in our cities in the United States than in Ecuador. At other times, however, we were moved to see young cargo hands and shoeshine boys covered with filth and worrying about their next meal, as well as the hungry old women waiting for us to finish our dinners so that they could gnaw at the bones. It was hard to tell them that anyone cared for them or wished them well.

It was hard, too, to reconcile the sight of the masses of workers and inhabitants of slums without end in Guayaquil and families living in prisons with the sight of ministers in Quito, who dress in European suits and eat in restaurants like El Rincón de Francia, where even we were not permitted to enter. What does this mean, we wonder, for the future of Ecuador?

At the same time, we came to love the beauty of the country — its natural splendor, its diversity of cultures, traditions, and peoples, and its moderate climate. We hope that Ecuador will always protect these assets.

Moreover, we appreciated the hospitality and warmth of Ecuadorians and their willingness to speak with us about their lives and perspectives, something we do not see enough of in our own country.

LIMITATIONS

Undoubtedly, a group of only five foreigners visiting a country for only three months, without an extensive background in economic development or in specialized fields (agriculture, forestry, geology, etc.) cannot cover everything or pretend to understand fully the reality of Ecuador.

Our Spanish is not perfect and we do not speak a single word of Quechua or any other native language. Moreover, as Americans we know that we hold certain prejudices. Finally, our resources were limited. We shared one telephone and we were unable to visit several areas of the country due to the lack of funds for special transportation. Most of our contacts we had to make ourselves.

Nevertheless, we visited several places where the majority of ministers, ambassadors, tourists, and other development researchers never go. Unlike these individuals, due to our independence, we were not limited by established restrictions nor by the necessity to maintain relations with specific sectors or to protect property or programs. Further, we were in the position to take a wholly inclusive perspective at the macrolevel. We have the liberty, too, to present suggestions for structural, political, and cultural reform, as well as economic reform, where these affect the economy.

We present our recommendations after a process of discussion and consensus. We come from several universities, disciplines, and experiences but we share in our conclusions.

THE FUTURE

We present this plan during the first month of the new Presidential Administration — a time of great hope and optimism in Ecuador. We share in this optimism.

We expect policy changes in the areas of decentralization, availability of credit, the role of the Armed Forces, and the accountability of government. One of our goals is to provide, not only a list of aspirations, but also practical ideas ready for implementation — a plan to transform the hopes that the majority of Ecuadorians have expressed into reality.

We hope also that this presentation does not signify the end of our connections with Ecuador. Rather, we hope that this will be the beginning of future joint efforts — between students of our country and Ecuadorian students — in research that is both more widespread and also in greater depth.

We hope, too, that someday funds will be available — from our universities, governments, corporations, foundations, or organizations in the United States or Ecuador — which that allow for the continuation of activities such as this one.

David Howard Lempert,
Thomas Abner Lewis III,
Kim McCarty,
Craig Ernest Mitchell, and
Shannon Wright

Quito, Ecuador, August 22, 1988

Overview

We highlight the urgent problems facing Ecuador and provide a capsule summary of our strategy below.

PRIORITIES: URGENT PROBLEMS FACING ECUADOR

The greatest threat to Ecuador is its rapid population growth. Instead of confronting the problem of population directly, Ecuador has adopted a strategy of "tossing its problem into the backyard." That backyard is the Amazon region, an area long disputed with Peru and the site of numerous border conflicts. Ecuador's policy is one of sending the problems of overpopulation and poverty elsewhere. The most probable result of this strategy, as Ecuador uses up all its own resources, will be a war against Peru perhaps within 10 years, and almost certainly within the next 40 years.

The phenomenon of internal migration in the country is connected to the problem of population explosion and presents a series of difficulties, not only for immigrants themselves, but also for their communities of origin and of destination. These problems touch on all aspects of Ecuadorian life. In the cities, the results are crime, social ills, destruction of the family, and emotional tensions. In rural areas, the results are a deterioration of the community and the loss of human resources. All these problems lead to an economic loss for the country and a rapid growth in government expenditures in its effort to manage the rise in social and economic problems and in social tensions that threaten to erupt in violence.

The concentration of political power and opportunities for its abuse, internal problems of government that prevent conflict resolution, and state bureaucratization threaten development, economic growth, and political stability.

The destruction of Ecuador's cultural diversity threatens the ability of the society to adapt to changing conditions and devalues Ecuadorian life. The loss of minority cultures is accompanied by a process of homogenization and is resulting in a loss of identity for large numbers of citizens, who are left disoriented and alienated. The resulting lack of diversity reduces the ability of the country to respond to change.

The most serious problems facing Ecuador's industrial economy are, first, the need to recover the confidence of the private sector and to reduce the flight of capital and the increase in monetary speculation through demonstration that investment in Ecuador is intelligent and profitable, *and second, the need to generate income through conversion of production from the internal market and nonmarketable goods to production for the foreign market.*

Food production in Ecuador is stagnant. The productivity of the agricultural and fish-farming sector in Ecuador has not grown in the 1980s and if this condition does not change, the country will encounter serious problems in the 1990s. An obvious governmental prejudice favors large and powerful producers, leaving the population of small farmers in the Sierran mountain regions without assistance.

STRATEGY SUMMARY

To Control Population Growth:

Create incentive mechanisms for population control:

1. <u>Provide financial incentives to women that reflect their number of children.</u>

2. <u>Provide social security benefits based on the number of children.</u>

3. <u>Make recognition of paternity by fathers and by the State obligatory.</u>

Create mechanisms of social infrastructure in order to link women to economic production in order to give them alternatives to early motherhood, to reliance on the income of their children and their husbands, and to boost productivity.

1. <u>Channel public and private investment toward productive initiatives initiated by women (particularly in artisanry, light industry and trade).</u>

2. <u>Reform the educational system in rural areas, making it accessible to women, particularly in regard to development of technology and forms of productive organization.</u>

3. <u>Improve the distribution of family planning services.</u>

To Address the Problems of Internal Migration and Community Disintegration:

Strengthen communities as attractive and advantageous places for development in various areas:

• Create more provincial universities.

• Reduce the number of inhabitants required for the authorization of high school construction.

• Reform curricula in order to promote discussions of local history, various Ecuadorian cultures, and current problems which the community or province faces.

• Establish a system of provincial banks in order to replace the national bank (Banco de Fomento) using the same capital base. Allow elected representatives from the community to serve as Directors, but still subject to outside audit.

• Increase the budget of the Ministry of Health and the portion designated for outreach and improvement of rural services.

• Establish local museums, artistic exhibits with work of members of the community, theatres, public movie theaters, and municipal projects which reflect community pride and identity.

• Require that at least half of the Armed Forces and National Police in each province come from the same province.

To Address Central Government's Inability to Respond Adequately to Local Needs and its Tendencies Toward Over-Centralization and Bureaucratization:

Strengthen the system of checks and balances within the Ecuadorian political system through:

1. <u>Decentralization</u>:

• Establish independent political authorities at the provincial, municipal and village levels.

• Establish a national formula for distributing national funds in and objective manner so that those communities with the greatest needs receive the most funding.

• Each level of government, with publicly elected leaders, should have the power to impose taxes and raise funds, establish its own laws, maintain its own police force, initiate programs and provide services in any area it chooses, enter into contracts with other provinces, with businesses or with individuals, and elect or appoint judges.

2. Professionalization

Establish a stronger system than that which currently exists of civil servants so as to create a body of professionals whose primary interest is carrying out professional responsibilities, without political pressure.

3. Establish an Independent Government Auditor at the National Level

4. Establish New Ministries for Natural Resources, Indigenous Affairs, and Fishing and Fisheries.

To Protect Ecuador's Threatened Minority Cultures

Encourage a dual economic strategy for Indigenous peoples which combines traditional subsistence agriculture with a second source of income; one which uses the traditional skills in which that group has a competitive advantage relative to other groups.

To Make Better Use of the Country's Human Resources

Encourage Initiative and Self-Confidence through reforms in the Educational System:

• Train teachers to prepare exams which do not require memorization, to ask questions in class for which there are no correct answers, and to ask questions and generate lists of ideas in any subject instead of seeking a correct answer.

• Use the experience of Ecuadorians in the community, and introduce students to new approaches which are successful as well as to individuals who can be role models.

Direct more attention to basic health and the promotion of personal hygiene.

Redirect medical schools more toward the promotion of basic health.

Implement a program of primary auxiliary health workers.

To Provide Revenues for New Programs:

Generate funds from all sectors without discrimination.

Eliminate the inefficient use of national resources through:

• Taxes with implications for health on tobacco, soda, alcohol, salt and meat.

• Taxes with implications for National Pride and Ecuadorian Culture on: imported ties, suits, perfumes and materials to manufacture them; and foreign films.

• Newforms of taxes such as a tax on luxury consumer goods in order to limit the consumption of goods which are non essential for development and which improves income distribution.

To Stabilize the Modern Sector

Make a since effort to combat inflation, not with price controls but with a reduction in the State budget deficit.

Support productive investment in production for export and for efficient domestic production.

Continue a policy of free exchange rates.

To Increase Food Production

Redirect available resources from large estates towards small producers of essential foodstuffs.

Increase technical assistance and associated research for food production.

Increase support for programs of land conservation.

Research the possibility of establishing cooperatives among small producers.

To Make Ecuador's Existing Institutions More Responsive to the Country's Development Needs

Request foreign assistance in the training and professionalization of the Armed Forces, National Police and Customs Police in order to enforce the law against those who are violating national laws and misusing national resources.

Maintain the separation of Church and State and protect the integrity of Indigenous Communities through restrictions on the establishment of new religious missions.

Summary

We propose an integrated strategy for dealing with the problems facing Ecuador. While we present our recommendations in priority order, to meet Ecuador's most urgent needs, the various components of this strategy complement each other. Each recommendation is designed to address a variety of needs as part of a coordinated approach to changing policy and institutional structures to promote development.

The details of our recommendations are summarized below.

SLOWING POPULATION GROWTH AND COMMUNITY DISINTEGRATION

We propose a strategy which addresses the root of the problem of population growth and community disintegration rather than its symptoms.

The problems of population growth and the explosion of urban areas are linked. Ecuadorians are leaving their communities because there are inadequate productive opportunities in rural areas. Women continue to bear children at a young age because they are not engaged in economically productive activities and because their status and security in Ecuadorian society depend on their child bearing.

We have designed a strategy to improve opportunities for production in rural areas — with particular attention to opportunities for women — to make communities more attractive and prosperous, and to provide women with greater security and status in the society.

POPULATION AND THE FUTURE

We propose two measures to deal with the population explosion which threatens the future of Ecuador. The two can be implemented separately or together.

First Alternative: Create Incentive Mechanisms for Population Control

This alternative consists of three parts:

1. Provide Financial Incentives to Women That Reflect Their Number of Children.

As an incentive to women to postpone having children in order that they may continue their education and pursue their careers, we propose to award women between the ages of 21 and 25 with a monthly stipend. We suggest an amount of 5,000 sucres (60,000 sucres annually) in 1988 sucres. We choose this level because it represents an individual's minimum living expenses. As a condition of receiving benefits, women will be obligated to come to a governmental office three times each year in order to declare that they are not pregnant and do not have children.

2. *Provide Social Security Benefits Based on the Number of Children.*

In recognition of the fact that in Ecuadorian society, children care for and support their parents in old age, and in order to avoid punishing (as well as to give incentives to) women who have few children, we propose to provide social security benefits directly to women with few children who cannot receive another source of support. We propose to pay a monthly benefit of 5,000 sucres (60,000 annually) to women over age 60 who do not have children. We propose a monthly benefit of 3,000 sucres (36,000 annually) to women over age 60 who have only one child. We propose a monthly benefit of 1,000 sucres (12,000 annually) to women over age 60 who have two children. (These proposals would be funded by new taxes described below.)

3. *Obligatory Recognition of Paternity by Fathers and the State.*

In order to protect young women and the Ecuadorian family, and recognizing that there are 711,000 unmarried women in Ecuador (30 % of all women) with 341,000 children (5 % of all children in the country) (Censo de Población 1982), we propose to encourage paternity suits instigated by the parents of the mother. We suggest that parents have the right to demand, not only expenses for the support of their grandchild, but also a fine that will be divided by the grandparents and the state.

Second Measure: Create Mechanisms of Social Infrastructure in Order to Link Women to the Productive Process

This alternative consists of three parts:

1. *Channel Public and Private Investment Toward Productive Initiatives by Women (Artisanry, Light Industry and Trade).*

Create more employment in the rural sector — particularly for women. This will occur through investment in small business in rural areas — industry that is labor intensive and, where possible, uses locally available materials. (See also the sections on migration and decentralization, in this chapter, where we explain our strategy for the distribution of credit and identification of rural industry in need of support.)

2. *Reform the Educational System in Rural Areas, Particularly in Regard to the Development of Technology and Forms of Productive Organization of Which Ecuadorian Women Can Take Advantage.*

Improve the system of rural education, especially opportunities for women. (This can be done using resources that already exist in local areas and that will become available through the decentralization of government functions.)

3. *Improve the Distribution of Family-Planning Services.*

Increase the provision of information and advice as well as the distribution of technology and resources for family planning. Currently, access to these services in rural areas is minimal. (The level of resources necessary to improve family-planning services is minimal.)

MIGRATION AND THE URBAN EXPLOSION

Our strategy for slowing migration to the cities is to boost the services and employment opportunities in local communities, foster community pride, and minimize the role that certain institutions play in taking young people out of their communities and socializing them into a national Ecuadorian culture which devalues their ethnic and community identity.

Education

University Level. We recommend that the Government of Ecuador decentralize the country's educational system, create more provincial universities and offer a larger variety of disciplines in each school. Curricula ought to be reformed in order to teach more practical skills, transfer knowledge that applies to the circumstances of local peoples and aid them in making better use of their available resources. Extension school programs could be established to reach those students who do not have the financial means or desire to move to areas where universities are located.

At the High School Level. The Ecuadorian government ought to reduce the number of students required in a locality to authorize construction of a high school or for implementation of an extension program, as a means of better reaching all youth. In addition to these measures, funds allocated for free school uniforms should be increased for needy families, and the distribution of such funds should be improved.

At the Elementary School Level. Elementary school curricula ought to include discussion and instruction on local history, Ecuadorian cultural diversity, and the current problems which villages and provinces face.

Agriculture

Loans and Assistance. We recommend that programs for offering loans and technical assistance to small farmers be increased and better managed and that the requirements for collateral should be more lenient.

One of the most effective ways of funding promising initiatives in rural areas would be to make public capital available at the local level instead of concentrating it in the hands of central government. We propose a system of provincial banks to replace the Banco de Fomento (with the same capital base) with representatives elected by communities to serve as Directors.

Furthermore, we support the development of alternative private banks at the local level.

At the same time, local financial institutions, including new provincial banks, ought to continue to be subject to audits at the national level. We propose, however, that these audits be conducted through more independent bodies than those that currently exist. (See "Decentralization" in Chapter 2.)

Health

In addition to increasing the budget of the Ministry of Health and the portion of the Ministry's budget designated for outreach and improvement in rural services, we support the establishment of a program of primary auxiliary health workers. (See "Health" in Chapter 3.)

Culture

The House of Culture ought to establish a program of cultural expression in rural areas that will provide funds to villages to *establish local museums, to promote artistic exhibits with members of the community, and to develop theatres, public movie theaters, and municipal projects which develop local pride and community identity. (See also, "Symbolism" in Chapter 7.)*

The Armed Forces and the National Police

The Ecuadorian Armed Forces and the National Police ought to require that half of their forces in each province come from the some province. Several communities have informed us that the loss and emigration of young people was a result of their obligatory military service. At the same time, we have heard it repeated several times that soldiers or members of the National Police lack knowledge of and respect for local needs and traditions. While we understand the importance of the presence of an outside force when local officials defy national laws, we believe that a balance between people from the community and from outside it will increase the respect for public authorities, prevent the emigration of young men from their communities, and improve the ability of the Armed Forces and National Police to understand local circumstances.

GOVERNMENTAL REFORM
AND COMMUNITY DEVELOPMENT

We propose a strategy for decentralization and governmental reform as well as a variety of initiatives to strengthen local communities; particularly Ecuador's native cultures.

Making rural communities and small towns more attractive and prosperous places to live requires not only a redirection of resources but also institutional changes in government. Such changes would place more powers at local levels and make government more accountable to its citizens.

At the same time, Ecuador's indigenous communities, which are not yet integrated into the mainstream of Ecuadorian life, can best strengthen their independence by building on some of their unique cultural attributes. In what would appear to be somewhat paradoxical, it is by developing their strengths and seeking commercial advantage from them that these groups can set up buffers between themselves and the national culture that will enable them to strengthen their hold on their resources.

DECENTRALIZATION AND GOVERNMENTAL REFORM

Decentralization

The government of Ecuador should clearly establish, by constitutional means, independent political authorities at the provincial, municipal, and canton levels. Provincial governments should have the power to initiate projects throughout the province, including the municipalities.

Powers

Each level of government (with publicly elected officials) should have the power to:

• *levy taxes and raise funds from any person or organization (with the exception of other governmental organizations) in the form of tariffs, licensing fees, fees for services, and so forth, without the need of prior approval from any other level of government;*

• *establish its own laws, which meet the needs and address the interests of the community;*

• *maintain independent police forces in order to enforce local laws;*

• *initiate programs and provide services in any area — such as education, health, public works, or social welfare — and prepare its own development plans, without the approval of or coordination with any other level of government;*

• *enter into contracts with other governmental bodies, organizations, and individuals (between provinces, for example) in order to coordinate affairs between regions, businesses, and individuals (but not with foreign sovereign governments) outside the locality or the country;*

• *elect or appoint judges to hear legal cases on local and national laws, with the exception of those that affect people or organizations outside of that level of government (where that level of government lacks sovereignty).*

Transfers

The government of Ecuador ought to establish a national formula for revenue distribution to local governments that adheres to objective standards. We suggest that this formula be based on categories such as the following:

• *the index of nutrition and caloric consumption,*

• *the rate of infant mortality,*

• *life expectancy,*

• *educational level, and*

• *level of median income.*

In accordance with this formula, communities with the greatest needs ought to receive a greater proportion of funds.

The government of Ecuador should establish a system of development banks ("Bancos de Fomento") at provincial levels in place of the publicly chartered national banks at the national level.

Directors of these banks ought to be elected from the communities where they are based. (This corresponds to our recommendations for combating problems of migration.)

Elections

At local levels (provincial and below) there should be at least one elected official for every 30,000 inhabitants. At other levels of government where this representation is impossible (at the national level in the election of deputies to the Congress, for example), the authority charged with administering elections —Tribunal Supremo Electoral (TSE) — ought to randomly select, from voter rolls, groups of citizens to serve in public functions (analogous to the selection of jury panels in the United States). These groups ought to have full voting power along with elected officials at these levels of government for a period of service of six months.

The majority of the members of the TSE should be publicly elected. All the employees of the TSE should be chosen through competitive examinations and should be protected against removal for political reasons.

Other Changes

The posts of governor (gobernador) and the administrative representatives of the Ministry of Government (tenientes políticos, intendentes and jefes políticos) should be eliminated. The functions of the gobernador should be carried out by elected prefetos at the provincial level.

Strengthening of the Civil Service System

All the employees of the state with the exception of elected officials, ministers, and officeholders appointed according to written constitutional provision, should be selected in accordance with the procedures of a strong civil service system. Government employees ought to be selected through a process of objective testing that is appropriate to the responsibilities of the positions for which they are applying. Increases in salaries and promotions should be objectively defined by pay and job scales and should be awarded on the basis of quality work, as measured by objective standards. The firing of an employee for political reasons should be prohibited under penalty of fine.

For the appearance of objectivity and for reasons of technical support, the government ought to request the assistance of one or more international organizations in establishing this system. This is particularly important with regard to the offices of the Tribunal Superior Electoral, as well as in the formation of districts and electoral bodies (suggested in the previous section on governmental reforms), and a national auditor (controlaría).

Independence of the National Auditor (Controlaría)

The Government of Ecuador ought to establish the independence of the National Auditor through the best available method. We suggest two alternatives.

First, it can contract with private groups to serve as independent auditors. The Congress can select these groups every four years (for terms of four years), beginning in the middle of the president's four-year term. The compensation of members of this auditing body should include, as an incentive, a percentage of all of those misappropriated funds that they are able to discover and recover for the government.

Alternatively, the government can implement the first alternative but establish the auditor as a public office underneath the Congress, and completely separate from the process of selection of presidentially appointed officials (generally appointed by the President and ratified by the Congress.)

Other Governmental Reforms

Ministry of Natural Resources

The government of Ecuador should reestablish the Ministry of Natural Resources with the mandate to preserve the natural ecological heritage of the country for future generations. In carrying out this task, the ministry ought to have its own police force.

Ministry of Indigenous Peoples

In order to demonstrate its interests in matters that affect one third of the Ecuadorian population, we recommend the creation of a ministry that will consider the special needs of indigenous peoples and maintain continual communication with the Confederación Nacional de

Indígenas del Ecuador, CONIAE, the national federal of indigenous peoples. Only through such direct contact can the government obtain a complete understanding of the needs of indigenous peoples.

Ministry of Fisheries

Due to the enormous, unrecognized potential both at the national and at the grassroots levels, of the cultivation of fish through fish farming, and due to the conflicts of interest that now exist in a ministry that oversees animal husbandry, agriculture, and fisheries, we believe that the government of Ecuador should establish a Ministry of Fisheries, independent of the current Ministerio de Agricultura y Ganadería.

CULTURE AND DEVELOPMENT

We recommend that the Ecuadorian government demonstrate its commitment to cultural pluralism and begin its battle against human rights abuses with the symbolic condemnation of genocide against indigenous peoples, which continues de facto to this day in Ecuador.

*   *The Government of Ecuador ought to reject proposals like that made by the Spanish government to participate in the celebration of the "500th Anniversary of the Discovery of America" in 1992, and other events, which follow. Such an occasion would be a celebration of conquest and of the principle of genocide of the Native American peoples who survive to this day.*

*   *The Government of Ecuador should support events like the celebration of 500 Years of Resistance of Indigenous Peoples organized by CONIAE and similar events, which follow. In addition, it should publicize the celebration in foreign countries, not only to raise consciousness about issues affecting native peoples, but also to strengthen the cultural identity of distinct Ecuadorian groups, thus contributing to Ecuadorian development.*

DEVELOPMENT AND INDIGENOUS PEOPLES

Because of the inevitable alienation and loss of identity caused by cultural extinction and absorption, we believe that optimal development options for Ecuador's many indigenous groups will be those which protect cultural diversity. Specifically, economic development will be most effective and efficient when traditions such as dress, language, dance, relationship to the land, family relationships and choice are preserved.

While the ideal development strategy would be to preserve local cultures as they are, the reality for most of Ecuador's cultures is that they have already had contact with the larger society and are being absorbed into national life. The strategy most likely to protect them is one which helps buffer their traditional values against the needs of the larger economy. After hearing the Otavalan's own reports of what they consider their success in making economic progress without losing their cultural identity, we note a number of strategies that mark their success and might be copies by other groups:

1. Use of a dual economic strategy to combine traditional subsistence farming with secondary sources of income, as part of a relationship with Ecuadorian society that strengthens both the local and national economy and serves as a political buffer: in the Otavalan case, the production of artisan goods.

2. Building on a traditional skill in which one has a competitive advantage over other groups.

3. Targeting a particular market niche. For the Otavalans this means specialty items which will appeal to wealthy customers.

4. Producing goods that are useful as well aesthetically pleasing, rather than simply decorative or of stylistic value, so as to reach a larger market.

5. Using a production process requiring little capital investment which allows for production in the households of even poor campesinos (peasant farmers.)

General applications by indigenous peoples of strategies to build on their strengths, increase their resources, and bolster their autonomy through economic and political power include the following:

• Groups (including the Otavalans) should survey foreigners as well as the Ecuadorian market, to discover new market openings. Knowing and understanding changing tastes in the Ecuadorian and international markets is, possibly, the single most important factor in

producing goods that will target a specific niche and generate sustained income over time.

A well-known case in point is the Panama hat industry in Azuay, which is estimated at some $8 million annually. The weaving of Panama hats was suggested by an outsider who recognized the tremendous market potential of this item and the special craftsmanship in the region.

• *Indigenous groups should seek others with experience in similar projects so as to learn from their experience. The U.S. Agency for International Development program that is sending Otavalan, Saraguran, and Salasacan representatives to trade suggestions with the Navajo people of the United States is a prime example of this type of cooperation.*

USING THE FULL POTENTIAL
OF HUMAN RESOURCES

We propose several key changes in Ecuador's system of education and health care. These recommendations fit in to the strategy of community development and decentralization outlined above. Strengthening the capabilities of individuals to be productive at the community level and empowering citizens to meet their own needs requires careful attention to education and health, the basic factors in developing a country's human resources.

In addition to decentralizing the educational and health care systems, we propose a number of qualitative changes to respond to individual needs and develop individual capacities for initiative and self reliance. Rather than merely redistributing resources, we call for redirection of the focus of the educational and health care systems to basic needs of the communities in which they are located.

EDUCATION

The problems of Ecuador's educational system go well beyond content and are rooted in methods and form of the educational process, itself. Teaching students how to think (how to apply knowledge to solving problems), to value themselves as individuals, and to seek rewards on the basis of merit rather than characteristics unrelated to performance, require changing the way in which students are taught and in which performance is evaluated.

Among the many types of changes which are possible, we propose the following:

Encourage Initiative and Self Reliance Through the Educational System

The government of Ecuador should establish special programs to train existing and future teachers in educational techniques and particular skills. Training should include the following skills:

* *how to design an exam that does not require the memorization of facts but the solution to new problems and the use of skills;*

- *how to prepare an exam that another teacher can correct without knowing anything about the students in the class where the exam is taken;*

- *how to ask students questions for which there are no established or prepared answers and encourage students merely to express their opinions and think for themselves; and*

- *how to prepare students to ask questions and generate lists of ideas and possible solutions to a given problem instead of seeking one "correct" answer.*

If there are not enough teachers in the country who already have these skills, or if it would be difficult to identify them, the government should request the assistance of a foreign assistance organization, such as the U.S. Peace Corps, which was founded in the 1960s to provide educational assistance to lesser developed countries.

In order to make the best use of Ecuadorians' own experience and to introduce students to new methods that have been successful and people who can serve as role models, the government of Ecuador should invite those individuals whose earnings from their own businesses have grown more than 200 % (in real sucres) in the last five years to spend five days in universities or high schools, speaking with students, answering questions, and giving lectures about their experiences. In exchange for this, they ought to receive a 10 % rebate on their taxes and the option to receive this reduction in exchange for five days of service in every year in the future.

Improve Distribution of Technical and Basic Education

The government of Ecuador should follow the models of several private stations in Ecuador in the presentation of educational programs and should prepare more radio and television programs for presentation on public and private stations.

HEALTH

We see health care as a central component of development and have made recommendations for health care and education throughout our report. Tax policies, the use of the educational system, population control, the development of opportunities for women, and use of the media for spreading messages about products and nutrition, are all part of a health care strategy and are elaborated at various places in this report. The most basic components are as follows.

• *The Ecuadorian Government should revise the budget proposed by the Ministry of Public Health and approve an increase in the amount to be allocated to the ministry by 50 %: approximately 10 billion sucres. We also recommend redirecting the appropriations within the ministry so as to serve the majority of Ecuadorians with primary health care, rather than concentrate resources on urban areas and expensive medical care for a few individuals.*

• *We recommend reorienting the program of study in medical schools toward basic health, and complementing it with opportunities for technical and specialized training. Until this occurs, medical education in the country will remain out of touch with the reality of current health care problems facing the country.*

• *The Ministry of Public Health should implement a program of primary auxiliary health care workers in the most isolated communities and in peripheral urban neighborhoods (marginal barrios).*

• *The Ecuadorian government should encourage the cooperation between the Ministry of Public Health and the Ministry of Public Education which was initiated through the meetings of OTIDES. The efforts to incorporate health education in the programs of public education in all levels, from primary school to university, should be encouraged.*

• *The Ecuadorian government should support health warnings on television and radio which inform the public about means of protecting their health.*

MACROECONOMIC FINANCIAL STRATEGY

We propose an economic strategy that not only meets the standards of sound fiscal and monetary practices set by the international community — providing revenues for new programs and stabilizing the economy's modern sector — but also serves many of the particular objectives of the development strategy.

Rather than propose taxes (or program cutbacks) which hurt specific groups in Ecuadorian society, we view taxation from the standpoint of development needs. We have designed a tax strategy which seeks to promote health, safety, and national identity, and to promote economic activities favorable for equitable development.

REVENUE GENERATION AND NATIONAL BUDGETING

We propose a variety of taxes in order to provide the necessary revenues for new social programs and to repay Ecuador's national debt. We estimate that they would generate revenue equal to more than 10 % of the current government budget.

Taxes with Implications for Health

<u>Specific Consumption Items</u>

<u>Tobacco</u>. A 50 % tax on tobacco would raise 15.5 billion sucres a year.

<u>Sodas</u>. A tax of 50 % would raise between 7.5 and 18.8 billion sucres annually.

<u>Alcohol</u>. A minimal increase in taxes on alcohol would generate sufficient funds for the treatment of alcoholism, for recreation centers to provide alternatives to alcohol consumption, and for the prevention and for the treatment of battered women and abused children.

<u>Salt.</u> A tax of only 20% would raise 1.47 billion sucres.

<u>Meat</u>. A tax of just 20 % would raise between 10 and 17.5 billion sucres annually. We suggest that half of these funds be earmarked for the new Ministry of Fisheries.

Taxes with Implications for National Pride and the Protection of Ecuadorian Culture

We propose a tax of 300 % on imported ties, suits, perfumes and the imported materials used to make these products domestically and an additional tax on motion pictures of 10 % (which would raise 150 million sucres annually and could be earmarked for a national film industry).

Improvements in the Collection of Taxes

We suggest that Ecuador accept the assistance offered in the past by international organizations in the training and professionalization of customs officials and in stemming the flow of illegal or untaxed items into the country. The Organization of American States is currently working in this area and we recommend that Ecuador request special assistance from the O.A.S. in its special capacity as an international organization.

New Forms of Taxes

Luxury Taxes. A tax on luxury consumer goods would reduce the consumption of items which are not essential to development and could improve income distribution since luxury goods are primarily consumed by the middle and upper classes. We conservatively estimate that a tax of 10 to 20 % on the sale of luxury consumer goods would reduce consumption of those items by 5 % and would raise between 6 and 12 billion sucres annually. An important advantage of a luxury tax on consumer goods of whatever origin is that it does not produce an incentive for substitution of these products with domestic goods. If Ecuador did wish to promote substitution for imports with internal production, it is clear that it would seek to promote substitution of goods essential for development rather than luxury goods.

Consumption Tax. In the long run, the Ecuadorian government should consider a tax on consumption in place of a tax on income. This form of taxation has the advantage of discouraging consumption of luxury items while promoting savings and capital formation.

EXCHANGE POLICY

We view the policies of exchange rates not as the center of an economic strategy, but only as one component of a development strategy with particular implications for growth of the modern industrial sector. Our recommendations for exchange policies, for balancing the government budget and for maintaining the balance of trade by promoting certain export sectors are complementary to the rest of our proposals.

We are in basic agreement with the calls of other development agencies in proposing the following:

In order to resolve the crisis in its exchange markets, Ecuador requires a policy of confidence, not of controls. This policy should consist of three parts.

1. Ecuador needs a sincere effort to combat inflation, not with price controls but with a reduction in the government budget deficit. We cannot deny that inflation moves the exchange rate upward. From the experience of the antiinflationary programs of Argentina (1985 — Plan Austral), Brazil (1986 — Plan Cruzado), and Bolivia (1985 — New Economic Policy), it appears that the first two countries failed in large part because they did not reduce the state budget deficit, while Bolivia succeeded because its policies were accompanied by a significant reduction in the state budget. The basic structural inflation in Ecuador is much less than it was in those other countries. It is likely, therefore, that a policy of combating inflation will be successful if it is accompanied by deficit reduction.

2. The policy must support productive investment in production for export and for efficient domestic production. The most important goal is to recover the confidence of the private sector by demonstrating that investment in Ecuador is prudent and profitable. The result will be a reduction in the flight of capital and speculation, two forces that significantly affect the rate of exchange.

3. The policy must leave the exchange rate to the free market, as is currently the case. If inflation returns to normal, low levels and the private sector has confidence that the probability for success is high, the pressures that force the exchange rate upward will disappear.

Whatever government does, it has to do immediately. Recently, we have seen an enormous amount of monetary speculation in Ecuador because the public does not know what the new government will do. If the government does not announce its economic programs quickly, the Ecuadorian people will lose confidence in it.

MACROECONOMIC PRODUCTION STRATEGY:
SECTORIAL FOCUS

We choose to make recommendations in two sectors which we were able to survey in a reasonable amount of time — agriculture and tourism. Were our team larger, or if we are able to produce a follow-up study, our analysis would include studies of Ecuador's major export industries — oil, fishing (shrimp), and agricultural exports (bananas, cocoa) — as well as attention to the country's growing industrial base.

In examining the production of foods for domestic consumption and the tourist industry, we tie our recommendations in these areas to several of our other objectives — promoting local production, strengthening communities, and increasing local use of resources.

FOOD PRODUCTION

If Ecuador does not change its strategy for agricultural development, the country will face a grave crisis in food production. To avoid this crisis, the government must do the following.

Redirect available resources from large farms to small producers of essential foods, where there is greater potential for increased productivity (considering the primitive levels of technology used today in the majority of small farms and the potential for improvement). The production of essential foods currently receives only a fraction of available credit for the agricultural sector.

Increase technical assistance and research for the production of foods, with a particular goal of strengthening these programs to assist small producers. The government must take strong action to stimulate improved methods of cultivation, not only to improve the distribution of superior varieties of seeds and inputs, but also to improve methods of cultivation and land preservation. Resources provided for agricultural research must be directed away from expensive programs (e.g., atomic energy laboratories) and toward those programs that are more cost effective, will identify more productive uses of particular lands, and will result in improved methods for the producers of foodstuffs.

Increase support for land conservation programs that already exist, such as reforestation and special cultivation methods, since land erosion will be one of the most serious problems that Ecuador will face in the coming years.

Research the possibility of cooperation (the formation of cooperatives) among small producers as a means of improving the capacity of those producers to ensure that government programs truly help them. It is possible that the failure of some of these programs in the past was due to mistakes in the policies on which they were based.

Overall, it is very important that the government not return to the policies of the past, which involved trying to implement a program of food price controls. Such controls produce market distortions and serve as a negative incentive to production (as the history of such programs in Ecuador has shown), whereas at this time the country needs significant increases in production to satisfy a growing demand for food.

In contrast, programs that increase productivity and production could diminish the growth in prices if the supply of basic foods grows more rapidly than the demand.

TOURISM

• *Foreigners should be charged significantly more than Ecuadorians for museums, anthropological sites, domestic airline flights, and so forth.*

• *Localities should establish more museums displaying local traditions, history, and artwork.*

• *Ecuador should open more archaeological sites to tourism. By charging foreigners admission fees to these sites, part of the additional revenues could be allocated to preserve these sites as educational resources and sources of cultural pride.*

• *Reserves should be designed for high-budget, nature-conscious tourists (such as those who visit the Galápagos), which would serve the dual function of preserving the ecosystem and providing revenues through "ecotourism."*

• *DITURIS, the government travel agency, should publish a weekly bulletin describing local special events and listing artesanía (crafts) shops in the cities.*

• *DITURIS should also distribute a guide to museums, historic buildings, and churches to make them more accessible to tourists.*

THE APPROPRIATE ROLE OF THE MAJOR
INSTITUTIONAL ACTORS IN DEVELOPMENT

We propose that the most powerful institutions operating in the country — the Armed Forces and National Police, the Church, and foreign governments (we examine the role of the United States) — reevaluate their roles and their effect on development.

While it would be naive to believe that Ecuadorians could change the role of institutions which exert unequal influence on the country's policies, we hope that the moral authority of objective policy analysis will carry some weight and will influence the world community and strengthen the hand of those organizations committed to development in Ecuador.

As U.S. citizens, it is in our power to appeal to our government and to international religious organizations to make more appropriate contributions to Ecuador's development, and to urge Ecuadorians to seek the help of international organizations to assist in meeting their development needs where domestic institutions interfere with their abilities to achieve equitable and sustained growth.

THE ARMED FORCES AND THE NATIONAL POLICE

Although we had hoped to study the important role of the Ecuadorian Armed Forces and the National Police in greater detail and heard throughout the country several suggestions and recommendations for reform in these areas, we are restricting our suggestions to realms in which the U.S. government and embassy can offer assistance.

We have dealt with several problems that we observed in the nation's military in other sections — on population (regarding policy in the Amazon region and with relation to Peru; see Chapter 1), migration (Chapter 1), communities (Chapters 1 and 2), and symbolism (Chapter 7).

In addition to those recommendations, we propose that the government of Ecuador request the continued assistance of the United States in the training and professionalization of the Armed Forces, the National Police and the Immigration Police, and that such training be conducted with close and constant civilian oversight from both countries with attention to issues of accountability and control. We recommend that the government of the United States and the Organization of American States provide the resources and assistance necessary in this area through the U.S. Department of Justice and development agencies, and particularly to aid in enforcing the law against those who are misappropriating national resources.

RELIGION AND DEVELOPMENT

Separating Church and State

Representatives of religious institutions should not participate in official government ceremonies and events in a role other than that of private citizen. Moreover, officials of the government should not receive or accept special honors or awards from religious institutions or their representatives.

Protecting the Integrity of Indigenous Communities

The government of Ecuador should not allow the establishment of new missions except in cities with populations of more than 25,000 persons. In order to protect the religious liberties of Ecuadorians, we define "mission" as a religious organization that has funds or people from outside the country.

THE ROLE OF THE UNITED STATES IN ECUADOR

The Governmental organizations of the United States in Ecuador should assist Ecuador in meeting its most pressing needs and widen its focus to include assistance in the following areas:

U.S. Agency for International Development (USAID)

We recommend that USAID focus its resources on assisting the government of Ecuador in:

- *transferring responsibilities and powers to local governments, and providing the necessary training at those levels;*

- *meeting the needs of the "poorest of the poor" through systems of rural credit (see the section on migration in Chapter 1),* infrastructure, and assistance to children so that they have the resources to attend school; and

• improving the civil service system at all levels of government. (See the section on decentralization and governmental reform in Chapter 2).

The Peace Corps

We believe that the Corps ought to:

• work with USAID and the Ministry of Education in the training of Ecuadorian teachers in order to develop methods of instruction which encourage initiative and self reliance. (See the section on education in Chapter 3);

• increase the number of volunteers working in small rural communities identifying needs for integrated rural development,and see that these volunteers coordinate their work with those working with government ministries in provincial capitals; and

• develop and provide funds for a new technical assistance organization staffed by U.S. citizens who are of Ecuadorian descent.

The Cultural Section of the Embassy and the U.S. Information Service

We urge USIS and the cultural section of the U.S. Embassy to make better efforts to inform Ecuadorians about the realities of life in the United States.

The U.S. Armed Forces

The U.S. Armed Forces hould offer assistance in the training and professionalization of the Ecuadorian Armed Forces, the National Police, and the Immigration Police in order to stem the violation of laws by certain members of these organizations. (See also the section on the Armed Forces in Chapter 6.)

CHANGING STATE OF MIND

We propose a strategy designed to combat feelings of dependency on major industrialized nations and to raise the self-esteem of those groups of citizens which have been viewed as second-class in Ecuador.

Our recommendations in this area reinforce our goals of building the pride of local communities and of empowering Ecuadorian citizens, particularly women and minority peoples.

DEPENDENCY

The Ecuadorian government should encourage the formation and strengthening of popular organizations which empower citizens. We recommend the following measures. In general, and as part of our overall strategy to be reiterated and echoed in all aspects of planning:

- *Government decentralization. and*
- *Cultural autonomy.*

In new structural changes:

- *Coordination and education of national and international development agencies.*

In specific application:

- *The utilization of appropriate technology,*

- *Local control of bank credit,*

- *Local control of environmental and natural resources, and*

- *Redirection of local education to regional needs.*

SYMBOLISM

Removing Old Symbols

The Ecuadorian government ought to announce an immediate moratorium on signs that attribute the construction of public works to a particular public official and should reduce the number of signs that announce the construction of public works to a minimum.

Promoting New Symbols as Sources of Pride

We recommend that the government make a special effort to recognize the achievements of women, as well as of indigenous communities and their leaders, in the construction of monuments and murals and the naming of new governmental districts and streets.

Regulating the Effects of Advertising

The Ecuadorian government ought to impose a tax on all commercial advertisements of tobacco, soft drinks, products containing sugar, and other products that threaten public health, in the amount of 1.5 times the cost of the advertisement.   These funds should be earmarked directly for the Ministry of Health for the creation of advertisements of equal size and distribution in order to inform the public of the risks of, and possible substitutes for, these products.

REPORT

1

Slowing Population Growth and Community Disintegration

We begin with the most urgent problem facing all societies: that of balancing population with resources. The key to economic development is to match population to resources, and in that equation, we believe the most important component is population. Unlike other planners, our approach is to look at population not as a problem resulting from lack of contraceptive technology or information or slow urbanization and transition to patterns of population growth in industrial societies. We focus instead on the underlying reasons why societies seek to expand their population and on the psychological regions for childbearing, and we place population growth in the context of other population issues, like rural-urban migration and the explosion of urban areas.

Many development agents have been afraid to confront issues of population control directly because of the political implications of challenging organized religions opposed to it, as well as the political ideologies that are attached to pronouncements on population and population control in a number of the developed countries of the West. Indeed, in countries that share this view, it has been difficult to delink traditional religious opposition to limiting population growth from the traditional policies that the same organized religions have often supported, namely, colonial and military expansion into already populated regions as a prelude to the rapid extraction of the resources in those areas.

More recently, with the difficulties of trying to convince the populations of the developing world to voluntarily limit their reproduction, population growth has increasingly been viewed as the dependent variable in the development equation rather than something that development agents can quickly influence. Many development planners now place less effort on population policies than in the past, arguing that birthrates naturally fall as societies industrialize and that the top priority must be to industrialize poorer nations in order to slow population growth.

While threats of famine or instability must be met as a top priority, development strategies that postpone population planning in an effort to raise living standards in the short term — by rapidly depleting resources or creating massive debts — only postpone the problem of population growth and magnify the potential for devastating future consequences.

In our view, many planners are not only turning away from the most important problem in development, they are failing to look deeper, at the root causes of population growth. Both those who recognize the importance of slowing population growth and those who do not could achieve greater success by adopting new strategies to address the root causes of population growth, and in doing so they could also begin to solve a number of other development problems that are closely related to it.

Aside from the inability to predict a natural disaster, not only is every development problem, at its center, also a population problem, but every choice in development has implications for population. Cultures in harmony with their surrounding environments have long had mechanisms for regulating population to keep it consistent with economic productivity. The shift of societies to new methods of productivity or to expansion is what has tipped the balance. Once expanding societies reach the limit of their resource base — or run into their neighbors — or once stable societies find their resource base exploited and their previous modes of survival disrupted, the synchronization between population and productivity will also be disrupted. The task of development is to recreate societies to best restore that balance.

The connection between population growth and a variety of problems in developing countries is undeniable. A rapid increase in the number of people living in environments that sustained a much smaller population in the past — namely, on the land — has resulted in displacing rural populations, sending the overflow into the cities (to which people have to migrate due to lack of resources in rural areas) or into forest land, which is being destroyed and converted into fields for farming or forcing them to more intensely use existing land to the point of destroying areas that were once fertile.

This chapter focuses on the issue of population growth by placing it in context with its social and psychological causes. A population policy must be linked, not only to economic growth, but also to the economic and social roles of women and men in society, to the changing family, and to means of providing care and security in old age, as well as to policies for community expansion and rural versus urban growth. We reject strategies of rapid industrialization as a means of controlling population growth and turn the causal arrow in the other direction.

Our solutions take a broader view than that of either improved family planning technologies, education, or economic growth. In our view, forcing people out of their communities and into urban areas when the original communities can actually be a source of productivity and stability is part of the cause of the problem rather than the solution. It is through increased productive opportunities in communities where people are rooted, greater security, and a closer understanding from the ground level, of how societies work, that these problems can be more effectively addressed.

This chapter addresses the issue in two sections — one on population and the context in which population growth occurs and one on the impact of population on urban and rural areas — with recommendations for community and national life.

POPULATION AND THE FUTURE

The focus of development efforts in the area of population has been in two areas: providing the technology of birth control and promoting its use among women, and modernizing economic productivity while improving public health so as to create the demographic conditions in which women choose to bear fewer children.

While several decades of experience with these approaches have resulted in some successes at slowing the rate of population growth, there still seems to be little agreement on the underlying reasons for childbearing and population growth, both from the perspective of families and from the underlying mechanisms of societies. In our view, development planners misunderstand both the link between economic productivity and demographic decline and the reason why women choose to bear fewer children. We looked more closely at the underlying reasons people choose to bear children and discovered that:

• the decision to bear children is an economic as well as a social one— for their ability to provide financial security, protection, and comfort in old age;

• an emphasis on childbearing reflects the status of women as homemakers with no other productive economic or social role providing them with self esteem and contribution; as well as the minor role and lack of obligation that men have in child rearing;

• population growth, on a national level, is often linked with strategies of nationalism and expansion; a cultural strategy of taking neighboring resources rather than living within the constraints of existing resources; and,

• rapid birth rates among marginal groups in a society may actually benefit elites in the society, even while hurting the country as a whole, by keeping certain groups at a disadvantage and available as cheap labor (both children and adults).

It is our conclusion that an effective population policy, therefore, must be linked to other strategies of sociocultural change. Policies for effective population control must go beyond industrialization and family planning outreach to:

• find security for families, and particularly for women, in old age, in order to reduce the need to "self-insure" by having more children;

• create a more significant role for women — as educated and productive members of society with higher economic and social status;

• create greater incentives for men to acknowledge paternity and participate in child rearing, thus changing the role and responsibility of men as well as women; and

• be part of a strategy of demilitarization and expanded productivity on an existing resource base without expansion or warfare as means of regulating population (through death) or increasing access to resources (through conquest).

These efforts are not a substitute for increasing efforts at family planing or creating the "demographic transition" from rural to urban families. They are a means for laying the ground work for these other efforts; all of which must be combined for the effective control of population growth.

RECOMMENDATIONS

We propose two measures to deal with the population explosion which threatens the future of Ecuador. The two can be implemented separately or together.

First Alternative: Create Incentive Mechanisms for Population Control

This alternative consists of three parts:

1. <u>Provide Financial Incentives to Women That Reflect Their Number of Children</u>.

As an incentive to women to postpone having children in order that they may continue their education and pursue their careers, we propose to award women between the ages of 21 and 25 with a monthly stipend. We suggest an amount of 5,000 sucres (60,000 sucres annually) in 1988 sucres. We choose this level because it represents an individual's minimum living expenses. As a condition of receiving benefits, women will be obligated to come to a governmental office three times each year in order to declare that they are not pregnant and do not have children.

2. <u>Provide Social Security Benefits Based on the Number of Children</u>.

In recognition of the fact that in Ecuadorian society, children care for and support their parents in old age, and in order to avoid punishing (as well as to give incentives to) women who have few children, we propose to provide social security benefits directly to women with few children who cannot receive another source of support. We propose to pay a monthly benefit of 5,000 sucres (60,000 annually) to women over age 60 who do not have children. We propose a monthly benefit of 3,000 sucres (36,000 annually) to women over age 60 who have only one child. We propose a monthly benefit of 1,000 sucres (12,000 annually) to women over age 60 who have two children.

3. <u>Obligatory Recognition of Paternity by Fathers and the State.</u>

In order to protect young women and the Ecuadorian family, and recognizing that there are 711,000 unmarried women in Ecuador (30 % of

all women) with 341,000 children (5 % of all children in the country)
(Censo de Población 1982), we propose to encourage paternity suits
instigated by the parents of the mother. We suggest that parents have
the right to demand, not only expenses for the support of their
grandchild, but also a fine that will be divided by the grandparents
and the state.

Costs. *We estimate that the cost of this alternative will be a*
little more than 15 billion sucres annually (an increase of less than 4%
of the national budget.)

Second Measure: Create Mechanisms of Social Infrastructure in Order to Link Women to the Productive Process

This alternative consists of three parts:

1. Channel Public and Private Investment Toward Productive Initiatives by Women (Artisanry, Light Industry and Trade).

Create more employment in the rural sector — particularly for
women. This will occur through investment in small business in rural
areas — industry that is labor intensive and, where possible, uses
locally available materials. (See also the sections on migration and
decentralization, in this chapter, where we explain our strategy for
the distribution of credit and identification of rural industry in need of
support.)

2. Reform the Educational System in Rural Areas, Particularly in Regard to the Development of Technology and Forms of Productive Organization of Which Ecuadorian Women Can Take Advantage.

Improve the system of rural education, especially opportunities for
women. (This can be done using resources that already exist in local
areas and that will become available through the decentralization of
government functions.)

3. Improve the Distribution of Family-Planning Services.

Increase the provision of information and advice as well as the
distribution of technology and resources for family planning. Currently,
access to these services in rural areas is minimal. (The level of
resources necessary to improve family-planning services is minimal.)

Costs.   If the government invests the same 15 billion sucres as in the first alternative, this would create 9,080 jobs for women.

• In order to reduce the number of births by 25,000 (which we estimate would occur through an investment of 15 billion sucres in the first alternative), the government would have to spend almost 45 billion sucres in employment creation.

• Note that this is an investment. We can estimate conservatively that roughly 50 % of the costs will be recuperated. Therefore the real costs will be about 25 billion sucres, and probably these costs will have other beneficial indirect effects — encouraging the development of services to provide these new industries, increasing national demand which will spur the growth of already established industries, and so forth.

REPORT

The most severe problem that confronts Ecuador is that of rapid population growth. Despite this, for several cultural, historical, and political reasons, the country has tried to avoid and postpone the problem, hoping it would disappear. However, this is a real problem, and it is the root of many difficulties that confront Ecuador at this moment in history. It is a problem Ecuador cannot ignore.

Because of the severity of the problem, it is one that we choose not to explain in delicate or polite terms. The manner in which Ecuador is currently dealing with rising population presents a grave danger, not only to Ecuador but also to its neighboring countries and the rest of the world. We would prefer to avoid presenting our conclusions and observations so brusquely, but it is unavoidable as all of our data leads us to the same conclusion.

By not directly confronting its problem of population growth as a national priority, Ecuador has adopted — consciously or subconsciously (it does not matter which as the result will be the same) — *a strategy of "throwing its refuse in the backyard."* That backyard is the Amazon region, and particularly the site of contested territory and border disputes with Peru. *The policy of colonization is a policy of throwing the problems of overpopulation and poverty elsewhere rather than dealing with them, thus building pressure for future conflict.*

Without measures to control it, Ecuador's population will continue to increase. The result of the strategy of colonization of uninhabited or tribal lands without a strong population policy will be the degradation of the Amazon region, a change in the world climate, the loss of the production of much of the globe's oxygen, the disappearance of many medicinal and nutritive plants not yet discovered, and the pollution of the rivers of Brazil and Peru.

Perhaps within 10 years or perhaps in forty (depending on the statistics), but inevitably, Ecuador will have two options after its arable land runs out. Without more land on which to place more people, Ecuador will have to either look for a way to acquire more land or accept an internal struggle between classes, generations, and ethnic groups. It appears that Ecuador is preparing for the first option. *The probable result of current strategy will be the escalation of border disputes into a fullscale war against Peru.*

ANALYSIS

When Will Ecuador Fill Its Land?

In order to estimate when Ecuador will fill all its land, several factors must be taken into account. The data are complex, confusing, and contradictory, and the method of prediction requires several assumptions. What, for example, does it mean to completely fill land? Does this recognize the existence of reserves and indigenous territories? Is this a use in which every grain of earth is cultivated with the same intensity as in certain parts of the Sierra today?

It is obvious that there is little interest on the part of the Ecuadorian government in doing this type of analysis because the implication of filling the land conflicts with other preferences and needs of the Ecuadorian people. Perhaps it would be impossible even to make this type of calculation, given all the assumptions that could distort the results, even if the government wished to do so. The fact is, however, that pressure on land is increasing with enormous speed. According to our calculations, Ecuador will completely fill its land in the next 10 to 40 years; in other words, during the lifetime of most living Ecuadorians.

How Much Land Is There?

The figures on the extent of land are contradictory. The total land area of the country is 70 million acres (around 28 million hectares.) Estimates made in 1972 of the potential of land for cultivation and grazing vary between 6.2 million hectares and 20 million hectares (70 % of the total). (Weil, et. al. 1973) Another land measure made in 1968 by the Ecuadorian government described a potential of 8,475,000 hectares (World Bank 1979).

Estimates of the Ecuadorian Ministry of Agriculture in 1986 are 50 % higher. In 1986, they believed there were 12,446,791 hectares of potentially usable land. (The rest, some 13 million hectares in forest, is not specified as to whether or not it is potentially usable in the future.) Most of this land is in the Amazon region (Banco Central del Ecuador 1986).

Land Use — A Simple Model

A simple model of land use would calculate the growth in the use of

Table 1.1   Extent of Land Use, Including Agriculture and Animal Husbandry

1954 — 5,999,700 hectares (Censo Agropecuario Nacional 1954) (Note that this figure is problematic. Before agrarian reform, with the existence of large estates (*haciendas*), much of the land described as utilized was not well cultivated, which the figure may represent.)

1968 — 6,937,500 hectares (Encuesta Agropecuaria Nacional 1968)
1968 — 4,170,000 hectares (World Bank 1979, figures from the Government of Ecuador). (Note the contradiction between the two figures for 1968.)

1980 — 5,539,200 hectares (Ministerio de Agricultura; see Economist Intelligence Unit 1987)

1984 — 5,934,900 hectares (Ministerio de Agricultura; see Economist Intellligence Unit 1987)
1984 — 5,956,592 hectares (Ministerio de Agricultura, Dir. Sec. de Planificación, División de Informática y Estadística)

land in fixed relation to the growth of population. This model is problematic because it ignores changes in the technology of agricultural production, the quality of the land, and the number of people who can be supported by a parcel of land. It also ignores the growth of other sectors of the economy. (Less than half of Ecuadorians who are economically active work in animal husbandry, hunting, fishing, and agriculture, and the sector counts for only 20 percent of gross domestic product.) This model assumes that Ecuador is an agricultural nation, that other economic sectors are stagnant, and that there is a fixed relation between land use and population.

In which of these conflicting land use figures can we have confidence? The last four figures together, representing a steady increase in the use of land, are consistent with each other and probably do not represent other effects of land utilization that existed before Agrarian Reform Program. Thus, we can say that between 1968 and 1984, the use of land grew by 43 % (whereas between 1968 and 1980, it grew by 33 %).

In the same period, the population grew about 52 % (37 % between 1968 and 1980). The use of land grew less than population, probably because of the growth of the petroleum industry and other businesses. If we project that the economy will continue along this path (an optimistic prediction), we can estimate a growth in land use by 43 % for every population increase of 52 %.

• If there are only 8,475,000 hectares potentially available for use, land use can only increase. With a population growth rate of 3.0 % per year, this would occur by 1998 — *in 10 years*. (The actual population growth rate is between 2.8 and 2.9 %, but we are using 3.0 % in order to simplify the calculations.)

• If the potentially available land is 12,447,000 hectares, land use can grow by 108 %. According to these figures, the land will be full after the population grows by 131 %. This would occur in 2013 — *in 25 years*.

• If the potentially available land includes the entire forest, land use can increase by more than 300 %. Thus, the land will be full after the population grows by 360 % This will occur in 2013 -- *in 39 years*.

• If we say that nonagricultural sectors are going to stagnate and suggest that the utilization of land will grow at the same rate as population, according to the same array of estimates for potentially available land, we can estimate that the land will be full in either 1996 (*8 years*), 2009 (*21 years*), or 2022 (*34 years*).

Improvements in the Model

To assume that agricultural production will neither improve nor worsen as more land is brought into use — holding technology and land quality constant — deviates slightly from the observed reality. With the increase in land use of the period between 1968 and 1980, as land use increased by 33 %, the value of production in constant sucres (between 1970 and 1982) rose by 50 %.

However, at the same time, the percentage of people living in rural areas or working in agriculture also fell. Thus, production can support more people, but it could be that there are more people in urban areas who are unemployed. (It is unclear whether the increase in agricultural production will be reflected directly in more employment in urban areas.)

With a few changes in our original assumptions, we can try to make a model that is slightly more complex and thus find that the rural

Table 1.2.1 Percentage of the Population and Number of Inhabitants in Rural Areas

Year	Percentage of Population	No. of Inhabitants
1950	71.5%	2.2 Millions
1962	64.7%	3.0
1971	61.1%	4.0
1987	46.5%	4.6

Sources: Instituto Nacional de Estadísticos y Censos 1983; Banco Central del Ecuador 1988; Economist 1993; Weil et. al. 1973.

Table 1.2.2 Percentage of the Working Population in Rural Areas

Year	Percentage of Working Population
1962	65.9%
1970	62.6%
1980	56.9%

Source: Redclift (1979, p. 12; compiled from Ecuador Bureau de Estadísticos y Censos).

sector is shrinking rapidly (see Tables 1.2.1 and 1.2.2).

If we use the figures for 1970 and 1987 and conclude that in 17 years, the population in rural areas will increase by 15 %, this is an increase (uncompounded) of 1 % per year. At the same time, with these statistics, we can see that production is growing more rapidly than the increase in land use (150 % to 133 % in 12 years, which is 17 % more rapidly than the land or about 1 % per year, uncompound).

In rough calculations, when the number of people increases by 1 %, the use of land increases around 2.4 % and production increases by 3 %. Thus, when land use doubles (up to 12 million hectares) — in 24 years, or quadruples (to 24 million hectares) — in 38 years, the production on the land (at current rates of use) will support 1.77 times the 1984 population of 9.09 million (growing at 2.4 % per year), and 2.47 times the 1984 population (16.09 and 22.42 million, respectively).

As a result, with the two estimates of potentially available land, the land will fill in either 2004 (16 years) or in 2016 (28 years.) (As before, this assumes a growth rate of 3.0 % per year, which is used for rough calculations.) However, we need to consider at the same time that production is growing. Thus, land will not only be utilized, it will support a greater population.

If production increases by 3.0 % per year and population grows at the same rate, 12 million hectares can support twice as many people as 6 million hectares supported in 1984. (Population and productivity grow together.) This would occur *in 20 years — in 2008*. Thus, 25 million hectares could support four times as many people as 6 million hectares did in 1984. By this calculation, the land would be at capacity in 35 *years — in 2023*.

Another Model

In the majority of underdeveloped countries, projections of population and resources compare growth in employment with growth of the economically active population. In these countries, with land already utilized, the projections deal with the agricultural sector, the nonagricultural sectors, and the availability and growth of employment in each. In such cases the estimates for the future are not of overpopulation of land but rather of projected unemployment and potential for instability (inability to absorb young people into the labor force).

We can adopt a similar method for Ecuador, but in reverse. If we assume that in Ecuador the available resources for nonagricultural sectors are fixed (actually, dropping or stagnating) and that all the available resources in Ecuador exist in the form of potential, but currently unutilized, land, we can estimate when the land will reach its limits by estimating the number of people who will not be absorbed in the nonagricultural sectors. In such a case, we assume that those who cannot find employment in nonagricultural sectors will use the available land as their only means of economic survival.

Unfortunately, to estimate the growth of the nonagriculture sector is not easy. One method is to assume that the future will be similar to the past (which is simple but not reliable). The graph on the next page includes four data points (the census years) between 1950 and 1982. (Note the jump in the 1982 figure — probably the result of the oil boom. Data are from the Banco Central del Ecuador 1986 and International Monetary Fund 1986.)

Figure 1.1 Employment in Nonagricultural Sectors between 1950 and 1985

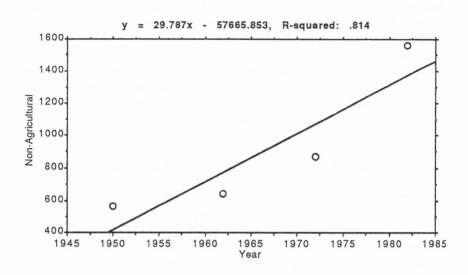

Note: Employment is measured in thousands.

Figure 1.1 shows the best line fitted to these points by a simple regression and projects that the number of jobs in these sectors would grow at a rate of 29,800 per year. With census figures, we can project that in 1990, for example, the number of people in the labor force would be 2,932,500 (a growth of 586,000). New positions in the non-agricultural sector would number 238,400 according to the regression projections. Thus, 348,000 people would view work in the agricultural sector as their only alternative to unemployment. This is half as many people as those working in agriculture in the 1980s. In other words, it is possible that the use of land would increase by 50 % by 1990!

Using simple assumptions and rough figures, we estimate that Ecuador will use 12 million hectares of land (the 1986 estimate of the total amount of potential land) by the year *1998 — that is, in 10 years.* If we assume that Ecuador can use its entire forest for agricultural production (25 million hectares), all the country's land will be in use by the year *2013 — in 25 years!*

PROPOSAL

We propose two measures to deal with the population explosion that threatens the future of Ecuador. The two can be implemented separately or together.

Without more research into the effects of these alternatives and the effectiveness of each, we are divided in suggesting one over the other. However, we are in complete agreement that Ecuador cannot avoid the adoption of solutions with some of these characteristics in order to prevent the destruction of its natural resources and avoid the potential for civil war or imperialistic conflict.

First Alternative: Create Incentive Mechanisms for Regulating Births

Although this alternative may appear somewhat unusual, we believe it merits careful consideration because of its attempt to incorporate the principles of the free market with a respect for Ecuadorian values, with the goal of directly confronting the problem of population.

This alternative consists of three parts

1. Provide Financial Incentives to Women Which Reflect Their Number of Children.

As an incentive to women to postpone having children in order that they may continue their education and pursue their careers, we propose to award women between the ages of 21 and 25 with a monthly stipend. We suggest an amount of 5,000 sucres (60,000 sucres annually) in 1988 sucres. We choose this level because it represents an individual's minimum living expenses. Woman will be obligated to come to a governmental office three times each year in order to declare that they are not pregnant and do not have children.

2. Provide Social Security Benefits Based on the Number of Children.

In recognition of the fact that in Ecuadorian society, children care for and support their parents in old age, and in order to avoid punishing (and to give incentives to) women who have few children, we propose to provide social security benefits directly to women with few children who cannot receive another source of support. We propose to pay a monthly benefit of 5,000 sucres (60,000 annually) to women over age 60 who do not have children. We propose a monthly benefit of 3,000 sucres (36,000 annually) to women over age 60 who have only one child. We propose a monthly benefit of 1,000 sucres (12,000 annually) to women over age 60 who have two children.

3. Obligatory Recognition of Paternity by Fathers and the State.

In order to protect young women and the Ecuadorian family, and recognizing that there are 711,000 unmarried women in Ecuador (30 % of all women) with 341,000 children (5 % of all children in the country) (Censo de Población 1982), we propose to encourage paternity suits instigated by the parents of the mother. We suggest that parents have the right to demand, not only expenses for the support of their grandchild, but also a fine that will be divided by the grandparents and the state.

We believe that the adoption of this alternative would have several advantages.

Future Budgetary Savings to Government.

It may seem like the cost of this alternative is high, but we believe that over time it will actually result in substantial savings to the government.

Expenses During the Life of a Woman Who Supports One Less
Child. We estimate that for every three women between the ages of 21 and 25 who receive the monthly stipend, one will decide to have one less child during her life. Perhaps the program will be more successful than this; perhaps less so. However, we believe that this estimate is realistic. Thus, over a five-year period the expenditure of 60,000 sucres per year for three people would amount to 900,000 sucres.

When the woman who bore one less child reaches age 60, she can receive a monthly social security benefit for the rest of her life (about 13 years, assuming that life expectancy in Ecuador will rise to 72). Thus, this woman would receive 2,000 sucres monthly, which amounts to 312,000 sucres.

At the same time, other elderly women will receive monthly benefits in this program. Ten percent of all women who now are between the ages of 40 and 44 do not have children. They will receive 5,000 sucres each month for 13 years. Five percent have one child and would receive 3,000 monthly. Seven percent have two children and would therefore be entitled to receive 1,000 sucres per month (Ecuador 1983).

We estimate that there will be two women receiving 5,000 sucres (s) monthly, one receiving 3,000 s monthly, and one receiving 1,000 s monthly (22 % of all women) for every two women with one fewer child who will be eligible to receive the monthly benefit. Therefore, for each woman who receives the stipend as an incentive, the State at the same time pays out 1.092 million sucres to those who have made no changes in child bearing.

In sum, for each birth avoided in Ecuador by this plan, the government would pay out 2.304 million sucres (over the 52 adult years of the life of a woman).

Savings in Education. The education budget in a recent year was 44,506.3 million sucres (Banco Central del Ecuador 1986). During the same year, 2,760,340 students attended public schools at all levels (Ministerio de Educación). In other words, the government spends 16,123 sucres per student per year. If each student receives 15 years of education, this amounts to public expenditures of 241,845 sucres.

Savings in Health. In 1985, central government spent 12,541.2 million sucres on public health. We estimate that the use of public health resources in Ecuador are double for young people under 15 years of age than for the rest of the population. If there were 3,920,023 persons under 15 years old and 5,457,957 over 15 in 1985, the use of health services would amount to 1,886 sucres annually for children under 15 years old and 943 sucres annually for people over 15.

Thus, someone who lives for 52 years would receive 15 years of health services at a cost to the government of 1886 sucres per year (28,290) and 37 years at a cost of 943 sucres per year (34,891). Total health benefits to that individual would cost the government 63,181 sucres .

Savings in Other Government Services. We can consider, too, the use of other services per capita. (Actually, the rest of the national budget of 133 billion sucres, besides expenses on health and education, represents 15,000 sucres annually per person, or 780,000 sucres over a period of 52 years. It is difficult to say that these costs vary directly with population, however. Thus, we have decided not to include them in the calculations. Nonetheless, it should be kept in mind that there are savings here.)

Savings per Child. Currently, an Ecuadorian who reaches the age of 52 will reproduce himself 2.6 times. There were 247,000 Ecuadorians between the ages of 50 and 54 in 1982, with a total of 635,000 children currently alive, according to the Censo de Población (Ecuador 1983, pp. 50, 322).

If, during this period, a child reaches 30 years of age, he or she can be expected to reproduce himself almost 2 times (he will have an average of 1.6 children). If a second child reaches age 22, he or she will be expected to have, by age 22, an average of .9 children. Therefore, we can assume descendants who will be 30 years old, 22 years old, 16 years old (with a frequency of .6), 10 years old, 3 years old (with a frequency of .6), and 2 years old.

If we calculate using this example, it will result in costs to the government of

$$15 + 15 + (11 \times .6) + 5 \text{ years of education} = 41.6 \text{ years at } 16,123$$
$$\text{sucres}/ \text{ year} = 670,717 \text{ sucres.}$$

Costs would also amount to

$$15 + 15 + (15 \times .6) + 10 + (3 \times .6) + 2 = 52.8 \text{ years of public health}$$
$$\text{costs at } 1,886 \text{ sucres per year} = 99,581 \text{ sucres;}$$

and

$$15 + 7 + (1 \times .6) = 22.6 \text{ years of health cost at } 993 \text{ sucres per year}$$
$$= 22,442 \text{ sucres.}$$

Thus, total health costs would be 122,023 sucres, meaning that after 52 years, the government would save (avoid expenditures) of 1,097,766 sucres in 1985 sucres (the total of education, health, and calculations for descendants). With an inflation rate of 223 % in this period, in 1988 sucres (with estimates by the government of 23 % in 1986, 29.5 % in 1987 and 40 % in 1988), future governmental savings would amount to 2,448,018 sucres (3,147,438 sucres if we use an inflation rate of 80 % as measured by the World Bank for Ecuador for 1988).

In other words, after subtracting the costs of 2,038,000 sucres, *this program would save roughly 140,000 sucres (2,800 sucres per year,* or 840,000 sucres at 16,000 each year if we use the inflation rate measured by the World Bank) *for each woman who chooses to have one fewer child.*

Improvements in the Life and Status of Women: Resources for Education and Investments.

Statistics show that the equality of women in Ecuadorian society exists only up to a point. For women who are intellectually gifted, that point is the third year of higher education. In urban areas, 88,089 men and 77,299 women have received one to three years of higher education. In rural areas the figures are 77,537 and 69,719. However, by the fourth year of higher education and beyond, for every 89,963 men in urban areas, only 49,545 women receive the same level of education. In rural areas the situation is the same — 81,942 to 45,896 (Ecuador 1983, pp. 144 and 177).

We believe that this reflects both the lack of available resources for women and, related to this, the pressures imposed on women over age 20 to accept the social role of marrying, raising children, and taking an inferior position in the labor force.

We believe that one method of establishing the importance of the female role in Ecuadorian society and fulfilling the guarantees established in the constitution for equality and equal opportunity for women is to make this equality a reality by providing the resources that women need in order to improve their status — resources for education (or for investment).

Given that women confront difficulties in receiving the same financial support from their families that their brothers receive, and as we are conscious of women's difficulties in receiving loans or capital advances from banks, financial institutions, family, and other male-dominated institutions in Ecuadorian society, we believe that the best method of providing resources to women is directly by the state.

Social Status.

We note that the inferior position of women in Ecuadorian society is tied both to their unequal access to resources and to the fact that they marry older men. In our opinion, the traditional difference in age between married women and their husbands contributes to the inequality and inability of women to participate as equal members in the labor force. Women living in households where their fathers control family resources and make the majority of decisions leave to marry as young women and enter a situation where, for reasons of age, they are unequal to their husbands. After having a child, the accepted role — and one imposed by their husbands and society — is one in which they lack access to resources (they are tied to the household and do not earn an income) and are saddled with the responsibilities of child rearing and household labor.

From the perspective of economic development, this represents an enormous loss in potential and human resources. The most effective economies are those that identify the individuals who are most skilled — with intellectual ability, new ideas, and willingness to work hard — and channel resources to these individuals. This is directly opposite the path that Ecuador has chosen in respect to women (and minorities and the lower classes, as well).

Access to greater resources during ages 21 to 25 will allow women to postpone marriage and choose more equal mates, as well as to live independently and improve their educational level and have fewer children, something that will also grant them more freedom and opportunity. This will alleviate the double burden of raising children and serving other economic roles in the household (housework, earning extra income for the household in urban areas, or working in the fields in rural areas).

In the long run, the development of skills and opportunities for women will result in an advantageous drop in the birthrate because women who are more highly educated play a more important role in the labor force and usually limit their families to two or three children (Ecuador 1983).

The Role of Men.

It would be impossible to change the social role of women without also changing the role of men. This is difficult for the state to do in any way other than symbolically. (See "Symbolism" in Chapter 7.)

Nevertheless, besides giving resources to women in order to raise their social position in relation to that of men, the imposition of fines on men who abuse their superior position in ways that are harmful to society is one method of creating a new sense of responsibility.

Since we are not able to identify many economic incentives that the government can create in order to encourage men to take a greater role in family planning or the raising of their children, the strengthening of legal rights to paternity suits is one way of making men more conscious of their responsibility in these areas.

Costs.

We estimate the costs of this alternative at slightly more than 15 billion sucres (an increase of 4 % of the national budget). Although this appears to be a large increase, in relation to the enormity of the problem of population and the great steps this alternative would take

Table 1.3 Costs For Development Strategy One

Compensation for women over 60 years old without
   children:
33,600 women x 60,000 s annually   <u>2,016</u>   million s

Compensation for women over 60 with one child:
15,000 women x 36,000 s annually   <u>540</u>   million s

Compensation for women over 60 with two children:
17,000 women x 12,000 s annually   <u>204</u>   million s

Compensation for women 21—25 years old who currently
   have no children:
181,508 women x 60,000 s annually   <u>10,890.48</u> million s

Estimate that 50 % more women (half of women aged
     21—25 who now have children) will decide
   not to have children. This would mean that
   50 % of those who are now entering the age of
   21 who do not have children will not have
   children. This is 50 % of 50,000 or 25,000.
25,000 women x 60,000 s annually   <u>1,500</u>   million s

   Total Costs (1988 sucres)   15,150.480 million sucres

Source: Censo de Pobación 1982 (Ecuador 1983).

toward resolving it, as well as the savings to the government over time
and other advantages for women in the economy, we believe it to be a
worthwhile investment.

Second Alternative: Rural Investment.

This alternative consists of three parts:

1. Channel Public and Private Investment Toward Productive Initiatives by Women (Artisanry, Light Industry and Trade).

Create more employment in the rural sector — particularly for women. This will occur through investment in small business in rural areas — industry that is labor intensive and, where possible, uses locally available materials. (See also the sections on migration and decentralization, in this chapter, where we explain our strategy for distribution of credit and identification of rural industry in need of support.)

2. Reform the Educational System in Rural Areas, Particularly in Regard to Development of Technology and Forms of Productive Organization of Which Ecuadorian Women Can Take Advantage.

Improve the system of rural education, especially opportunities for women. (This can be done using resources that already exist in local areas and that will become available through the decentralization of government functions.

3. Improve the Distribution of Family-Planning Services.

Increase the provision of information and advice as well as the distribution of technology and resources for family planning. Currently, access to these services in rural areas is minimal. (The level of resources necessary to improve family-planning services is minimal.)

Theory and Advantages.

In contrast to the first alternative, with its focus on direct economic incentives to women to have fewer children, this alternative assumes that the problem Ecuador faces is more than just a problem of population growth.

This alternative assumes:

- that the problem of population growth is interconnected with unemployment and underemployment;

- that the problem of population growth is in part a result of great differences in the provision of education, health, and family planning services between urban and rural areas;

• in accord with the first alternative, that economic incentives affect birthrates but also that the economic incentives have to be accompanied by better employment opportunities for women and improvements in the services of education and family planning in rural areas where the birthrate is highest;

• that under the current system, equal opportunities do not exist for productive investment in rural areas as they do in urban areas due only to the prejudices of government which favor major cities; and

• that women in rural areas, even when they have access to resources, will not be able to obtain the education they desire because it is not available.

In order to change this situation, the second alternative proposes that what is necessary is a major investment in rural areas and in small cities. In the past, the majority of government funds have gone to two metropolitan centers — Quito and Guayaquil. Now, however, the country is faced with a crisis — of employment and rapid population growth. In order to resolve this crisis, investment must be directed to rural areas and to small cities. Why is this the case?

It is undeniable that the birthrate is lower in big cities. In Quito, the average number of live births per woman is 3.9 (Ecuador 1987), and in the rural Sierra, it is 7.5. Why is there a difference? This alternative assumes that the two important factors are education and employment opportunities.

The level of education plays a significant part. The national rate of live births for women without education is 8.6, while for women with primary education it is 5.6, and for women with high school education or more, it is 3.0 (Ecuador 1979).

We also find a relation between birth and employment. The average number of live births for women in the labor force in 1982 was 2.2 while it was 3.5 for women who were not in the labor force (Ecuador 1979).

In accordance with these statistics, a program of rural investment that stimulates the creation of jobs for women and improves opportunities for their education would lead to a reduction in the birthrate.

Costs of the Second Alternative.

Statistics for the period between 1972 and 1981 confirm that capital investment in small industry in Ecuador created five times as many jobs as investment in large industry. An investment in small industry of 5.3 billion sucres in capital (1981 sucres) resulted in the creation of 31,600 jobs (Zuvekas 1982). If we convert the 5.3 billion sucres in 1981 to current sucres, using an index of 4.93 (Banco Central), and assume that the same relation between investment and employment in small industry exists today, it would cost 26.1 billion sucres to create 31,600 jobs. In other words, an investment of 825,949 sucres would create employment for one worker in small industry.

If we say that for every two jobs newly created as a result of government investment, one job would be for a woman, and if the government invests the same 15 billion sucres as in the first alternative, this would create 9,080 jobs for women (and the same number for men). For every additional woman in the labor force, we estimate that there would be one fewer child — this would be a reduction of 9,080 births.

To reduce the number of births by 25,000 (which we estimate will occur with an investment of 15 billion sucres in the first alternative), the government would have to spend roughly 45 billion sucres in creating employment. However, the advantage of this alternative is that at the same time, it creates employment for 50,000 people. With approximately 88,000 people entering the labor force annually, this would guarantee a solution to the problems of employment in the country.

An investment of 45 billion sucres would be approximately an increase of 10 % in the national budget; this is not much, considering the results. Recall, too, that this is an investment. We can estimate conservatively that roughly 50 % of the costs would be recovered. Thus, *the real costs would be around 25 billion sucres, and it is likely that these expenses would also create indirect effects* — encouraging the development of services to provide these new industries, increasing national demand, which will spur the growth of already established industries, and so forth. It is difficult to measure the extent of the indirect effects, but there is little doubt that they would be significant.

Complementary Nature of the Two Alternatives

The first alternative has the objective of creating employment — to provide resources to women in order that they educate themselves and become part of a more highly skilled labor force — that is, more attractive to investors of capital and better qualified to make use of their own resources, and also to provide resources that can be used for their own investments or to free them from certain tasks so that they can invest their time in other activities (freeing the resource of labor itself).

The second alternative assumes that in many cases, what is necessary is capital, in slightly larger concentrations and distributed in a more specific manner, for direct investment in the creation of rural industry and improvements in the system of rural education for women. This alternative also would encourage the education and transformation of women into a more highly skilled labor force — and in so doing it compliments the first alternative — because the first alternative provides resources to women so that they can pay for education, while the second develops the educational system itself. The first alternative assumes also that the birth rate can be changed through economic incentives that directly change the status of women. It could be that the two types of investments would be advantageous for different groups.

The second alternative assumes that in order to change the status of women and reduce the size of the family, women must be working; when they are working, their social roles and their use of time are different as a result of their activities. Thus, a more direct approach would be to encourage employment for women in areas where the birthrate is highest — in rural areas.

Statistics show the following: in the course of their lives, women in urban areas have one child less than women in rural areas.

Table 1.4 Average Number of Living Children

Age Group	Urban	Rural
15-19	1.3	1.3
20-24	1.9	2.1
25-29	2.5	3.0
30-34	3.1	4.0
35-39	4.0	5.1

Source: Calculated from Censo de Población 1982 (Ecuador 1983).

There is no doubt that women who live in cities have fewer children, but it is not completely clear what the most important factor is. Is it that women can leave the house and thereby improve their status? If this is the case, giving women a monthly stipend and helping them to attend universities would be the appropriate solution. Is employment itself the important factor? The figures show that the number of children nationally for women who do not work is 5.48 compared to 3.07 for women who do work. Alternately, is it employment outside the house that is most important? In this case, giving a monthly stipend to women in rural areas to improve their lives would not solve the problem. The statistics show that in rural areas, the birthrate for women who work in the home is 5.09, and for those who work outside the home it is 3.38 (ESMIVD 1982). The second alternative would encourage employment in rural industries for women in order to take advantage of the relationship between births and employment outside the house.

Finally, is the access to family planning and education the significant factor? According to Instituto Nacional de Economía figures (Informe General 1979), the global birthrate for women without education is 8.6, for women with primary education, 5.6, and for women with high school or college education, 3.0. Statistics also show that six of seven women between ages 20 and 24 in Ecuador who are students do not have children, and 60 % of those between 25 and 29 who are students also have no children (in comparison with 37 % and 15 % of the entire female population in these two groups) (Ecuador 1983). If it is access to education that ought to be promoted, the two alternatives can complement each other. The first gives women the resources to educate themselves, and the second provides resources to improve the system of education in rural areas.

The assumptions that favor one alternative over the other are different with respect to the cause and effects of having a smaller family. If these factors could be separated, it would be easy to choose one of the two alternatives. However, if cause and effect turn out to be mixed and inseparable, a combination of both strategies would be necessary.

Family-Planning.

There is an emphasis on the distribution of family-planning information in the two alternatives because both assume that the problem of family planning in Ecuador is more than just the lack of social and economic status of women to enable them to demand that their male partners accept birth control. It is a reflection of the fact that many women still do not have information or access to methods of family planning.

We have visited communities, for example, where we heard women express fears about using methods of family planning that were due to misconceptions.

Food Production and Population.

The program of increasing the production of basic foodstuffs (described in the section on food production in Chapter 5) is quite complementary to a population program that uses economic incentives. Each of the two alternatives, and particularly the second, increases rural income. In low-income families (the majority of the rural population), the portion of the family budget that goes towards food purchases is high. With an improvement in rural income, the demand for food products will rise. If this rise is not accompanied by an increase in the production of these products, the majority of the gains from a population program will be lost. For this reason, it is best that the two alternatives be adopted simultaneously.

MIGRATION AND THE URBAN EXPLOSION

Development planners from the industrial centers of the First World and the developing worlds have long held unquestioned the assumption that *development* is synonymous with urbanization and industrialization. For many planners, the guiding theory has been that development was fueled by agricultural "surplus," forcing people off their lands and creating a pool of labor to staff the factories of industry. The assumption in development has been that the "efficiency" of agroindustry and factory production in cities was the essence of growth and that the healthy productive societies were those in which displaced and diverse rural peoples would merge in a new national urban culture. In many respects, this thinking was the same in countries under U.S., Russian, or other influence.

Given our observations, we think there is now enough evidence to prove that assumption wrong. The reality is that one of the key problems in the developing and much of the developed world is the havoc caused by migration to the cities and outmigration from rural communities. These problems touch all aspects of life: in the cities, there is crime, poverty, marginalization, urban sprawl, social diseases, destruction of the family, and emotional tensions; while rural areas experience a disintegration of the community and the loss of human resources, which strip these communities of their best minds, of investment capital, and of resources for education and cultural development, which are at the root of their productivity. All these factors result in an economic loss to the country, a rapid growth in government expenditures in efforts to manage the rise in social and economic problems, and the growth of social tensions that threaten to erupt in violence.

In short, the evidence is that:

- "brain draining" communities of their best minds and recruiting local leaders to the industrial centers, thus assimilating them into the national culture and cutting their ties to their roots and allegiances to their communities, is short-sighted and not sustainable.

- promoting agro-industry and other capital-intensive forms of production in which people lose their land, their other forms of capital, their social networks, their dignity, and their political power can be ruinous in the long run even though overall productivity may increase in the short run.

• More recently, the policies of industrialization — of agrobusiness, export-processing zones, and factory towns — have created new vulnerabilities and social problems. These large enterprises now have the political clout to manipulate public policies through their control of vast amounts of resources and laborers. Enterprises can and do leave communities at will, (often leaving hazards in their wake), causing areas to economically or environmentally decay and giving residents no choice but to abandon them en masse without much potential to develop other economic opportunities in those areas.

The effects of the migration that these policies have triggered are severe and they are felt at a variety of levels:

Effects on the Country

In terms of national security and efficient production, urban migration leaves countries economically and socially vulnerable. The concentration of industry and resources presents a great danger in the case of natural disaster (an earthquake in mountainous regions or a hurricane on the coast) or foreign attack. In addition, the distance between the production of resources and the industry that uses them, results in a loss of income due to transportation costs.

For reasons of national security, the disintegration of communities represents a loss in national experimentation with various strategies at local levels which could serve as models to apply to other communities. Moreover, urbanization threatens the private property, integrity, individualism and pride of every citizen. The flight to cities and the development of large factories threatens to convert diverse societies into masses of factory workers who are homogenized and stripped of their personal differences.

Effects on the Immigrants

Leaving their original communities creates psychological tension because the individual or family loses the assistance and intimacy that the familiar surroundings and community offered. The organization of the extended family insures that each member is included and none go uncared for. With the distance caused by migration, the advantages of economic and emotional support are lost, resulting in the alienation of the immigrant from the means of stability to which he or she is accustomed.

With the high rates of unemployment and underemployment in urban centers, there is a high likelihood of not finding work or only finding a low-level position with a minimal salary. Without the help of the extended family and with few job opportunities, immigrants often find themselves plunged into poverty.

The change that immigrants feel in moving from a rural environment to an urban one can result in a sharp alienation from their surroundings (particularly if an individual comes from an indigenous community where the country's official language is rarely or never spoken), an intense depression (which diminishes the ability to work effectively), and sicknesses caused by changes in surroundings, food, and weather.

Effect on the Community Losing People to the Cities

Communities lose their networks of support, just as do their emigrants, thus diminishing their sense of unity. When the members of a community who are the younger, most productive, and energetic individuals, are motivated to leave because of a lack of means of subsistence or quality education, the community will feel its inability to give its citizens a better life. Thus disappears part of its unity and pride.

In losing its most dynamic individuals, the community is weakened and loses its confidence in being able to resolve its problems and progress. This weakness increases the community's sense of powerlessness; it affects its ability to organize cooperatively, use its local resources, and make claims on central government.

The predominance of male immigrants has resulted in a proliferation of families headed by single women. Although these women may feel a new authority and control normally prevented by the presence of the husband, the quantity of work and responsibilities left to them are overwhelming. Often, the absent male head of household returns temporarily or sends money to his family, but the single mother will be responsible for the raising and care of children, the cultivation of land, attending to the store or business, household chores, and so on. With such a burden of activities, which is often too great to fulfill, the family slips into poverty. Thus, the migration of the husband does not always benefit the rest of the family.

Effects on the City Receiving Migrants

The rapid growth in the cities requires that municipal governments expand the infrastructure in order to tend to the needs of the recently arrived population. The expansion of slums in the peripheries of urban centers indicates that as people arrive, the cities have been unsuccessful in their efforts to efficiently incorporate these areas into the network of city services. Thus, the slowing of rural-to-urban migration would allow municipalities to respond more effectively to the expansion of the cities and avoid the creation of slums.

In large cities, income and living standards of the new immigrants prove to be less than the average for the rest of the city. This is explained by the lower level of education of the immigrants, which makes it difficult to find well-paid work, as well as the scarce resources they have on their arrival, their disorientation and lack of understanding of urban life, and their relocation into neighborhoods in the city where infrastructure and state services are insufficient. The increase in the low-income population threatens the stability of the city and the well-being of the country in general, for the following reasons.

The cities are centers of political organization due to the concentration of people and the existence of well-developed means of communication and transportation. With the ease of organization (in comparison to rural areas), distinct interest groups strengthen. Although the force of such groups contributes to pressures on the government to provide social service and address their complaints, it also can contribute to political instability. As the cities increase in size, the disparities intensify, both in absolute and relative terms: the number of poor and their relative percentage in the population increase every year. With the possibility of organizing themselves, friction between urban classes can intensify. The effect of this increased friction is difficult to predict, but it is probable that it will cause more conflicts between socioeconomic groups. This can lead as much to a resolution of grievances as it can to a riot, thus preventing harmonious and equal development.

At the level of the individual, high rates of immigration will result in the proliferation of crime. It is the conditions that the immigrant confront that lead to crime. The lack of emotional and family support, the difficulty of finding adequate employment, and the tension of urban surroundings can make individuals desperate, leading them to robbery as a last resort. Given this, municipalities ought to first react to the problem with measures of creating more employment or systems for incorporating immigrants into the urban community, rather than with police measures. The budgets of the police, courts, and jails will ultimately increase with the rise in crime, leading to an economic loss to the country that could be avoided by other, preventative types of spending.

It is for these reasons that we reverse the assumptions of previous development planners and follow a different set of policies and priorities, which flow from doing so. In our view, development policies must be oriented toward balanced growth and healthy communities, recognizing the strength of social institutions and support systems in traditional communities and the harms that come from stripping communities of their resources or promoting rapid change. Past policy approaches must be reversed.

Rather than centralize resources in urban areas, a more effective strategy is one of decentralization and linkage — placing resources in local communities and building development upward from within those communities, while creating communication networks between them to increase the availability of intellectual resources and the sharing of useful ideas among them.

This means rooting all the different forms of capital — intellectual and human resources, education, investment capital, health resources, and cultural activities — at the local level in developing countries that have yet to make the urban transformation, and placing them in the hands of citizens with greater authority to oversee and administer industrial enterprises in the creation of a new kind of community in countries that are already further developed along the lines of the urban industrial model.

RECOMMENDATIONS

Education

University Level. We recommend that the Government of Ecuador decentralize the country's educational system, create more provincial universities and offer a larger variety of disciplines in each school. Curricula ought to be reformed in order to teach more practical skills, transfer knowledge that applies to the circumstances of local peoples and aid them in making better use of their available resources. Extension school programs could be established to reach those students who do not have the financial means or desire to move to areas where universities are located.

At the High School Level. The Ecuadorian government ought to reduce the number of students required in a locality to authorize construction of a high school or for implementation of an extension program, as a means of better reaching all youth. In addition to these measures, funds allocated for free school uniforms should be increased for needy families, and the distribution of such funds should be improved.

At the Elementary School Level. Elementary school curricula ought to include discussion and instruction on local history, Ecuadorian cultural diversity, and the current problems which villages and provinces face.

Agriculture

Loans and Assistance. We recommend that programs for offering loans and technical assistance to small farmers be increased and better managed and that the requirements for collateral should be more lenient.

One of the most effective ways of funding promising initiatives in rural areas would be to make public capital available at the local level instead of concentrating it in the hands of central government. We propose a system of provincial banks to replace the Banco de Fomento (with the same capital base) with representatives elected by communities to serve as Directors.

Furthermore, we support the development of alternative private banks at the local level.

At the same time, local financial institutions, including new provincial banks, ought to continue to be subject to audits at the national level. We propose, however, that these audits be conducted through more independent bodies than those that currently exist. (See "Decentralization" in Chapter 2.)

Health

In addition to increasing the budget of the Ministry of Health and the portion of the Ministry's budget designated for outreach and improvement in rural services, we support the establishment of a program of primary auxiliary health workers. (See "Health" in Chapter 3.)

Culture

The House of Culture ought to establish a program of cultural expression in rural areas that will provide funds to villages to establish local museums, to promote artistic exhibits with members of the community, and to develop theatres, public movie theaters, and municipal projects which develop local pride and community identity. (See also "Symbolism" in Chapter 7.)

The Armed Forces and the National Police

The Ecuadorian Armed Forces and the National Police ought to require that half of their forces in each province come from the some province. Several communities have informed us that the loss and emigration of young people was a result of their obligatory military service. At the same time, we have heard it repeated several times that soldiers or members of the National Police lack knowledge of and respect for local needs and traditions. While we understand the importance of the presence of an outside force when local officials defy national laws, we believe that a balance between people from the community and from outside it will increase the respect for public authorities, prevent the emigration of young men from their communities, and improve the ability of the Armed Forces and National Police to understand local circumstances.

Between 1974 and 1982, the growth of population in Ecuador was only 31 %, but the growth in urban population was 42 % in the Sierra and 51 % in the coastal region. The growth in fertility remains highest in rural areas: in 1979, the rate of fertility was 5.5 in the urban Sierra and 6.6 in the urban coastal region, compared to 7.5 % in the rural Sierra and 8.3 % in the rural coastal region. Assuming that the rural population has a higher reproductive rate than the urban population, it is obvious that the growth in urban population was the result of migration. A large portion of the rural population migrates to the cities because of unfavorable conditions in rural areas. (It should be noted that the differences in urban and rural growth rates are also partly explained by the lower death rates in the cities.)

For Ecuador, the situation is particularly acute, not only because of the threat to its extraordinary cultural diversity, but also because of the challenge to its emerging political democracy. Unlike many countries, Ecuador remains a country of individual proprietors. One-third of all economically active Ecuadorians have private capital or are owners or active members in managing agricultural production or private business. Statistics show that 45 % of those in rural areas control their own means of production, in comparison to only 30 % in urban areas (1982 Population Census). The flight to cities and the development of large factories threatens to convert Ecuador into a country of factory workers who have been homogenized and stripped of their personal differences.

As explained in the previous section, it is essential that government address the problem of population as a key contributor to migration and that it do so both in urban as well as in rural areas. El Centro de Estudia de Población y Pataernidad Responsable, (CEPAR) recognizes the conclusion of *Population Reports 84* that "family planning is one of the 'indisputable' measures needed to discourage migration in the long run" (p. 14). If the government is not prepared to initiate extreme measures, at the very least it must adopt a stronger and more progressive approach than it has taken thus far.

At the same time, migration policies must include strategies that promote the economies and communities of rural and indigenous areas. We propose to develop communities into attractive and advantageous places through reforms in several areas.

Education

Many aspects of the school system actually promote migration, to both small and big cities. While the full outline of educational reforms are presented in a separate section, detailed below are particular changes designed to slow outward migration.

At the University Level.

We recommend decentralizing the educational system for the purposes of creating more provincial universities and offering a larger variety of disciplines in each school. The curricula must be reformed in order to teach skills and transfer knowledge that apply to the life of local peoples and encourage them to make better use of their available resources. Extension school programs should be established in order to reach those students who do not have the financial means or desire to move to areas where universities are located.

In traveling through the country and speaking with villagers and residents of small cities, we heard repeatedly that young people have to leave their households to continue their studies at the university level. When the continuation of education requires young people to leave the community, they lose the daily support of their families, while the families lose the labor and education of the children. Worse, once the young people have left they generally do not return, due to a lack of opportunities in their communities in which they can use their newly acquired skills or because they have begun to adapt to urban life. Of the population over age 6 who migrated to Quito, 16.4 % (16.4 % of women and 16.3 % men) left for reasons of education.

At the same time, the concentration of universities in urban areas has created an incentive to students to remain in the cities after graduating. The focus of university disciplines is on urban life and makes it more likely that students will remain in cities. Medical schools, for example, focus mostly on urban health and teach models of medicine that frequently do not correspond to the reality of life in rural communities. These prejudices in medical education and the status given to urban life result in many doctors not returning to their own communities or avoiding work in rural communities where the needs are greatest.

At the High School Level.

The number of students required in a locality to authorize construction of a high school or for the implementation of an extension program to reach all youth, ought to be reduced. In addition to these measures, funds allocated for free school uniforms should be increased for needy families and the distribution of such funds should be improved.

The success of a high school cannot be judged only by reading evaluations, noting its proximity to other communities on the map, or visiting and speaking with teachers and students. These measures are important but do not take into account those people who are not served by schools because they are too poor or live far away and cannot attend. In rural areas, frequently students have to commute to a neighboring village to attend school because the small number of young people in the community does not, in the opinion of the state, justify the investment in providing them with their own school. Although there are advantages in large high schools, such as the opportunity to offer more subjects and a large variety of teachers, there are also several disadvantages to the concentration of educational centers. First, the time that a student spends commuting can be three or four hours each day in the most isolated regions. These hours nonproductively consume the energy of young people who, ironically, constitute one of the poorest sectors of the Ecuadorian population. In addition to the expenditure of calories, the time spent commuting results in a loss of labor for the family as well as a loss of time for study.

In speaking with parents who live in rural areas and have children who are not attending high school, we heard various explanations. In addition to not being able to sacrifice the labor of their children (necessary for the harvest, hunting, or caring for younger siblings), parents noted the lack of money to purchase the obligatory uniforms and the high cost of land and water transportation. They explained to us that in reality, the education is not "free" because of the additional expenditures they must make and the loss of the household help of the children.

At the Elementary School Level.

Curricula ought to include discussion and instruction on local history, Ecuadorian cultural diversity, and the current problems that villages and provinces face.

In promoting local consciousness and the value of unity and importance of their existence as a distinct and integral part of Ecuador, such steps increase the students' sense of local pride. This fosters a concern for the well-being of the community, which can contribute to people remaining in the villages. Out of pride and local concern, people will become more motivated to solve the community's problems within the community itself rather than moving to the cities. Discussing real concerns and seeking answers in the schools can lead to the adoption of solutions in real future circumstances.

Loans and Assistance.

Programs for offering loans and technical assistance and finance to small farmers need to be increased and better managed. We propose a system of provincial banks to replace the Banco de Fomento (with the same capital base), with representatives elected by communities to serve as directors. We propose that the requirements for collateral should be more lenient and we support the development of alternative private banks at the local level.

Many Ecuadorians migrate due to the lack of available land for cultivation. This scarcity can be explained by three major factors: population growth, inequitable distribution, and the lack of technical and financial assistance. The problem of population growth is dealt with by family planning, while the problem of land distribution has been recognized and somewhat alleviated since the Agrarian Reform Plan of 1964. *Population Reports 84* explained that "Agrarian Reform could diminish rural migration 'but without technical and financial assistance for small farmers, new disparities have arisen between large and small farmers'" (CEPAR 1984). These disparities promote the same migration that the Agrarian Reform Plan tried to avoid and again result in the concentration of land in the hands of wealthy absentee landowners. Frequently, we hear that many peasants leave their lands during times of crisis (the droughts in Loja or Manabi, for example). Due to the lack of emergency assistance or technical resources, they sell their land as the alternative for survival. Since the law covering land reform does not prevent the concentration of land but rather the concentration of its use, this presents a large danger for the agrarian sector and for the stability and economic growth of the country. With the increase in lands of absentee owners, the disintegration of communities can only accelerate.

Thus, the extension of assistance is critical for improving the conditions of peasants as well as decreasing their incentives to move to the city. (See "Food Production" in Chapter 5 for a detailed explanation of other assistance programs.)

Many people explained to us that the problem of rural credit for local communities is more a social problem than an economic one. There is a widespread belief in the country that the neglect of small communities represents prejudice against indigenous groups and favoritism of the upper classes (local friends of the political administration and members of the oligarchy). Such a system of allocating financial assistance violates the Constitution and makes a mockery of the country's political system.

In this case, we suggest that merely changing a few restrictions will be inadequate to solve the most basic prejudices against certain sectors of the population. It is well known that the small farmers are those who most need loans but they cannot receive credit due to a lack of sufficient lands to serve as collateral. We see no reason why banks cannot secure their loans with the land that small farmers do have and with their harvest, in which their loans are invested. In the long run, such revisions in credit policies will benefit, not only the peasant, but also the entire country, because they will lead to increased agricultural production and reduce urban migration.

Credit Policies

We cannot confirm the existence of discrimination in loan policies, but the fact is that 60 % of those who live in rural areas are indigenous peoples (U.S. Agency for International Development 1984), and the government's lack of statistics on indigenous groups in the census (an omission that seems unusual to us) and other incidents that we observed directly suggest that this merits serious consideration. In several conversations, we heard Ecuadorians use words like "savage" or "animals" in referring to certain groups of indigenous peoples, while we witnessed bus drivers (of public "colectivos") fail to stop for indigenous peoples. A number of officials told us that the central government insults and mocks indigenous groups shamelessly.

For these reasons, we believe that the best solution would be to place available credit at the local levels rather than concentrate it in the hands of the central government. We propose that these credit institutions be managed by directly elected representatives of the rural communities that they serve.

Several indigenous groups have formed institutions like credit cooperatives because, they say, of the difficulties in getting bank loans. Unfortunately, these cooperatives are undercapitalized and do not have a large impact on development.

Health

In addition to increasing the budget of the Ministry of Health and the portion of the budget designated for outreach and improvement in rural services, we support the creation of a program of primary auxiliary health workers.

One of the advantages and attractions of cities is the concentration and access to medical services, in contrast to the lack of these services in rural areas; this is a factor that can influence migration.

One program in particular that has been successful in the state of Chiapas, Mexico, involves primary auxiliary health workers and was implemented by the Ministry of Health in 1985. Each community elects a member to be the primary health worker to serve his or her village. The worker has to participate in a two month course in the capital, learning to promote basic health and personal hygiene, give injections, and administer primary care and certain drugs. After the course, the worker returns to the village to tend to community health and act as the intermediary between the people and the employees of the Minister of Health. This system of medical assistance offers three advantages to decrease migration. First, the basic necessities of the rural population can be supplied within the villages, with little need to go to the cities other than for the treatment of serious problems. Second, in obtaining medical services from a member of the same village, the community gains confidence in its ability to resolve local problems and improve its way of life. Medical service is not seen as a paternalistic gift provided by the state, but as a function of the community. This promotes self-sufficiency. Finally, the program of community health workers creates employment for a person within the community.

Culture

The House of Culture ("Casa de Cultura") should establish a program of cultural expression in rural areas that will offer funds to villages to establish local museums, artistic exhibits with members of the community, theaters, public movie theaters, and municipal projects that develop local pride and community identity.

We have visited several communities that are beginning museums of their archaeological heritage or recent history, and found there a great amount of community spirit and local pride. The expansion of these centers and institutions creates the cultural stimulus and the recreational opportunities that give young people an incentive to stay in the community and give others an incentive to visit. The expansion of a system of interlinked libraries between regions in order to share books and materials also merits consideration. We have heard a great deal about the lack of technical resources, information, and connection with centers outside the rural areas — a need that libraries can fill with a small investment.

The Armed Forces and the National Police

The Armed Forces and the National Police ought to require that half their forces in each province come from that province.

Several communities have informed us that the loss and emigration of young people was a result of their obligatory military service. At the same time, we have heard it repeated several times that soldiers or members of the National Police lack knowledge about, and respect for, local needs and traditions.

While we understand the importance of the presence of an outside force in cases where local officials defy national laws, we believe that a balance between people from within the community and outside it will increase the respect for public authorities, prevent the emigration of young men, and improve the ability of the Armed Forces and National Police to understand local circumstances. We believe this will also encourage the participation of these organizations in projects of building infrastructure (the construction of bridges, roads, water systems, fisheries in farming communities, etc.) that will benefit those communities.

REFERENCES

Banco Central del Ecuador. *Memoria Anual* Quito: 1988.

Banco Central del Ecuador. *Cuentas Nacionales del Ecuador, 1977-1986* Quito: 1987.

Centro de Estudia de Población y Paternidad Responsible. *Population Reports* Quito: 1984.

Economist Intelligence Unit. *Country Profile: Ecuador* London: Economist Publications, 1987.

Ecuador. *Censo Agropecuario Nacional* Quito: 1954.

Ecuador. *Encuesta Agropecuaria Nacional* Quito: 1968.

Ecuador. Instituto Nacional de Estadística y Censos. *Censo de Población 1982* Quito: 1983.

Ecuador. Instituto Nacional de Estadística y Censos. *Anuario de Estadísticas Vitales, 1986* Quito: 1987.

Luzuriaga, Carlos, and Clarence Zuvekas, Jr. *Distribución del Ingreso y Porbreza en las Areas Rurales del Ecuador, 1950-80* Quito: Banco Central, 1982.

Redclift, Michael R. "The Influence of the Agency for International Development on Ecuador's Agrarian Development Policy" *Journal of Latin American Studies*, 11: 1 (1979): 185.

United States Agency for International Development. *Country Development Strategy Statement: Ecuador: FY 1986* January 1984.

Weil, Thomas E., et. al. *Area Handbook for Ecuador* Washington, D.C.: U.S. Government Printing Office, 1973.

Zuvekas, Clarence, Jr., and Carlos C. Luzuriaga. "Ecuador: A Macroeconomic Assessment of Trends in 1982 and Projections for 1983-87" Quito: United States Agency for International Development (USAID), 1982.

2

Governmental Reform and Community Development

While issues of governmental reform, social and cultural environment, and the protection of indigenous peoples are often viewed as only secondary concerns in current development planning efforts, we see political and social reforms as inextricably linked to economic development. We also see current politico-economic systems which centralize authority and seek to homogenize and rapidly urbanize national cultures, as one of the greatest impediments to economic growth. Efforts in these areas are among the most important components of a strategy of community and national development

Only recently have major development agencies begun to openly recognize the important links between structural reforms in political and legal institutions — concerns for decentralization, human rights, and the protection of community and individual difference — and economic growth, and start to address what are delicate but critical issues of power. However, despite attempts, for years, to avoid dealing with these issues, it is no secret that one of the key obstacles to development is corruption and the abuse of power. Corruption and misallocation of resources, the inability to peacefully and equitably resolve conflicts between different groups, and overbearing bureaucracies threaten development, economic growth, and stability. Effective political reform to protect the rights and opportunities of individuals, communities, and cultural minorities is critical to creating the incentives for innovation, experimentation, and joint effort that underlie the productive use of resources in a stable environment.

Unfortunately, in many cases, the inability of development agents and governments to address these issues has made existing problems worse, since development assistance has often worked to the advantage of existing elites; allowing them to tighten their control over potential competition and weaken or destroy minority cultures within their borders. Indeed, it often makes no economic sense to provide aid to countries without pressures for structural reform when as much as *ten times* what is given may be taken out by the elites of those countries and placed in foreign bank accounts or invested overseas. Such has been the case in many dictatorial regimes in the past — often places where the same leaders are toppled or flee, with little of the money ever returning — and is occurring now on an unprecedented scale in many of the Newly Independent States of the former Soviet Union, with the lesson apparently unlearned. Where the key to reform would be real political and legal change, including real efforts to try to step the theft and outflow of capital by elites, there has been little substantive change in the thrust of development policy.

On the one hand, while development agents have often presented themselves as powerless, the truth is that the leverage of financial assistance, military aid, and moral authority are considerable if they are exercised properly. At the same time, human rights and steps toward "democratization" are now standard prescriptions in the tool kits of government development agencies, but there is often little understanding of what they mean and few guidelines as to how they are to be implemented. An effective theory of legal and political reform lags well beyond the recognition that changes are needed.

To understand the changes that are necessary in developing countries (and in many cases, developed countries as well) is just to work through the basic and simple theoretical principles of efficiency and then to apply them to countries from the level at which they find themselves. The failure of many development agencies is that they simply project existing procedures in wealthy countries onto developing societies, thus limiting the kinds of changes they advocate to minimal and inadequate reforms and often being satisfied with promoting elections and political parties rather than seeking to meet overall objectives. Given the importance of this area of development, its long neglect, and the lack of developed theory, it is worth laying out these principles in some detail.

Most simply, economic efficiency requires a political process that is equally efficient. Not only must government structures be set up to optimally meet particular needs — to address specific interests and problems within a country and place expertise and resources at the appropriate levels — but the system itself must work toward the kind of openness to citizens and their needs that will make it flexible and adaptable. To create an efficient economic system with sufficient opportunity requires a political system that also allows a full expression of preferences, processes for free and fair negotiation of those preferences, equal access to the system, and the ability to enforce agreements and rights.

BASIC CONCERNS

To create economic efficiency requires keeping in mind four overall, but basic, concerns and then applying the basic theories of economics. These concerns are as follows.

Political Accountability of State Institutions

Formal governmental institutions — the machinery of the state — must be efficient and representative. Indeed, they must be reinvented to place the appropriate people and technical resources at the site of issues and problems with the proper incentives to provide services. This is the "supply side" of government — the ability to meet a country's needs.

Accountability of Economic and Other Nongovernmental Institutions That Make Political Decisions

Beyond formal governmental institutions, nongovernmental institutions increasingly make political decisions regarding the allocation of capital, community resources, and environmental and labor conditions. These institutions are considered "private" in some countries (subject only to outside regulations), and "public" in others, though the distinctions and the reasons behind them are often blurred. Establishing mechanisms for internal and direct public oversight, coordination of decisions with public needs, and the applicability of political and economic rights is a matter of concern in countries where large institutions play a major role.

Creating mechanisms for the accountability of economic institutions is most important in societies that are in transition to a market economy (particularly the industrial nations of the former Soviet Union and Eastern bloc) and developing countries that have begun the transition from subsistence economies to manufacturing, export processing, or other industry. In many developed countries that have been lax in holding nongovernmental institutions responsible, these concerns may also be critical. While countries like Ecuador, where much of the economic activity is still subsistence farming, might not need to pay immediate attention to holding nongovernmental institutions accountable as a top priority, accountability is particularly important in institutions that allocate capital (the commercial banking system), as well as in major export industries with large domestic and transnational "private" employers.

Political Equality and Equal Opportunity for Citizen Input

The "demand side" of an effective political system is just as important as the "supply side," since the efficient provision of services must also match public preferences. Mechanisms of citizen participation must be efficient to insure that the preferences of all citizens are heard equally in oversight, decision making, and enforcement. In most developing, and many developed, countries, to do this requires eliminating financial, cultural, informational, and structural barriers to participation. It means expanding the resources available to citizens to participate in the full array of political and legal processes through which decisions are made and implemented.

Cultural Protection

The basis of a politically and economically efficient system must recognize and uphold the inviolability of community and indigenous culture as part of a system of basic rights. In order for individual preferences to have meaning, the basic subunits of community and ethnic differences must be protected from invasion by majorities or by minority interests with greater resources.

PRINCIPLES OF "COMPLETING THE MARKET"

Within this larger framework of structural government reforms, political reforms, and the protection of communities and cultures are a number of economic principles that can serve as guidelines for reforms. Simply stated in economic terms, to make an economy more efficient is to correct "market imperfections" that prevent perfect competition. To do so requires an efficient political system, which requires "perfecting" or "completing the market" in the political arena as well.

The important conditions for perfect markets in political and economic systems are analogous. They are:

• preference allocation mechanisms in which all citizens have equal bargaining power, free from threats or coercion;

• low barriers to entry into the fray of competition;

• minimal "transaction costs" of organization so that the many individuals with small interests can compete effectively with the few who have large, concentrated interests;

• enforceability of agreements; and

• the free flow and availability of "perfect" information to aid in proper choices.

MECHANISMS OF REFORM

The art of political and legal development is to appropriately choose from a full set of mechanisms in each of these five areas. A list of those mechanisms, which can serve as guidelines for developing (and developed) countries, as well as a list of aspirations follows.

Mechanisms for Citizens to Express Preferences

Voting directly for representatives weights all participants equally and is particularly effective in small systems where there is a personal relationship between citizens and representatives and few issues.

Competitive elections through political parties creates conditions for at least expanded choice. Similarly, "best loser" seats, minority districts, or "lotteries" from among voters or announced candidates are means of attempting to improve representation.

Referenda are another method of equal participation for all citizens and generally include the right of citizens to recall officials and to suggest and approve of constitutional changes.

Jury representation is also a method of selecting a valid representative sample equally from all citizens, with an even higher quality of information and decision making than the other methods. Juries can be used not only in several areas in the court system — civil and criminal — in place of the powers of appointed judges, but also in a legislative role and in the oversight of economic institutions. The larger and more complex the political system, the more important are jury mechanisms in administrative functions of oversight and legislation as well as in decision making in the civil law system.

Minimizing Barriers to Political Participation

The greatest barriers to effective political participation are those that deny access to capital. Denying access to resources — money, education, or raw materials — prevents political competition in the same way that it hinders economic competition. Competitive and efficient political and legal systems must not be marketized; in other words, sold or made available only to those with the leisure — the time and money — to run for political office or influence leaders and other citizens. Among the mechanisms necessary to make a political system competitive are:

Equal justice (equal access to lawyers, regardless of wealth),

Equal education, regardless of the parents' social standing,

Equal access to media, regardless of the ability to pay to be heard and independent of the reliance on those who manage or fund mass-communications media, and

Openness of courts to citizens (a wide latitude for standing — recognition of when people can claim to be affected parties — and justiciability — when and at what level an impartial body will resolve an issue — particularly in civil and constitutional courts) who wish to test legislation, constitutional interpretation, and government and private actions against public standards.

Minimizing the Costs for Citizens to Express Preferences

Competitive elections are only one of the potential mechanisms for citizens to organize and voice their preferences in an effort to compete against institutional interests — public or private entities.

Class action suits and wide incentives for rewards to those who institute and win such suits (e.g., contingency fees and common fund recoveries) are important means of minimizing costs of citizen participation.

Giving autonomy and authority to communities and minority regions within decentralized federal systems is an additional mechanism in this realm which allows minority cultures and subcultures to create and protect their independence with their own financial and policing powers as means of maintaining individual differences.

Creating Enforcement and Accountability to Citizens

In a competitive and efficient political system, enforcement depends on neutral bodies, and not on a centralized executive power. The power to make legal decisions, to prosecute the laws, and to uphold standards must be shared with the public.

Jury mechanisms take decision making power out of the hands of appointed judges and place them with citizens.

Openness of courts to larger numbers of civil suits (e.g., giving victims of criminal activities — from anti-trust violations to assaults — the ability to sue on civil claims) and wider rules on standing and justiciability (e.g., through low-level constitutional courts, where individuals can attempt to enforce the guarantees of their constitution), increase citizen participation.

Private attorney general laws, in which attorneys can act on their own initiative to bring enforcement issues before the courts and the public (with the ability to present cases before public juries), act as a check on power and a guarantee that governing authorities, themselves, will be held accountable and that enforcement will reflect the values of the society rather than of the institutions or elites.

Constitutional rights in large organizations must cover workers in nonstate institutions in the same way they cover those working in public bureaucracies in order for those rights to have meaning. Guarantees and freedoms that apply to a worker in one context must apply in all similar contexts (e.g., large private enterprises) regardless of the exact capital source for those operations.

Improving the Flow of Information to Citizens

The key to holding institutions accountable is to establish mechanisms of direct citizen oversight and to open channels of information.

Jury mechanisms — representative citizen groups with investigatory power — can serve as effective watchdogs of large governmental and private institutions as well as a greater means of expressing legislative and judicial preferences. "Grand juries" or citizens' panels within the military, police, political agencies, and large economic institutions can serve as a means of ferreting out information to aid in legal action and improve political decision making.

Equal access to media must be provided to make the mass media available to any member of the public on a random selection basis, upon request, with funds available to citizens for program development as a means of establishing equal opportunity of expression and increasing the flow of information.

•

In incorporating these principles, recommendations for governmental reform and strengthening communities are closely linked with the strategy of alleviating tensions in the country that were produced by the population explosion and rapid migration.

The next three sections describe how this approach can be implemented in a developing country, beginning with decentralization and other governmental reforms to increase political and institutional accountability, next turning to the issues of cultural development, and finally presenting a strategy for the protection of indigenous peoples through strengthening communities and helping them to build the resources to bolster their own rights. These changes all require long-term commitments, with increments at every step following the guidelines above. Each movement to strengthen community, local governments, and resources should lay the groundwork for more inclusive changes to follow.

DECENTRALIZATION AND GOVERNMENT REFORM

In almost all less-developed countries, the issue of governmental reform is controversial and one that most planning agencies and international aid organizations prefer to avoid. Indeed, international development agencies are much more likely to work with the leadership of developing countries than recognize obligations to the peoples of those countries. Most often, it is voluntary organizations and other non-governmental organizations that try to fill in the gaps with their limited resources, making whatever inroads they can.

In our view, political and economic reform, beginning with steps to decentralize authority and strengthen communities, is one of the most critical areas for effective development policy. Decentralizing power is not only a means of providing a challenge to the concentration and abuse of power at the national level, it also represents a tremendous stimulus to initiative and self-reliance. In doing so, planners must distinguish between delegation — in which authority still remains centralized but only its administration becomes more localized — and decentralization, which implies a transfer of authority.

Most former colonial regimes are centralized unitary systems, built on administrative models of provincial governors and other central government appointees, who serve in strict hierarchies. Such systems, which are often based on military authoritarian model of politics, are characterized by:

• weak or nonexistent local governments;

• little separation of powers or overlapping powers at any level;

• no real system of independent audit or accountability to oversee decisions and no citizen watchdog function to prevent or punish corruption;

• a poorly developed civil service system (i.e., professional public servants with technical skills and allegiances to tasks and standards rather than politics);

• weak judiciaries with few opportunities for citizens to institute processes against government or to decide such disputes, and little enforcement through civil actions. In such systems, enforcement is usually centralized in the hands of government prosecutors and police, through the criminal justice system; and

- minimal citizen participation and civic or democratic consciousness.

We believe that one of the first tasks of developing countries (with other potential changes in institutional oversight and access to follow) is to address these deficiencies through immediate governmental and political reforms to:

- decentralize government functions and shift the provision of services, decision making, and administrative authority — with tax and police powers — downward to the grassroots level;

- recognize the autonomy of different regional and ethnic areas;

- redesign the structure of ministries so they can deal more effectively with the tasks facing the country, including those of structural reforms;

- build and train a cadre of civil servants;

- establish independent auditors and an oversight system;

- establish a more open, accessible, and representative court system; and

- begin, to build and strengthen new institutions of citizen participation and see that political processes and government are representative, inclusive, and open.

RECOMMENDATIONS

Decentralization

The government of Ecuador should clearly establish, by constitutional means, independent political authorities at the provincial, municipal, and canton levels. Provincial governments should have the power to initiate projects throughout the province, including the municipalities.

Powers
Each level of government (with publicly elected officials) should have the power to:

• levy taxes and raise funds from any person or organization (with the exception of other governmental organizations) in the form of tariffs, licensing fees, fees for services, and so forth, without the need of prior approval from any other level of government;

• establish its own laws, which meet the needs and address the interests of the community;

• maintain independent police forces in order to enforce local laws;

• initiate programs and provide services in any area — such as education, health, public works, or social welfare — and prepare its own development plans, without the approval of or coordination with any other level of government;

• enter into contracts with other governmental bodies, organizations, and individuals (between provinces, for example) in order to coordinate affairs between regions, businesses, and individuals (but not with foreign sovereign governments) outside the locality or the country;

• elect or appoint judges to hear legal cases on local and national laws, with the exception of those that affect people or organizations outside of that level of government (where that level of government lacks sovereignty).

Transfers

The government of Ecuador ought to establish a national formula for revenue distribution to local governments that adheres to objective standards. We suggest that this formula be based on categories such as the following:

- *the index of nutrition and caloric consumption,*

- *the rate of infant mortality,*

- *life expectancy,*

- *educational level, and*

- *level of median income.*

In accordance with this formula, communities with the greatest needs ought to receive a greater proportion of funds.

The government of Ecuador should establish a system of development banks ("Bancos de Fomento") at provincial levels in place of the publicly chartered national banks at the national level. Directors of these banks ought to be elected from the communities where they are based. (This corresponds to our recommendations for combating problems of migration.)

Elections

At local levels (provincial and below) there should be at least one elected official for every 30,000 inhabitants. At other levels of government where this representation is impossible (at the national level in the election of deputies to the Congress, for example), the authority charged with administering elections —Tribunal Supremo Electoral (TSE) — ought to randomly select, from voter rolls, groups of citizens to serve in public functions (analogous to the selection of jury panels in the United States). These groups ought to have full voting power along with elected officials at these levels of government for a period of service of six months.

The majority of the members of the TSE should be publicly elected. All the employees of the TSE should be chosen through competitive examinations and should be protected against removal for political reasons.

Other Changes

The posts of governor (gobernador) and the administrative representatives of the Ministry of Government (tenientes políticos, intendentes and jefes políticos) should be eliminated. The functions of the gobernador should be carried out by elected prefetos at the provincial level.

Strengthening of the Civil Service System

All the employees of the state with the exception of elected officials, ministers, and officeholders appointed according to written constitutional provision, should be selected in accordance with the procedures of a strong civil service system. Government employees ought to be selected through a process of objective testing that is appropriate to the responsibilities of the positions for which they are applying. Increases in salaries and promotions should be objectively defined by pay and job scales and should be awarded on the basis of quality work, as measured by objective standards. The firing of an employee for political reasons should be prohibited under penalty of fine.

For the appearance of objectivity and for reasons of technical support, the government ought to request the assistance of one or more international organizations in establishing this system. This is particularly important with regard to the offices of the Tribunal Superior Electoral, as well as in the formation of districts and electoral bodies (suggested in the previous section on governmental reforms), and a national auditor (controlaría).

Independence of the National Auditor (Controlaría)

The Government of Ecuador ought to establish the independence of the National Auditor through the best available method. We suggest two alternatives.

First, it can contract with private groups to serve as independent auditors. The Congress can select these groups every four years (for terms of four years), beginning in the middle of the president's four-year term. The compensation of members of this auditing body should include, as an incentive, a percentage of all of those misappropriated funds that they are able to discover and recover for the government.

Alternatively, the government can implement the first alternative but establish the auditor as a public office underneath the Congress, *and completely separate from the process of selection of presidentially appointed officials (generally appointed by the President and ratified by the Congress.)*

Other Governmental Reforms

Ministry of Natural Resources

The government of Ecuador should reestablish the Ministry of Natural Resources with the mandate to preserve the natural ecological heritage of the country for future generations. *In carrying out this task, the ministry ought to have its own police force.*

Ministry of Indigenous Peoples

In order to demonstrate its interests in matters that affect one third of the Ecuadorian population, we recommend the creation of a ministry that will consider the special needs of indigenous peoples and maintain continual communication with the Confederación Nacional de Indígenas del Ecuador, CONIAE, the national federal of indigenous peoples. Only through such direct contact can the government obtain a complete understanding of the needs of indigenous peoples.

Ministry of Fisheries

Due to the enormous, unrecognized potential both at the national and at the grassroots levels, of the cultivation of fish through fish farming, and due to the conflicts of interest that now exist in a ministry that oversees animal husbandry, agriculture, and fisheries, we believe that the government of Ecuador should establish a Ministry of Fisheries, independent of the current Ministerio de Agricultura y Ganadería.

We believe Ecuador is now ready for open discussion and dialogue on the issues involved in the reform of its political institutions. In fact, the new government has invited open debate in this area.

We commend the Ecuadorian people and their elected leaders for their great steps in the last nine years in bringing about a rapid and successful transition from military to civilian government. This is a process that is still occurring, day after day, with a gradual evolution of the Ecuadorian constitution and in governmental institutions; moreover, it is a process that will eventually result in transforming public's aspirations into reality.

Popular Goals for the Ecuadorian Political System

We believe that the Ecuadorian people are united in several of their hopes for their political institutions:

The Desire to Avoid "Velasquismo" — Strongman Leadership Ecuadorian Style — and the Threat of "Populism."

There is a strong sentiment in the country for creating stable and effective political institutions that can resist personal ambition, demagoguery, and symbol manipulation. In part, it is a desire to strengthen a system of checks and balances. There are provisions in the constitution that already try to deal directly with this (the prevention of immediate reelection, for example).

The Goal of Preserving Civilian Government.

President Rodrigo Borja espoused the hope of most Ecuadorians when he told the nation that the Armed Forces should not enter into politics and should remain under the authority and control of elected leaders.

The Depoliticization of Government.

President Borja also expressed this sentiment with calls and promises for honesty and integrity in government. We could not find a single person in the country who would vouch for the general honesty of elected national leaders. We heard complaints everywhere about corruption in government at the national level.

The Demand for a Government That Encourages Initiative and Provides Incentives to Local Levels.

Ironically, most Ecuadorians believe that the stimulus for initiative at the local level depends on orders and decisions that come from above; from central government. Despite the lack of energy from the grassroots, to make these changes, there is a feeling that these reforms are necessary.

The Desire That Government Reflect the Popular Will.

Ecuadorians everywhere express their hope for a government that listens to the needs of the people. A government that is not accountable or responsive cannot hope to be one that will promote economic development because resources will never reach those areas where they can be used efficiently or should be distributed justly to meet the wants of the people.

The Desire for Stability.

The wish to avoid a return to a military regime exists alongside the desire to establish governmental institutions that can balance interests and resolve conflicts. Government must anticipate problems and crisis in advance and act in the interests of all classes, races, and sexes, without favoritism or neglect.

Hidden Dangers in the Existing System

Although the political and governmental system is still developing, there remain enormous gaps between the hopes of the public and the current reality. The greatest danger built into the current system is the concentration of power, which threatens the abuse of power, not only by a single person, but by a party.

Potential for Abuse of Power by a Political Party.

We heard worries in several parts of the country about the current political situation. The concern was not with the specific goals of the Izquierda Demócrata (ID or Democratic Left), the new governing party in 1988, but with the potential for abuse in a system where the majority of local positions, deputies of the Congress, and the President all belong to the same party. Many people told us that they, or people they knew, voted against Rodrigo Borja, the presidential candidate of the ID party, not because they are opposed to his ideas or dislike him personally, but because they feared his victory would encourage a party dictatorship.

Although we have no reason to doubt the integrity or ability of the ID party, in consideration of the Ecuadorian political system from an objective perspective, the fact that the party does possess the plurality of governmental positions makes this fear justifiable for the following reasons.

The Ecuadorian Constitution gives the government the power to eliminate political parties with which it is in competition. In order to be legally recognized and to participate in the public life of the state, a party ought to "uphold basic doctrines . . . in consonance with the democratic system . . . and obtain a set electoral quotient in the elections" (Constitution of Ecuador, part 1, title 2, section 6).

Who will interpret and apply this provision of the Constitution? The Tribunal de Garantías Constitutionales, a tribunal made up of three members elected directly by Congress and eight selected from lists sent by the President (two selections) and the Supreme Court (two) as well as other bodies (four). Thus, if the President and Congress represent one political party, they can together directly pick a majority of the Tribunal. (Note that the President and Congress also select the members of the Supreme Court.)

Who has the power to change the constitution? This power resides in the hands of the Congress. It needs only a two-thirds vote to change the constitution, change the laws, and, if the President is from the same party, enforce the laws.

What remedies are there against Congressional and presidential action? The fact is that if the President and Congress are from the same party, there is no remedy. The Supreme Court is elected by the Congress every four years, with the participation of the President.

Even when the national government does not have the power to eliminate a party, could it still maintain itself in power through the electoral system? It could do so by controlling elections. Of the eight members of the Tribunal Supremo Electoral, which monitors elections and announces election results, one is elected by Congress, two are nominated by the President and two are nominated by the Supreme Court (Constitution of Ecuador, title 4, section 1, article 109).

If the government (President or Congress) violates the law or the constitution, who can prosecute it? The procuraduría general (attorney general) has the power to start proceedings when there is a violation of the law. The Ministry of Government has the right, with the help of the National Police under its authority, to enforce national laws. Both the attorney general and the minister of government are named by, and friends, of the President of the Republic.

Many believe that with the plurality held by the ID party in Congress and a presidential administration from the same party, there will still be splits between deputies and changing coalitions that will eliminate the threat of a party dictatorship.

We believe that in the abstract, a President who serves with a Congress in which two thirds of the members are from his party, or even when at least one-third of the seats in Congress are held by his party, still represents a potential threat to democracy, given the enormous powers of the President and the way in which the Ecuadorian political system is constructed.

The Potential for Abuse of Power by the President.

The President has the responsibility of maintaining public order and has at his disposal the attorney general and the Ministry of Government. More than this, he has the power to "declare a state of emergency" in case of "serious commotion or internal catastrophe." This power to use Public Forces includes the power to establish prior censorship and suspend the existence of constitutional guarantees. In fact, this includes the power to imprison his political enemies — including members of Congress and the Supreme Court.

Instead of, or before, imposing this type of violent control, the President has at his disposal other, more subtle powers. He is in charge of public spending — 400 billion sucres of national budget — which he can appropriate to use for favors and bribes. It is not necessary to corrupt many officials in order to control government. In fact, 28 deputies in all constitute the Plenario, which takes the place of Congress during its periods of recess.

Besides being able to try to convince Congress to change the constitution in his favor, the President has the power to channel funds to areas of the country where deputies and voters promise their loyalty and to punish those who do not. In a poor country, this is a major source of authority. Further, a candidate for national deputy told us without hesitation that in order to win an election for deputy, he would need to spend 40 million sucres. Without independent resources, in order to have a chance a candidate must affiliate him or herself with a strong party and request funds from above.

In order to prevent the misappropriation and embezzlement of funds for the purposes of enriching the President and his friends, there is a National Accounting Office — a body in which the key positions are named by Congress from lists of individuals nominated by the President.

In theory, Congress can legislate against the President, but the President's power to respond is strong. According to the constitution, "The laws approved . . . which are objected to by the President of the republic can only be reconsidered by Congress after one year from the date of the objection" (Constitution of Ecuador, part 2, title 1, section 2, article 69). In reality, the power to legislate against the President does not exist.

In the case of presidential violation of constitutional rights (during a state of emergency), the sad fact is that there are rights but no remedies. The constitution provides the rights of habeus corpus, access to courts, free education, prohibition against all forms of discrimination, and so on. However, as long as the President nominates the judges, where is the remedy?

The Weaknesses of the System Below the Level of Central Government.

The measure of the strength of a democracy is the power that resides in other organizations or levels of government and is available to challenge the branch of central government that abuses its authority. In the case of Ecuador, the only organizations that have the power to challenge the central government are the Armed Forces (military power) and the Catholic Church (moral authority.) In either case, these groups are not representative of the Ecuadorian people and are not accepted as political actors in the Ecuadorian system.

In other democratic countries, there are at least two systems that provide some protection against abuse of power — the civil service and federalism. In Ecuador, however, the power of the President of the Republic or the power of Congress can be extended directly to local levels without opposition. In fact, the unitary centralized system imposed by the kings of Spain five centuries ago — with its anachronistic vestiges, which impede development — has not disappeared despite the liberation of the country by Simon Bolivar and the development of an electoral and constitutional system. As in the past, the power of central government from on high continues to extend all the way down to the provinces, municipalities, cantons and even parishes.

Governors (Gubernadores) are personal friends of the President. (As one governor told us, they are people whom the President has to reward in return for favors) and exercise political-military authority through a system of *intendentes, political chiefs*, and *political lieutenants*. This system exits in order to assure "conformity" with national laws and policy at the local level.

In the province of Morona Santiago, for example, 110 employees of the national government work solely through this form of control under the Ministry of Government and the authority of the governor. In all — including 90 construction workers — the provincial government itself only hires 124 employees. In the capital of the province, Macas, there are only 45 paid administrative employees and 103 construction workers. In other words, in the entire Province of Morona Santiago, there are more central government representatives working in the area of political control (90 administrative employees) and under the orders of an appointed official not from the province than there are administrators working under locally elected officials working to provide services at the provincial and municipal level (79).

Besides control, the role of the Governor is to "coordinate" the hundreds of administrative employees and day laborers working in the province under the authority of central government. In some cases, this coordination means that the provincial government cannot carry out electoral promises to the people of the province or that it has to await the approval, and sometimes tedious clearance, of central government before beginning any development projects.

It is interesting that governors justify their role with the explanation that they are "more objective" than elected prefects, who directly represent their provinces. They maintain that this is because they maintain no political connection with the province, having been sent from outside. They describe locally elected governments as demagoguic. However, while the experiences of other countries with strong local landowners may be different, most people with whom we spoke believe that the truth is exactly the opposite in Ecuador. In villages and provinces with few inhabitants (less than 50,000), people believe that they get to know political candidates quite well. This close link between the people and their leaders, they believe, reduces the potential for populism and diminishes the influence of money such as they claim exists at the national level. They trust more in their elected local officials, who have no power, than in their national leaders, whom they consider corrupt.

As in the time of the Spanish kings, the governors justify their role as representatives of ultimate authority in their power to receive petitions for special favors from people who are neglected by government programs at any level. This is a role that symbolically strengthens authority and dependence on the central government.

Most administrative employees and laborers of the ministries work at the President's disposal. We heard several times of the power of the President to replace officials in all the ministries and to use his authority to fire public employees at lower levels who do not follow orders from above, even when it would violate the exercise of their professional responsibility.

There is a need for an extensive professional civil service system with people chosen on the basis of competence through exams (for their qualifications and not for their contacts or political beliefs), leaving them secure in their positions without regard to their connections or ideology and with the chance to rise and increase salaries through a system of objective measurement of their work.

The fact is that central government controls the budgets of all locally elected governments. The National Planning Administration (Consejo Nacional de Ecuador, CONADE), under the authority of the Vice President, has to approve all local government budgets. It seemed strange to us to see that a budget in a municipal office was sent to the mayor by CONADE.

Half the funds for local government budgets come directly from transfers from central government (51.9 % in 1973, 50.0 % in 1983) (World Bank 1982). According to our findings, this has not changed.

In the province of Morona Santiago, for example, almost the entire budget (an amount equal to the municipal budget of Macas, as well) comes from the central government and is earmarked for specific, predetermined and preapproved construction projects. The role of the prefect, in short, is merely to administer central government programs.

In effect, the prefect administration does not have the powers of an intermediate level of government between municipalities, cantons, and parishes, and the central government at the national level. The prefect level exists merely to fill in gaps in services that are not provide at these lower levels.

At the same time, the distribution of funds from the central to the local governments is at the discretion of the President. There is no objective formula for the distribution of these funds in a just or objective manner. Thus, the President has the opportunity to award his supporters and punish his opponents.

The central government controls the income of all municipalities and prefects. Besides controlling transfers, central government sets all laws on local taxes and licensing fees. All new taxes proposed by local governments must be approved by CONADE in Quito.

Statistics summarizing the relation that exits between central government and local governments are shown in Table 2.1.

Table 2.1 Governmental Revenues and Expenditures (Percent of Gross Domestic Product)

	1973	1983
Income of Central Government	19.9%	17.3%
Income of Local Governments	4.5%	4.1%
Expenses of Central Government	14.2%	16.5%
Expenses of Local Governments	3.1%	3.7%

Source: World Bank (1982), p. 28.

The power of central government rests not only in Executive and Legislative Power which extends down to local levels, but also in the power of the Judiciary. All of the judges in the country, beginning with the Supreme Court, are appointed from above, named by the President, and approved by the Congress. Down to the lowest levels, judges are appointed in a chain starting from above. The result is that more than half, and in some provinces the majority, of judges come from outside the province and lack any understanding of local traditions, cultures, or economic circumstances or the ways of life of the people they are judging.

The protection of individual liberties that exists in other democratic states — trial by a jury of one's peers, for example — does not exist in Ecuador. There are no juries of persons from the same community who understand local traditions or who can sympathize with and interpret actions within their context.

Almost no one with whom we spoke in the country has confidence in the judicial system nor in the system of legal representation. Most believe that both judges and attorneys take bribes, succumb to political pressures from above, and have no understanding of local realities. Only judges and lawyers were in disagreement with this opinion.

Advantages of Our Proposed Reforms

We believe that our recommendations will strengthen the system of checks and balances within an Ecuadorian political context, and at the same time will greatly unleash the potential for economic development.

Separation of Powers.

The best way to prevent a dictatorship or the abuse of power by a party or an individual is to establish multiple sources of representative political power that can balance each other in the political process.

Professionalization. In a recent address at a conference on the Armed Forces, Doctor Fernando Bustamante suggested that the readiness of the Ecuadorian Armed Forces to assume political power in Ecuador in the past was the direct result of the politicization of the government. In his view, the Armed Forces are seen as the only organization in the country with a sense of professionalism and objectivity. The establishment of a stronger civil service system than what currently exists would create a corps of professionals whose primary interest is in carrying out their professional responsibilities free of political pressure.

Independent Auditors at the National Level. The complete separation of the national auditor from the Office of the President is the first step toward accountability of the executive branch. Government officials at local levels told us consistently that *corruption at the national level involved funds that approached 30 % of the entire national budget. The ability to prevent this corruption would in itself be enough to pay off the national debt!* Such a step can be taken only through an independent comptroller.

New Ministries. The creation of new ministries is not only a symbolic act. The establishment of a Ministry of Natural Resources with police powers would result in a body with the authority to challenge other ministries (such as the Ministry of Agriculture) in order to protect the soil, forests, and rivers of the country. A ministry like the Ministry of Agriculture, that has two objectives — increase production in the country and protect natural resources — cannot always fulfill both objectives. We have heard of mines and mining companies receiving licenses in national parks and of the cultivation of land in "protected" national forests. A separation of functions would help to prevent such use of the national resource endowment.

Decentralization.

Those who believe that centralization and "coordination" at the national level are more efficient than decentralization have never tried to receive approval for even the smallest act. Frustration with government bureaucracy has served as an incalculable disincentive to development — particularly to small entrepreneurs and small communities which lack the resources to make constant trips to Quito to receive approval for every decision.

The Power to Raise Funds. The complaint of almost all local governments is that while sources of income to develop their communities exist right in the community, they are unable to tap them without the approval of the central government. Therefore, they must wait several months in order for decisions to be made in Quito.

In other cases, they believe that they already have the legal power to solicit funds — as for example, with the power of governments in the Amazon region to collect a tax of .15 % on corporate capital from companies, such as Texaco, that do not contribute anything directly to the communities in which they are located — but they are prevented from doing so without receiving approval from the central government.

With the current system, it could be years before local governments have the power to impose taxes on the use of local roads or to try to tax businesses for the pollution and destruction of their communities so that they can obtain funds to try to repair some of these damages.

The Right to Receive Transfers from the State That Reflect Conditions and Needs in the Province. The reality that we witnessed in Ecuador is that "those who have, get more, and those who don't have, get nothing." Lacking political power or elected officials from the President's party, some regions are completely neglected. We believe that the best way of correcting this inequality in national development is to establish an objective formula for revenue sharing.

The Right to Conclude Contracts Without Central Government Approval. There are several opportunities for industrial expansion in various regions of the country, of which local governments cannot take advantage due to lack of the power to conclude contracts.

Inter-regional Agreements. As Ecuador is a country with coast, mountains, and jungle, with various climates, soils and conditions, it would be advantageous for each province to form connections with others for their mutual benefit. Some of these ties already exist, having been promoted by central government through organizations such as the Center for Economic Revitalization of Azuay, Cañar and Morona Santiago, and Predesur (CREA), which links Loja, Zamora and El Oro. Other ties, such as improved roads between Ambato and Tena, have enriched all participating communities. The advantage of such links lies in the ability to connect productive areas (agriculture or natural resources) with markets or manufacturing centers.

Other links — between Ibarra and Esmeraldas for example, through improvements in transportation in order to increase trade of products between the coast and the Sierra, or between Esmeraldas and other provinces in order to provide access for exports to world markets through the port — would be advantageous to all involved.

The Power to Form Industrial Parks. Although we do not support all of its activities, in the industrial park in Cuenca we saw a productive use of private foreign capital in a manner that could serve as a model for other regions of the country. The success of this idea in Cuenca required, however, prior approval of the central government, a step that delayed the development of the park as well as the spread of the idea to other regions.

The Power to Make Agreements with Foreign Investors. National laws prevent the investment of foreign capital in any initiative which would prevent majority ownership by Ecuadorian interests. These laws certainly do protect Ecuadorian interests in investments. At the same time, however, laws like these may not reflect the reality in specific cases. An underdeveloped province like Esmeraldas, for example, cannot introduce any outside investment because it lacks the capital that would enable it to provide the requisite 51 % of the funds for a project. The result is that there is little investment at all — local or foreign — in such provinces.

Police Power. Although local governments already have the right to maintain a police force, this power is not sufficient to present a challenge to police powers of the State nor to create a sense of pride and confidence in the way in which national laws are enforced at the local level. The elimination of the position of governor would create a new balance of power and accountability in the Ecuadorian political system.

Local Laws and Judges. The establishment of local laws and judges would create another check against the power of the state and also encourage development through the promulgation of laws and legal decisions that reflect local circumstances. The increase in confidence in the legal and judicial systems would spur development in the sense that they will increase confidence in a fixed system of laws and established norms that are not subject to change by political interests from above.

Accountability of Elected Officials. The great distance that exists between the people and their elected officials (when there are thousands of voters for each office) has resulted in what one Ecuadorian citizen called "formula politics" (personal communication, 1988). In his opinion, there is a "formula" for offices like mayor (*alcalde*) of the biggest cities in the country. For each campaign contribution and for each expenditure made by a candidate on his or her own campaign, if the candidate wins, he or she will receive ten times what was invested, which is returned in the form of embezzlement and kickbacks.

Although we cannot either confirm or deny these rumors, we believe that the election of deputies from electoral bases of 100,000 inhabitants or more can only encourage populism, the influence of money in politics, and a lack of accountability of elected public officials.

Where a close connection between elected officials and the public is impossible (due to the vast populations of large nation-states), we prefer forms of representation that directly place groups of citizens — randomly selected juries, for example — in positions where they can directly express their beliefs. This is why we propose for Ecuador a second level of representation, through a random selection of citizens, to supplement the system of elected representation at these levels.

Given the size of electoral bases in the country, the quality of representation and the accountability of government varies greatly. Provinces, for example, vary between 30,000 (Pastaza) and more than a million (1.382 million in Pichincha). It is for this reason that we recommend the strengthening of local governments at the canton level (cantons currently have a maximum of 300,000 inhabitants, with the majority having about 10,000) and considering a redistricting of other areas to make them more manageable.

CULTURE AND DEVELOPMENT

One of the consequences that frequently accompanies the process of development, and particularly urbanization, is the loss of cultural diversity. Culture defines a population just as it defines its members, by providing them identity and pride in their uniqueness and strategies to fit into their surroundings.

Planners and governments often fail to recognize the inherent value of cultural diversity. Often, they see ethnic groups as relics, representing ancient and abandoned traditions that do not belong in modern life and are not appropriate to the challenges that modern society faces. Actually, however, the protection of all ethnic groups is critical to the process of development.

It is important to protect the undeniable value of various cultures and their contributions.

With the destruction of a culture, its strategies for survival are also lost; strategies that are not only particular to one group but could be adapted by the general population. The loss of cultures is accompanied by a process of cultural homogenization of the population. The lack of diversity that results reduces the ability of the country to respond to change. A good example of the usefulness of traditional knowledge is the rediscovery of grains harvested by the native Andean populations in pre-Columbian times. During the following centuries, the natives were dissuaded from continuing their cultivation and adopted other varieties of grains. Today, the high quality of protein in the old grains and their potential to contribute to improving the health of peasant families, are just being rediscovered.

Culture provides a feeling of identity and village unity, an inclusive environment in which people hope to remain. With the loss of this environment, members of villages have less motivation and desire to stay. Thus, strong cultures help people remain in their villages, while cultural disintegration leads them to abandon them. This is what has led to the rural-urban migration that has characterized many countries' recent development, along with the problems it brings, including threats to national security, the rise in crime, and the increase in marginality within the cities, which weaken political stability. Development does not have to mean urbanization but rather the concern of people in all regions to improve their lives within their communities and cultures of origin, where they feel most comfortable.

The loss of cultural identity is accompanied by a loss of personal identity. These two phenomena affect family dynamics and can result in the weakening of the family. With this disintegration, the government must take on more responsibility in playing the role of socialization and support which, earlier, belonged to the family. Self-respect builds confidence, and generally a personal who is confident can contribute more to society and be more productive rather than having to spend energy dealing with internal confusion. A healthy individual is able to direct his or her energies to outside activities. When the traditional sources of self-respect disappear, the state has to provide them to individuals through means of increasing support for schools and social and cultural safety nets. Programs for encouraging self-respect would solve these problems, but they hardly exist in the developing world. The result of this lack is a visible rise in social problems such as domestic violence against women and children, juvenile delinquency, crime, and drug addiction.

The disappearance of culture promotes the loss of identity for the individual, which results in disorientation and alienation from his or her surroundings. In this state of confusion and insecurity, the individual cannot function as efficiently or be as productive in the society as when there is an equilibrium between the person and the environment. The process of deculturization affects the country as much as the individual because internal problems reveal themselves in one's ability to function with others. Thus, in terms of labor, it is more efficient to avoid a loss of identity, which can only lead to a loss in the level of production.

Democracy rests on cultural pluralism and the ability of individuals to fully express their identities. It is a failure of democracy and development when the process of modernization results in the loss of cultures. In countries that are considered models of democracy, the government should be capable of assuring that the rights of all are protected and include the right to maintain one's own culture. True democracy is a process of inclusion, not exclusion. Thus, the protection of distinct cultures should be celebrated as a victory of a well-managed democracy. When a group cannot maintain its traditional way of life — clothing, dialect, cultivation of land, or child rearing — because of a lack of resources that other sectors of the country control, because of racism that affects the distribution of state services and the administration of technical and financial assistance, and because of pressures from the "modern" sectors (both of the right and the left) for groups to be a part of national development at a cost to their heritage, it reveals a serious weakness of democracy. A country that values the democratic political process also has to value and protect different national cultures.

RECOMMENDATIONS

We recommend that the Ecuadorian government demonstrate its commitment to cultural pluralism and begin its battle against human rights abuses with the symbolic condemnation of genocide against indigenous peoples, which continues de facto to this day in Ecuador.

*   *The Government of Ecuador ought to reject proposals like that made by the Spanish government to participate in the celebration of the "500th Anniversary of the Discovery of America" in 1992, and other events, which follow. Such an occasion would be a celebration of conquest and of the principle of genocide of the Native American peoples who survive to this day.*

*   *The Government of Ecuador should support events like the celebration of 500 Years of Resistance of Indigenous Peoples organized by CONIAE and similar events, which follow. In addition, it should publicize the celebration in foreign countries, not only to raise consciousness about issues affecting native peoples, but also to strengthen the cultural identity of distinct Ecuadorian groups, thus contributing to Ecuadorian development.*

Several highly placed Ecuadorians hold the opinion that indigenous peoples are a burden to development because they have not adapted to the modern world and maintain their customs at a cost to the country's progress. This view could not be more wrong from the point of view of encouraging a diversity of strategies and experimentation as a means of improving the capacity for human survival.

Several types of life-styles and means of environmental adaptation exist today among the distinct Ecuadorian populations. If a major change in climate occurs, for example, not all people would be affected in the same way. Some would adapt better, not only for genetic reasons, but also because of their ways of relating to the land and elements. If there is an emergency and the country loses its access to a resource, such as hard wood, electricity, or oil, the country as a whole will be much better off if there are cultures that employ distinct survival strategies that other groups in the country can copy. Another potential scenario is a change in the international market (for political or economic reasons), in which the demand for Ecuadorian products falls. It could happen that the country will have to depend entirely on internal production. In such case, the existence of various cultures — some that know how to survive solely on the land, others that depend on weaving, and so on — offer a diversity of national schemes apart from the single model of modern industry and technology.

It is this diversity that is a sign of Ecuador's strength, not only as an economy but also as a polity, and that the country must take special steps to encourage and preserve.

The Ecuadorian government ought to reject proposals like that made by the Spanish government that it participate in the celebration of the "500th Anniversary of the Discovery of America" in 1992. Such occasions are a celebration of conquest and of the principle of genocide of the Native American peoples who survive to this day.

One of the proclamations of the new government in its political campaign was its concern for human rights. The most fundamental right is the right to life, something that has been denied to millions of indigenous people during the past five centuries. *Thus, it would be appropriate if the government began its battle against human rights abuses with the condemnation of the mistreatment and, in many cases, the de facto genocide against indigenous peoples, which continues to this day in the Americas.* By celebrating the 500th anniversary of the "Discovery of America," the government is symbolically betraying the Ecuadorian people whose rights it promised to defend.

It is disturbing that Latin American governments have not immediately rejected Spain's proposal but considered it and, in many cases, accepted it. There are two possible explanations for the actions and attitudes of these governments. One is that they maintain the historic vision that Spain brought "civilization" and "culture" to a backward continent and that they welcome that nation for having begun the process of modernization in Latin America. This opinion denies the value of native cultures and their contributions to Latin American identity. The second possible explanation is that the governments reject the 90 % of their populations that are native. Latin American governments, including that of Ecuador, are dominated almost entirely by people who, though they may be of mixed ancestry, are more of European origin than indigenous. Their rejection of their indigenous roots because of the belief that Europeans are superior facilitates the justification of discrimination against the native peoples. This is how the European and mestizo population maintains its domination. Perhaps most important, we perceive both explanations as racist and believe that *the government must condemn the celebration of the "Discovery of America."*

The Government of Ecuador should support events like the celebration of 500 Years of Resistance of Indigenous Peoples organized by CONIAE, and similar events. In addition, it should publicize the celebration in foreign countries, not only to raise consciousness about issues affecting native peoples, but also to strengthen the culture identity of distinct Ecuadorian groups, thus contributing to Ecuadorian development.

While the recounting of the discovery of America celebrates killing, the "500 Years of Resistance" celebrates survival. The Discovery promotes the European domination, while the resistance promotes pride in the Americas. In bringing CONIAE into the celebration, the government hope to unify Ecuadorians under a pretense of mutual recognition of past sins.

The most attractive aspect of the celebration of events like the Discovery of America is the hope for profits, yet, events commemorating the 500 years of resistance also promise financial success. If the government is motivated to partake in the activities of the discovery for financial reasons, it ought to consider the multiple possibilities for profits and other advantages that can accompany the resistance celebration.

- *Tourism* — CONIAE is in contact with various foreign organizations with mutual efforts to organize and publicize this event in Ecuador.   If the government works with them in programming regional festivals, fora for discussion, and exhibitions in archaeological sites, they could attract tourists, scientists, politicians and artists from across the world.

• *International Links* — The celebration can serve as an information network and exchange of ideas. Calling attention to Ecuador and its historical riches would also result in increasing international funds for excavating and preserving Ecuadorian ruins and archaeological sites.

• *Political Gains* — In leading this celebration, Ecuador would be recognized as a world leader in the fight for human rights. This fame would increase respect for Ecuador in the international community. It would also help to strengthen the reputation of Quito as an international and intellectual city.

In addition, there should be an ongoing revision of history that includes the role and contributions of cultures native to America. There should also be a recognition of the physical and cultural destruction of indigenous peoples that began with the Conquest, continued with Independence, and continues in more subtle forms today. The history that is taught in schools ought to include these tragic truths and the significance of native cultures for Ecuadorian development.

These goals will help to strengthen the unity and identity of the country's distinct cultures. Through the celebration of the resistance, the diverse Ecuadorian populations will gain a deeper appreciation for the country's cultural variety and, perhaps, attempt to protect it.

INDIGENOUS PEOPLES AND DEVELOPMENT

While the ideal development strategy would be to preserve local cultures as they are, the reality for most of the world's remaining indigenous cultures is that they have already had contact with the larger society and are being absorbed into national and international life. Even where there are laws to protect them, the laws themselves prove inadequate when indigenous peoples find themselves sitting on resources or territories coveted by groups with greater power.

Sadly, the strategy most likely to protect indigenous peoples is one of compromise — an approach that helps buffer their traditional values against the needs of the larger economy and enables them to generate the resources needed to create their own basis of power. It is one of the unfortunate ironies that in order to best protect their differences, they must choose a strategy that commercializes their unique attributes and uses them to compete in the world economy. One of the best ways to save cultural differences is to take advantage of the economic benefits that these cultures have over others and to develop them even more strongly in dealings with the outside world.

In studying one highly successful indigenous group in Ecuador — the Otavalans of the Ecuadorian Andes — who not only have preserved their traditional language, dress, and ceremonies but also has acquired economic and political power — we note a number of strategies that mark their success and might be copied by other groups.

Five factors that have been critical to their success are:

1. Use of a dual economic strategy to combine traditional subsistence farming with secondary sources of income, as part of a relationship that strengthens both the local and national economy and serves as a political buffer;

2. Building on a traditional skill in which one has a competitive advantage over other groups;

3. Targeting a particular market niche;

4. Producing goods that are useful as well aesthetically pleasing, rather than simply decorative or of stylistic value, so as to reach a larger market; and

5. Using a production process requiring little capital investment, which allows for production in the households of even poor *campesinos* (peasant farmers).

In applying these factors, it must be remembered that these are a means — to the goal of trying to protect cultural integrity — and not an end in themselves. The measure of success is not how well an indigenous culture can compete in the world market and how many resources it can accumulate. To do this is to merely mimic and adapt the processes of the outside world. The real measure is how well an indigenous group can minimize its participation in these activities and shield itself from the processes of globalization; how well it can use its knowledge of the outside world to restrain its influence.

RECOMMENDATIONS

General applications by indigenous peoples of strategies to build on their strengths, increase their resources, and bolster their autonomy through economic and political power include the following:

• *Groups (including the Otavalans) should survey foreigners as well as the Ecuadorian market, to discover new market openings. Knowing and understanding changing tastes in the Ecuadorian and international markets is, possibly, the single most important factor in producing goods that will target a specific niche and generate sustained income over time.*

A well-known case in point is the Panama hat industry in Azuay, which is estimated at some $8 million annually. The weaving of Panama hats was suggested by an outsider who recognized the tremendous market potential of this item and the special craftsmanship in the region.

• *Indigenous groups should seek others with experience in similar projects so as to learn from their experience. The U.S. Agency for International Development program that is sending Otavalan, Saraguran, and Salasacan representatives to trade suggestions with the Navajo people of the United States is a prime example of this type of cooperation.*

Given the combination of the Otavalans' combined fame for their entrepreneurial spirit and proud adherence to their traditional dress, we chose to investigate them as a potential model for other groups. After hearing the Otavalans' own reports of what they consider their success in making economic progress without losing their culture, we describe how they have relied on five key means of increasing their resources while protecting, as well as possible, the unique attributes of their heritage. We believe that this approach can be applied to other Ecuadorian groups as well.

Dual Economic Strategy

Rather than being drawn away from their lands and into textile factories in cities, Otavalans used their skill in weaving to develop their own cottage industry, using traditional patterns and techniques and improving them to meet the demands of the market. In doing so, they have combined subsistence farming with a secondary source of income, and they continue to own both their farms and their manufacturing equipment.

Build on a Traditional Skill in Which One Has a Competitive Advantage over Other Groups

Otavalans' unique attribute has always been their weaving — the ability to produce bright patterns and quality fabrics. Producing their traditional clothing, now modified for sale to non-Otavalans, has allowed them to maintain pride in their traditional skill and dress while producing it for sale, competitively, on national and international markets.

Target a Particular Market Niche

For the Otavalans, their savvy in marketing led them to produce specialty items that appeal to wealthy customers, as well as to make adjustments when economic circumstances warranted, to produce moderately priced textiles as well. Part of their success was that they remained in control of their own marketing, inviting purchasers to their village markets (which they developed as a tourist attraction and thus generate further revenue) and themselves traveling to urban centers to sell their own products.

Produce Goods That are Useful as Well as Aesthetically Pleasing

While some artisans are content to merely produce decorative items or locally used items (traditional cookware or instruments) that foreigners purchase as art objects or oddities but have little other use to buyers, the Otavalans produce items that can be used: hats, sweaters, blankets, and bags. When needs change — for lighter weight versus heavier weight or different sizes, cuts, or styles — the Otavalans have been able to adapt while maintaining the basic integrity and style of their products.

Use a Production Process Requiring Little Capital Investment

Such a strategy allows for production in the households of even poor peasant farmers.

•

Otavalo -- A Case Study

What follows is a case study of Otavalo and a discussion of adaptations of their strategy to the needs of several other Ecuadorian indigenous groups.

We spent several days in Otavalo interviewing many of the local artisan store owners, as well as most of the vendors in the Saturday market of August 6, 1988. We then traveled to nearby Peguche, where many of the products are made, and there interviewed most of the store owners, as well as several individual producers.

Present Economy. While traditional industrial development favors large-scale industrialization, the Otavalans have chosen to maintain a strategy of primarily cottage-based industry for their artisan production. The majority of the Otavalans work in one of two general production arrangements.

Many of the local store-owners in the city of Otavalo, as well as some of those who come in from the *campo* (countryside) for the weekly Saturday market, obtain their products by providing certain of the *campesinos* with the materials and then paying them for each item produced. Usually, this mode of production is supplemented by products that are made by the store owner's family.

Most other Otavalans (we think this is the majority, although our research has been too limited to be conclusive on this point) work in groups of five or ten families — often extended families — which work together as equal partners. Each family generally specializes in one product, such as tapestries or sweaters, and all the products are sold together in a common store or in the Saturday market. Some of these groups sell directly to other dealers who then market the goods in Quito, Europe and the United States. Sometimes, the production is arranged so that each family works in its own house, while other groups have begun using one location as a common workshop.

Quite a few of the Otavalans who either have stores in which to sell their goods or possess large stands in the market have begun selling sweaters made in Cuenca and in Peru. While the vast majority of the Otavalans seem to be involved in one of these two means of production, a few still produce one good within their own household and sell directly to businesses without cooperating with other families.

The Industry's Origin. The Otavalans have been recognized for their weaving ability since pre-Incan times. In 1917, however, the Otavalans began producing imitation tweeds, known as *casimires*, with which they were able to undersell expensive European imports. (Salomon 1973, pp. 442—43) At the time, most Otavalans were working in subsistence agriculture, weaving products for their own families and working on *haciendas* (plantations) to earn a small cash income. By marketing textiles made in their own households, they could earn enough income that it was no longer necessary to make the trips to do arduous, underpaying work on distant *haciendas*. Consequently, they were still able to spend time at home and continue to devote a great deal of time to agriculture (Buitrón and Collier 1971, 160—64). Thus, by employing this dual strategy of subsistence agriculture and artisan production, the Otavalans were able to maintain their traditional, agriculturally based life-style.

Future Trends. Recently, the Otavalans' international marketing of hand and loom-made blankets, sweaters, bags and belts has been supplemented by the machine manufacturing of certain items, such as hats and sweaters, targeted for lower-middle class Ecuadorian and Columbian markets. This introduction of machines, as well as of the additional targeted markets, suggests that in the next decade, some of the Otavalans may establish factories and move away from the decentralized cottage industry. At present, most Otavalans attribute the lack of factories to the lack of capital — a factor that is accentuated by the trend of economically successful Otavalans going into international marketing of the specialty crafts rather than investing in the production of goods for broader markets within Ecuador. In addition to this absence of investments, most Otavalans still take a great deal of pride in their hand and loom-made products and seem very reluctant to abandon this tradition in favor of lower-quality goods. This sentiment, combined with the cultural emphasis on economic independence and autonomy, further slows the emergence of large-scale production. Nevertheless, as land pressures grow, we expect that factories will begin to appear.

Effects on Traditional Otavalan Culture. Most important, despite the certain changes that have undeniably occurred in their culture, the Otavalans still maintain immense pride in their heritage. Virtually all the Otavalans we interviewed see being Otavalan as a vital component of their identity as well as being responsible for what they see as the success of the Otavalan *artesanía* (handicrafts) market. They realize that changes in the culture are taking place, but most individuals with whom we talked saw themselves as preserving the culture, even if others are not.

The most significant change in the traditional way of life seems to involve a very definite shift away from agriculture. Although most of the inhabitants of Peguche — a small village near Otavalo, where many of the *artesanía* products are made — still live on small plots of land, where they grow food for their own consumption, agriculture now plays a much smaller role in the life of most Otavalans than in the past. In 1973, Frank Salomon wrote that "the commitment to land is fundamental; other involvements in larger systems 'succeed' only insofar as they enhance and protect the family holding" (1973, p. 423). He indicated that one of the main ambitions of the Otavalans involved in *artesanía* was to acquire capital to buy more land. Today, however, it seems that goal has changed. In interviewing several Otavalans, both in the Saturday market and in Peguche, we found that at present, virtually no one is aspiring to buy more land. When asked why they were no longer trying to do so, most Otavalans explained that, first of all, there was no more land available. As the population has increased, plots have been divided into increasingly smaller shares and every piece of available land has been utilized. Here, we see overpopulation as probably the single most important factor forcing the Otavalans further and further away from their original cultural emphasis on land holding. Whether they like it or not, they are being forced to participate more and more actively in the market economy.

Another frequently mentioned disincentive to seek more land is the difficulty of making significant profits from agricultural products. Price increases are generally unable to keep up with the rate of inflation, and the sale of agricultural goods cannot match the regular income gained by the sale of *artesanía*.

As further evidence of the decrease in emphasis upon the ownership of land, we found that many of the dealers in the Saturday market had moved from the *campo* into town. Of 30 textile vendors interviewed in the Saturday market on August 6, 1988, 9 now lived in the town rather than the surrounding countryside or villages. Most had moved for reasons of economic necessity or convenience. While they claimed to miss the room and "comfort" of the *campo* , some felt it was worth the change for the sake of being able to easily run down the street to buy something in a store. Others, however, said they preferred the *campo* overall but were forced by the economic conditions to live in the town. This shift undoubtedly represents one of the most significant changes of this century in the traditional Otavalan culture. It is undeniably unfortunate but seems to be inevitable, given the land pressure due to population. Indeed, rather than evidence of decline, this may indicate the success of Otavalan culture; Otavalan population is growing and the culture now consists of agricultural and urban Otavalans.

In place of land as an economic goal, most respondents said that education for their children was their main objective. Although they did not specify exactly what level of education they wanted for the youth, it was a nearly unanimous goal to educate them. Showing a definite inclination toward Western culture, many mentioned radios and televisions as some items for which their savings would go, after education. Sounds of radios and televisions emanating from nearly every Peguche household on a Sunday afternoon clearly indicate the popularity of these items.

As the most noticeable evidence of their pride, the Otavalans have worked to maintain their traditional dress as a clear sign of their identity. Throughout the country, as well as in several foreign countries, it is not uncommon to see traditionally dressed Otavalans undisturbed by the predominance of Western dress in many of the circles where they conduct their business. Despite this remarkable trait, a number of Otavalans have begun wearing conventional Western clothes. Most who did so explained that the traditional clothing, such as the poncho was too expensive now to be affordable for everyday wear. Others, however, have abandoned items such as the traditional shoes simply because they prefer Western tennis shoes. Some parents with whom we talked had their very young children wearing jeans or sweatpants simply because the traditional white pants would get dirty too quickly. Most of these people plan for their children to wear the traditional clothes as they become older and no longer play in the dirt so often. This final example seems to us to be an excellent example of the Otavalans choosing for themselves how best to integrate the two cultures.

   Overall Success. For the most part, Otavalans seem to view themselves as choosing the changes that are currently taking place in their culture rather than as having their way of life forcefully destroyed by outsiders. Consequently, we see Otavalo as a culture dynamically adapting on its own terms to the changing conditions around it. As the most important evidence, we cite the strong Otavalan pride, which demonstrates that, regardless of certain material changes that are taking place, the sense of identity — which is one of the most valuable contributions a culture can make to an individual — is still very much a part of nearly every Otavalan's life.

   It seems clear to us that Otavalo has developed, while still maintaining much of its sense of culture. Further, it seems quite evident that the continued presence of this heritage as a prominent factor in most people's lives has, in turn, contributed very positively to the furtherance of this developmental process. As a result of this evidence, we feel that despite some changes that are currently taking place, Otavalo does offer a valuable model for other groups to adapt to their own situation.

•

Other Adaptations

   We propose several potential implementations of the Otavalan strategy for other Ecuadorian groups in two of the country's three ecological regions — the Sierra and the Amazon.

Sierra

   The *Saragurans* should investigate using their metalworking skill to expand from the production of *topos* (ornate pins) into silverware, bracelets, broaches, pendants, belt buckles, and other small metal items. These products could be effectively marketed to tourists as well as to many Ecuadorians and would require little further investment, given their current production of pins.

The *Salasacans* already have a healthy start in the textile industry. Perhaps they should stimulate their sales by establishing a market such as Otavalo's, which would attract more tourists. Another major factor that we noticed in Salasaca is that there seems to be much less cooperation among producers than in Otavalo. Having several families work together allows for greater specialization while also providing a more efficient marketing method than having every household work to sell on its own. There is already at least one cooperative established precisely for this purpose, but we think it is important to also encourage smaller groups, such as half a dozen families, to work together on a less complex basis than a cooperative.

Some of the many groups (including the Otavalans) involved in textiles should look into other products such as ties, socks, a wide variety of shirts, and so on. Cotton products, in particular, are difficult to find, even though the Otavalans were producing them in pre-Incan times.

Groups, such as the *Saragurans* and the *Quichua of Pastaza*, with experience in ceramics should diversify and market their production so as to include specialty items such as dinnerware, vases, and jewelry boxes.

Oriente (Amazon)

• Groups such as those around Puyo with experience carving balsa wood should expand from simply decorative birds to include children's toys, such as toy sailboats, as well as other decorative animals, such as butterflies and alligators. Some diversification can be important: a customer is much more likely to buy two different balsa products than two balsa birds.

• The *Shuar* should use their woodworking experience to expand from the marketing of only *chicha* (fermented yuca) bowls to making jewelry boxes and ornamental chests as well as a wide range of dinnerware. Such finely crafted items would be highly attractive to many Ecuadorians as well as tourists. Further, such production could encourage the Shuar to grow their own trees for the purpose. While we believe that the Shuar make sound ecological use of their land, we think this project could be well integrated with agricultural production to protect the land of the Oriente and stem the ecological destruction of the region.

Many groups from the Oriente have a great deal of knowledge concerning the medicinal, cosmetic, and nutritive value of many plant species of the region. The markets for these goods should be investigated and utilized by the groups themselves (with the help of intermediaries) rather than waiting for outsiders to come in and monopolize the profits by taking native crops and knowledge elsewhere.

REFERENCES

Buitrón, Aníbal, and John Collier, Jr. *El Valle del Amanecer* Otavalo: Instituto Otavaleño de Antropología, 1971.

Salomon, Frank. "Weavers of Otavalo" In Norman E. Whitten, Jr., ed. *Cultural Transformations and Ethnicity in Modern Ecuador*. Chicago: University of Illinois Press, 1981.

World Bank, *Ecuador*, 1982.

3

Using the Full Potential of Human Resources

The Romans' adage for a healthy society — "Sound mind in a sound body" — has, after two millennium, yet to become an accepted maxim or standard of development planning, or even of policies in developed countries. In the development community, World Bank plans for the funding of public infrastructure, for example, continue to identify human capital investment as being of lesser importance than investment in massive technologies, with their often disruptive social, economic, and cultural consequences. Building schools or hospitals still meets the standards of "public investment" set by outside lenders in World Bank policies, but student loans for higher education or subsidies to farmers to grow foodstuffs for nutrients, rather than addictive products like tobacco or narcotics, do not.

A healthy set of development priorities places a country's people — its labor force, its consumers, and its decision makers — ahead of machinery, economic sectors, or the existing institutional entities (government or business enterprises) and the needs that they identify for their own growth.

The measure of development in any society is the effectiveness by which that society maintains its communities and allows individuals to participate in voicing their own full set of preferences — not only consumer preferences and choices about work and working conditions, but also larger political, economic, and social choices. Unfortunately, it is from this range of choices, which by definition should be entered alongside other preferences in economic models but have not, that most individuals in developing countries have been excluded. While participation may be greater in developed countries, its scope and substance continues to be limited as well.

The ultimate goal of development efforts is a healthy and content populace that is actively pursuing the path it perceives as best for its own future. That is why we place this chapter third in this work, and ahead of discussions of government and institutional operations.

The previous chapter focused on community development and citizen participation as requisites for efficiency. This chapter focuses on what is essential to make that work — individuals need the education, skills, and energy to fully participate in their communities and contribute to their productive growth.

EDUCATION

More than anything, the future of a society depends on the next generation's skills, abilities, creativity, initiative, ability to solve problems, and courage to be persistent and not give up in the face of difficulty.

While most studies of development focus on skills training and the relation between education and specific jobs in society, they neglect giving equal consideration to the creation of attitudes and strategies of self-reliance, independence, and adaptability, which are as important if not more so. In our opinion, it is useless to have one focus without the other.

The issues facing developing countries are no different than those facing any other society seeking sustainable growth, be it a rural or an industrial nation. In fact, part of the problem facing developing countries is that they have adopted methods of education from industrialized nations; which are poorly suited in both places. Such methods, unfortunately, often serve as means of effectively warehousing young people until they are placed in the labor force or as a means of socializing them to be obedient as future employees in large organizations rather than confident innovators, owners, and participants in the economic and political decisions of a healthy society.

At the same time, the problems of education are not limited to the formal institutions of schooling. As societies develop, not only do they replace the family with public schools as the means of socialization and skills training, they rely on other institutions to serve these purposes as well. The inability, or unwillingness, to use alternate media effectively for educational purposes rather than to promote consumption or social control seems to affect societies at all stages of development, albeit to different degrees.

Overall, we believe that a dynamic educational system promoting economic growth must achieve several different goals. It must:

• encourage community pride in traditions and culture rather than seek to replace identity with a single standard;

• promote equal opportunity through equitable funding for all young people, regardless of accidents of birth. In industrial countries like the United States, the difference in funding between rich and poor children is as much as three to one. In many Third World nations, it is even greater;

- create stronger links between the community and schools so as to gear the educational process to real involvement in understanding and addressing community problems and to slow the process of brain drain, through which future community leaders are encouraged to migrate. In part, this requires attention to the curriculum, and in part it requires recognition that it is equally important to decentralize resources for schooling — from elementary school to professional education — to keep people close to their communities and make educational institutions a center of community life;

- revise teaching methods so as to recognize learning and individual development as the primary goal and essential stimulus to innovation and productivity, rather than uniformity, social control, and the creation of an undifferentiated national culture. In many multiethnic societies, building a national ethic is an important goal to prevent fragmentation, but the process must not be allowed to continue to the point where it begins to erode community pride and individual expression; a problem that seems to be occurring in societies regardless of their level of development; and

- recognize the role of mass media (and school curricula) as a form of public communication that should be more broadly open to public rather than commercial access and should serve a primary function of education and communication rather than entertainment or social control.

While many of these goals are too difficult to achieve in a single plan and would require a complete restructuring of the society, there are several steps that can reasonably be taken in the short run without a major struggle or dislocation.

RECOMMENDATIONS

Encourage Initiative and Self Reliance Through the Educational System

The government of Ecuador should establish special programs to train existing and future teachers in educational techniques and particular skills. Training should include the following skills:

- how to design an exam that does not require the memorization of facts but the solution to new problems and the use of skills;

- how to prepare an exam that another teacher can correct without knowing anything about the students in the class where the exam is taken;

- how to ask students questions for which there are no established or prepared answers and encourage students merely to express their opinions and think for themselves; and

- how to prepare students to ask questions and generate lists of ideas and possible solutions to a given problem instead of seeking one "correct" answer.

If there are not enough teachers in the country who already have these skills, or if it would be difficult to identify them, the government should request the assistance of a foreign assistance organization, such as the U.S. Peace Corps, which was founded in the 1960s to provide educational assistance to lesser developed countries.

In order to make the best use of Ecuadorians' own experience and to introduce students to new methods that have been successful and people who can serve as role models, the government of Ecuador should invite those individuals whose earnings from their own businesses have grown more than 200 % (in real sucres) in the last five years to spend five days in universities or high schools, speaking with students, answering questions, and giving lectures about their experiences. In exchange for this, they ought to receive a 10 % rebate on their taxes and the option to receive this reduction in exchange for five days of service in every year in the future.

Improve Distribution of Technical and Basic Education

The government of Ecuador should follow the models of several private stations in Ecuador in the presentation of educational programs and should prepare more radio and television programs for presentation on public and private stations.

REPORT

The Problems of Education

The problems of the educational system in Ecuador are a secret to no one. One needs only enter a classroom or pass by a school to find the following.

Students in high schools can remember dates of conquests in Ecuador's history but know nothing about:

• the current strength of the Armed Forces in the country and the relation that exists between civilian government and the Armed Forces;

• the history of most of the indigenous groups in the country, the record of their assimilation and exploitation, or the history of their own communities and a knowledge of the groups who live there;

• the role that the Catholic Church and missionaries play in politics and in Ecuadorian society;

• the economic and political power held by oligarchies, nationally and in particular regions;

• the conditions that exist in Ecuadorian institutions (prisons for instance);

• how to use the justice system;

• how to write applications for loans and to weave their way through the Ecuadorian bureaucracy; and

• how to manage a small business.

Students study English but cannot speak more than five words because no one taught them how to construct a sentence and they have only memorized words. Students shout in unison in response to their teachers in order to memorize a predetermined answer to every question. Overall, students sit in silence and never ask questions of their teachers or visitors; they only await instructions, orders and doctrines to memorize.

Education in nationalism seems to supercede everything else. Primary school students do not draw or sketch but paint in presketched pictures of white children carrying Ecuadorian flags. Children dress in military uniforms, carrying toy rifles for school ceremonies. Students in uniforms as if in military service never even think to ask why they cannot choose their own clothing or present themselves as individuals. Moreover, children not in school during school hours often cannot attend due to lack of resources to buy uniforms or money to buy a notebook or a text.

For many, the content of their education seems almost totally unrelated to their needs. Students in small communities are totally bored with the curriculum imposed on them (having been standardized in Quito), which is taught by teachers who come from outside the community. Students study only to receive good grades, not learning a single skill that they can use in their own communities but rather spending their days manipulating symbols that have no meaning to them, merely for the opportunity to leave their communities and live in the cities. High schools in rural areas make students sit, shut off from the world, in classrooms, without the opportunity to practice or learn practical skills in workshops or visit institutions of their country.

Artificially separated schools for boys and girls are due to false notions that co-educational schools promote promiscuity. In some cases there are high schools where, in the same building, girls are educated in domestic tasks and trained to fill anachronistic roles (sewing and cooking) while males are prepared for a more active life.

Higher education is similarly lacking. Libraries in, for example, medical schools of 7000 students may have a capacity for only 100 students (1.5%). "Free" education in medical schools means that students must buy books amounting to 75,000 sucres each year (four months of minimum wage). Moreover, in the educational system for doctors, hundreds will fail an exam after their first year and be given no chance to take another, nor allowed to use any of the skills they learned during the course of that year, despite crying needs for health care in rural areas.

Education for Initiative

Correcting most of the problems that currently exist in the educational system in the country is a matter solely of the will to change and to invest resources. To create a system that encourages initiative and produces students who are confident and self-reliant — the most important qualities for economic development — the solution is more complex but still worth trying. Among other possible alternatives, we recommend these steps in order to focus on this problem.

The government of Ecuador should establish special programs to train existing and future teachers in educational techniques and particular skills. Training should include the following skills:

• how to design an exam that does not require the memorization of facts but the solution to new problems and the use of skills;

• how to prepare an exam that another teacher can correct without knowing anything about the students in the class where the exam is taken;

• how to ask students questions for which there are no established or prepared answers and encourage students merely to express their opinions and think for themselves; and

• how to prepare students to ask questions and generate lists of ideas and possible solutions to a given problem instead of seeking one "correct" answer.

If there are not enough teachers in the country who already have these skills, or if it would be difficult to identify them, the government should request the assistance of a foreign assistance organization, such as the U.S. Peace Corps, which was founded in the 1960s to provide educational assistance to lesser developed countries.

In order to make the best use of Ecuadorians' own experience and to introduce students to new methods that have been successful and people who can serve as role models, the government of Ecuador should invite those individuals whose earnings from their own businesses have grown more than 200 % (in real sucres) in the last five years to spend five days in universities or high schools, speaking with students, answering questions, and giving lectures about their experiences. In exchange for this, they ought to receive a 10 % rebate on their taxes and the option to receive this reduction in exchange for five days of service in every year in the future.

Several educational methods have been used as part of attempts to train people to take more initiative, generate creative solutions, and act with confidence. We believe that the fastest way to achieve these objectives is to train teachers to prepare betters exams and ask different types of questions in their classes. More than the material — which in most cases students are going to forget anyway after a short period of time — what students must learn in their classes is to do whatever they need to do to succeed. What they need to do to succeed now is memorize, because their exams require memorization. The easy solution to this problem is to change the examination process and the types of questions that are asked in class. If teachers ask about things for which there are correct answers, there is no incentive to think and no interest expressed in the individuality of the students.

We believe that it is possible to train teachers to ask about things for which there are several different responses or that call for opinions. We cannot be certain, but we believe this might be an area where organizations like the Peace Corps can, and would, provide assistance if asked.

Second, we believe that Ecuador should take advantage of those people in the country who currently are not involved in the educational system but could serve as role models for the young people of the country. It is difficult to identify these individuals, but for a start we suggest that entrepreneurs who demonstrate their success in the rapid growth of their earnings be given an attractive economic incentive to share their experience and wisdom with the country's young people.

Distribution of Technical and Basic Education

Something that we heard in several areas of the country is that Ecuadorians need technical assistance and training but have no way to receive it. We believe that there already exists one means of improving the distribution of technical knowledge, but it is not well utilized. These are the media of radio and television. Thus, we suggest that the government of Ecuador should follow the models of several private stations in Ecuador in the presentation of educational programs and should prepare more radio and television programs for presentation on public and private stations.

HEALTH

One can judge the progress of a country by improvements in its levels of health, which is one of the most critical factors in economic development. Directing attention to health is an important productive investment that raises standards of living for everyone and will be returned several times over in a country's productive potential. However, it is an investment that, we believe, still receives inadequate attention.

Improving individual health improves mental and physical capabilities and the ability to contribute to economic production. When a child is malnourished during critical periods of growth, it will be impossible to recover mental capacity as an adult. Nor is it possible to make up for shorter stature and diminished strength caused by stunted childhood growth. By the same token, a person who is sick or in poor health is an economic drain on productivity, contributing fewer days at work, producing less on the job, disrupting those in the chain of output, and placing increasing demands on others for medical care and attention.

The problem of inadequate health care in developing and a number of more developed countries is one not only of lack of commitment but also of poor distribution. World figures reveal that 80 % of the world's health care expenditures are spent in cities and benefit 15% of the population. At the same time, only 20 % of health care funds are directed towards basic health for the other 85 % of the population (*Almanac of Women in the World* 1987).

At the same time, the problems of health care are not limited to the formal institutions of providing hospitals or health care workers in areas where they are unavailable. Rather, much of the problem of health care is a cultural one, brought on by rapid changes of modernization. For developing countries, many of the problems of health are those resulting from the disruption of traditional ways of life. Native diets have often been replaced with products of lesser nutritive value that are often heavily advertised to poorly educated consumers as having benefits they do not possess or that are nutrient rich but come to replace foods that may have filled special roles in an overall diet. New forms of economic organization, including changing patterns of agricultural productivity, have not only created new environmental and health hazards, putting carcinogens and toxins into the food chain, but have also disrupted traditional patterns of food collection and preparation, resulting in malnutrition. Changing forms of social organization have replaced important local knowledge and access to traditional medicines and health practices while disrupting traditional means of care giving within families and the community. The disruption of community and increased mobility has also tended to increase feelings of alienation and disorientation, leading to addictions, riskier health practices, and greater susceptibility to disease.

Overall, a health care system promoting economic growth and improving well-being for societies at any stage of development must achieve several different goals. It must:

• provide for universal access and coverage, seeking to make available the most basic services to populations that have been neglected — urban marginals or inner city dwellers as well as the rural populace;

• be tied to both strong environmental and safety policies and restrictions on industrial development so as to minimize the impact on traditional structures of health care and diet;

• focus on preventative aspects of health care through nutrition, improved mental health, and treatment. Part of this requires paying attention, not only to individual incentives, but also to those parts of society that actually benefit from poor health or have little incentive to change practices that disrupt existing ways of life. A policy of preventative health care must pay attention to the economic benefits that accrue to producers of junk foods and other low-nutrient or mass-produced products and benefit from changing dietary and nutrition practices. It must also recognize the large profits to farmers, distributors, and advertisers of both addictive and nonaddictive products that are deleterious to health — such as tobacco, narcotics, and alcohol. In many cases, these are cash crops fueling entire regions or economies;

• work with existing traditions and community health care practices;

• increase a commitment to education about the essentials of diet and the importance of certain practices for physical and emotional well-being; and

• recognize the importance of nontraditional sources of education for health campaigns. In many countries, the mass media continues to be used to disrupt health rather than promote it through the advertising of harmful products and minimal attention to consumer education in order to make appropriate choices about those products.

While this section focuses specifically on resources devoted to health care and to the quality and distribution of services, it is interlinked with policies in other sections — those promoting the strength of communities, education, use of the mass media, and tax powers to achieve important government incentives.

RECOMMENDATIONS

• *The Ecuadorian Government should revise the budget proposed by the Ministry of Public Health and approve an increase in the amount to be allocated to the ministry by 50 %: approximately 10 billion sucres. We also recommend redirecting the appropriations within the ministry so as to serve the majority of Ecuadorians with primary health care, rather than concentrate resources on urban areas and expensive medical care for a few individuals.*

• *We recommend reorienting the program of study in medical schools toward basic health, and complementing it with opportunities for technical and specialized training. Until this occurs, medical education in the country will remain out of touch with the reality of current health care problems facing the country.*

• *The Ministry of Public Health should implement a program of primary auxiliary health care workers in the most isolated communities and in peripheral urban neighborhoods (marginal barrios).*

• *The Ecuadorian government should encourage the cooperation between the Ministry of Public Health and the Ministry of Public Education which was initiated through the meetings of OTIDES. The efforts to incorporate health education in the programs of public education in all levels, from primary school to university, should be encouraged.*

• *The Ecuadorian government should support health warnings on television and radio which inform the public about means of protecting their health.*

REPORT

In the past few years, there have been great achievements in the average level of health in Ecuador. However, there are still great disparities in health between the most isolated areas of the country and the cities — between the humble people and those with money. *Ecuador has been successful in attending to some sectors of the population but still has not confronted the challenge of improving the health of its citizens in an egalitarian manner across the whole of its territory.*

Directing Resources to Health Care

The Ecuadorian Government should revise the budget proposed by the Ministry of Public Health and approve an increase in the amount to be allocated to the ministry by 50 %: approximately 10 billion sucres. We also recommend redirecting the appropriations within the ministry by allocating more to primary care, which serves the majority of Ecuadorians, rather than concentrating resources on urban areas and expensive medical care for a few individuals.

After spending several days in communities that received almost no medical attention or education on basic health or personal hygiene, we returned to Quito to find several public hospitals that seemed like luxury hotels in comparison. "Where do the priorities of the government lie?" we asked ourselves, wondering whether the government was interested only in serving its urban population or in improving the health of all citizens.

Reorienting Education and Training

We recommend reorienting the program of study in medical schools toward basic health and complementing it with opportunities for technical and specialized training. Until this happens, medical education in Ecuador will remain out of touch with the reality of current health care problems facing the country.

The majority of health problems in Ecuador could be avoided by improving education and basic services. The medical profession in Ecuador is simply biased against rural practice and rural health education. Doctors are concentrated in urban areas and few assume the responsibility of educating the population or attending to them. In various rural communities, we heard that the doctor who was promised by the Ministry of Public Health never arrived or left within a few months. We also noted that in those cases where the doctor remained, he or she merely attended to treating illness and never gave talks about basic health or met with the local people. Certainly, there are many doctors who work to improve community health by providing education in addition to medical services. Nonetheless, there is still a need to train medical students to concern themselves with the poorest sectors of the population and to value providing health education.

Medical education should focus, not only on local health problems, but also on methods to educate local communities, improve relations with those communities, and promote sanitation and basic hygiene. We often heard that doctors who are serving on year-long programs in rural areas frequently are not sensitive to local cultures and do not treat them with respect. Medical schools must take responsibility to educate their students in these matters. It should be reiterated that an integral part of being a doctor is to attend to the most basic needs of patients, with concern as much for their daily habits as with their illnesses.

Improving Primary Care and Access

The Ministry of Public Health should implement a program of primary auxiliary health care workers in the most isolated communities and in peripheral urban neighborhoods (marginal barrios).

In addition to the "year in rural areas" program for new doctors, Ecuador should strengthen rural health programs by establishing a network of auxiliary health care workers who are trained by the Ministry of Public Health in primary health care and the promotion of basic health. These workers could serve in their own communities as well as provide care in areas where there are no doctors. In larger communities, these local health workers could complement the services of the Ministry of Public Health and function as a link with the local people. In strengthening the effectiveness of these programs, the government should provide health workers with manuals on basic medicine and health promotion, such as the book *Dónde No Hay Doctor* (where there is no doctor) (Werner 1980).

The costs of such a program would be minimal, including only the expenses of training for the primary auxiliary health care workers, their income, and the costs of basic medicine. In the long run, these investments would be returned through an increase in the productivity of the population. (See also the discussion on health in "Migration and the Urban Explosion," in Chapter 1.)

Improving Overall Health Education

The government should encourage the cooperation between the Ministry of Public Health and the Ministry of Public Education, which was begun through the meetings of OTIDES. Government should also welcome efforts to incorporate health education in the programs of public education in all levels, from primary school to university.

The Ecuadorian government can take better advantage of its power to educate and socialize the population through education in improving individual health. Medical students from schools in Quito, Guayaquil, Loja, and Cuenca could be encouraged to share their knowledge and use their training at the local level as part of their professional training, while benefiting those areas at the same time.

Expanding Outreach

The government should support health warnings on television and radio that inform the public about means of protecting their health.

Almost all Ecuadorians have access to television or radio. These media can be used more effectively to disseminate useful information on health-related topics. The funding for health messages can be provided from taxes on salt, alcohol, and carbonated drinks. Further, government can encourage businesses and private organizations to participate in these promotions by offering reductions in corporate taxes.

REFERENCES

Almanac of Women in the World 1987.

Werner, David. *Dónde No Hay Doctor* San Jose, Costa Rica: Ediciónes Arneo, 1980.

4

Macroeconomic Financial Strategy

For development agents like the World Bank, International Monetary Fund, and area development banks, recommendations for economic development often begin (and sometimes end) with macroeconomic policies of stabilizing exchange rates, controlling inflation, and balancing budgets. Indeed, these are often considered the central concerns of economic development.

In our view, not only are these not the real starting points of an effective development policy, they are often completely misunderstood by the major players in development. Even though our recommendations in this area take into account the same practical considerations as do other development agencies and are based on the same base of empirical evidence and economic theory, we look at the larger picture, going beyond what is easily measurable or of most concern to foreign investors. In many cases, the numbers on which these other development agencies focus are only symptoms of larger problems and the solutions they offer leave the problems unaddressed. In other cases, the focus is not on a country's needs and concerns, as it should be.

The World Bank, the IMF, and other development agencies are either designed primarily as lending agencies or staffed by bankers. Therefore, it is not surprising that they view development as the ability to attract outside loans and copy foreign models of growth rather than indigenous ones. Nor is it surprising that they often view stable exchange rates and government budgetary policies as part of a development strategy based on attracting foreign investment.

The standard model of economic development as seen through the eyes of these development agents is one that promotes large, capital-intensive industries with the stated intention of making internal production more efficient and profitable, and thus providing countries with what they lack internally. Too often, however, the result is the growth of industries that are extractive of a country's resources and weaken local autonomy and cultural pride, combined with increasing international trade and growing purchases of luxury goods and other consumer products from the West.

Similarly, the "structural adjustment" policies advised by outside development agents focus on the wrong side of the equation. Such policies have the stated intention of balancing national budgets as a means of forcing efficiency in the public sector; in other words, creating pressures to streamline corrupt and costly bureaucracies that abuse their monopoly position. Too often, however, the result is that the pressures for budget balancing do little to reverse the imbalances in political power and instead end up sharply diminishing the services — education, social security, local culture, and legal and political access — that would allow the poor to compete economically and politically.

Often, the result of the policies is to encourage greater outside borrowing for capital-intensive investments, which results in a larger burden of debt and increased political and economic instability. With the debt to be paid, at the direction of foreign lenders, from further reductions in human investment, cultural investment, and more rapid exploitation of a country's natural resources, the result may not be development but rather a downward economic and political spiral.

In short, these are strategies of homogenization and dependency, which are good for First World countries and their representatives in developing nations but may be of little benefit to the majority of people in those countries.

An alternative model of development focuses on root causes and attempts fine-tuning rather than setting broad goals that are likely to be met with policy choices that reinforce existing problems. It is just as easy to combine sound financial policies with promoting cultural pride, making a commitment to human resources, helping the poor and weak to become strong, and achieving overall self-reliance as it is to advocate a policy of assimilating the country into the world economy and taking resources away from those who are politically powerless in the name of cutting costs.

Policies of budget balancing, controlling inflation, and achieving stable exchange rates are not only linked with each other, they are also linked to other underlying problems. Imbalanced budgets may not be the result of "too much" social spending but rather of inappropriate spending in other sectors, inadequate public oversight of government and the corporate sector, and poor strategies of investment. Trade deficits may not be the result of lagging raw material exports of resources that could be better exploited and of goods produced at too high a price because of "high" wages, but rather of a created demand for Western luxuries or unessential items, which foreign companies are overly eager to promote. Alternately, they may be the result of local elites hiding much of their gains abroad — in foreign banks and other assets — without any attempt by foreign institutions or governments to stop these outflows.

Indeed, there is more than one solution to the problem of balancing budgets. Cutting costs by eliminating programs that have a beneficial impact on development is the most short-sighted of any development strategy. Instead, it is just as easy to use tax policies to generate revenue from, and reduce consumption of, products that wipe out the gains of development or to target those specific areas of spending that are counterproductive. Likewise, it is just as easy to seek better enforcement of tax collection or alternative types of taxes in order to restructure incentives for saving and investment.

Similarly, the problem of foreign debt is not solved in the long run by punishing the weakest sectors and may only create situations in which debt will increase. The problem is best alleviated by addressing where borrowings have been invested and making sure that capital is directed to its most productive uses rather than to those who are politically powerful and represent interests or consumption patterns most similar to those controlling the lending.

At the same time, addressing the problem of foreign debt requires recognizing the cause of outward capital flows. In part, the flight of capital is the end result of years of policies that neglect the interests of a particular ethnic group or social class, resulting in instability and violence that could have been averted if investments had been made in those sectors all along. In part, it is the result of international banks and foreign governments doing little to stop elites in developing countries from taking a country's gains and placing it in their own accounts, abroad. Ultimately, these preferences are an artifact of the conditions and consumption preferences that development planners in the First World create and reinforce, whereas the real goal of development should be to encourage a more efficient investment of capital within developing countries. Particularly in times of instability, when there are even greater incentives for those who hold a country's wealth to take it abroad, it is the role of the international community to help strengthen domestic and international laws that prevent such large movements of assets other than for the protection of at-risk minority populations who are forced to emigrate to escape oppression or genocide.

Since policies of budget balancing and exchange policies are often linked — with balanced budgets reducing the demand for governments to print money to meet its obligations, thereby reducing inflation and keeping a country's currency stable and investor confidence strong — we begin with an examination of revenue generation and government budgeting and then turn to exchange policy to establish a macroeconomic financial strategy.

REVENUE GENERATION
AND NATIONAL BUDGETING

In the case of most developing — and many developed — countries, resources available from the public sector are diminishing, and the burden of debt often hangs above like the sword of Damocles. Since our recommendations for development initiatives demonstrate an unbridled optimism in countries' commitments to their future and call for tremendous investments in certain sectors that have previously received inadequate attention, we recognize at the same time that the practicality and reality of development is that it must be done within the constraints of limited resources.

Nevertheless, we believe that there are still ample resources in developing countries to support new programs and pay off domestic and foreign debts without the need to request additional outside funding, take extreme measures, or even take funds from one social class in order to help another. In this respect, we distinguish ourselves from several other planning organizations.

Usually, attempts to generate revenues are based on tax reforms designed to take the most from the business sector or the upper class. It is true that from an economic standpoint, this may be the most ideally efficient solution, particularly since the wealthy usually benefit disproportionately from government services and because higher taxes on those in the upper classes have little real effect on their incentives to continue to keep accumulating. The problem with progressive taxes is not that they are inefficient but that they fail due to tax avoidance or sabotage. Rather than create a zero-sum game that creates a political backlash from the upper classes and jeopardizes other reforms, it is best to create a "win-win" situation for everyone.

Our theory of taxes and revenue generation is based on two principles: *First, government should raise funds from all sectors without favoritism, and second, it should eliminate the inefficient use of national resources.* In our view, taxes should be used to change patterns of consumption and resource use as much as to meet government obligations. Taxes are not only means of raising revenue but also a way to demonstrate priorities and influence behaviors.

Development Goals of Tax Policies

Overall, we see tax policies as having three different development goals: to promote the right mix of consumption of products that are best suited to development, to create the right balance between savings and investment and to strengthen the capabilities of different levels of government.

1. *To promote consumption patterns best suited to development*, to finance our proposals, we have identified several examples of taxation that meet the two tests of fairness and efficient use of resources. Not only do they raise sufficient revenue for development programs, they serve at the same time to encourage improvements in public health and protection of the integrity of indigenous cultures. The taxes that we suggest are those that are most readily visible. We are sure there are other examples that would meet our criteria, which can be found through further study.

While the kinds of new taxes that we propose have incorporate what have been referred to as "sin" taxes, this is not an appropriate or a complete label for how developing and developed countries can use taxation as a meaningful tool in development policy. In addition to taxing what may be harmful or frivolous, taxation should be viewed more positively as a means of improving diets and health; promoting local products, culture, and pride; and making more efficient use of a country's resources.

Taxes on products can have different kinds of positive impacts on development that go beyond the protection of infant industries through taxes on foreign competitive goods:

Certain food products in developing countries — salt and soda, processed sugars — are not sinful but are merely not part of an indigenous or a healthy diet. Many of these products were introduced by outsiders as part of the process of colonization; they were traded to natives for their compliance in exchange for use of lands, with the effect of disrupting their traditional diets. Taxing these products is a means of trying to wean a country back to healthier, traditionally rooted, and, often, locally produced foods.

Addictive products in many developing countries — tobacco and refined alcohols, for example — were also introduced by outsiders or presented in more potent and addictive forms, with pernicious effects on peoples not used to them. Through sophisticated advertising practices, they replace a more healthful use of a country's resources and also replace more productive uses of foreign exchange for imports. Government policies through taxation can be used to reverse these harms while reducing long-term costs due to declining health and productivity of consumers.

Many products simply reflect a "created" demand for international status and replacing local culture with approval from those with greater wealth — such as luxury items from abroad, foreign clothes and

The authors submit the Ecuador development plan to Ecuadorian President Rodrigo Borja Cevallos in the Presidential Palace in Quito, August 1988. From left to right, David Lempert, Kim McCarty, Tal Lewis (member of original research team), President Rodrigo Borja, Shannon Wright (member of original research team), and Craig Mitchell. (*Photo credit: Craig Mitchell*)

Guayaquil. In efforts to emulate Western development, the harmful is often mixed with the good. We support strategies to limit certain cultural imports and protect local symbols. (*Photo credit: David Lempert*)

Ingapirca. These two remnants of ancient times, the Inca city of Ingapirca and the llama, stand against a backdrop of over-farmed hillsides. We support strategies to protect these historical sites while improving earnings from tourism and ecological tourism. (*Photo credit: David Lempert*)

Otavalo. Through a combination of entrepreneurial spirit and local pride, the Otavalan Indians have managed to protect much of their cultural heritage while holding their own in the new Ecuadorian and world economy. (*Photo credit: David Lempert*)

Baños. The influence of militarism runs deep, with these school children being prepared early for war and hierarchy, approaches directly counter to what they will need to be economically successful. (*Photo credit: David Lempert*)

Shuar Region. Once the fierce headhunting peoples of the Amazon (among them, the old man with a tattoo on his forehead), the Jivaro are losing their land and must compromise in order to survive. We recognize the needs and difficulties of adaptation of groups like the Shuar and support a variety of strategies and solutions from which they ought to be able to choose in pursuing their own path of development. (*Photo credit: David Lempert*)

Guaranda. The road to development ought to be one which combines traditional and new. (*Photo credit: David Lempert*)

Shuar Region. The newlywed Jivaro couple (center) celebrates their wedding in the Amazon home, in a mix of old and new. (*Photo credit: David Lempert*)

accessories, and foreign films. It is sad that many people in developing countries now feel a psychological need to keep up with wealthier neighbors, now that they have been brought into the world market. Spending on such items offers no real value to the natives other than status. Too long it has been overlooked in development policies and assumed to be a healthy sign of "free choice" and "modernization" when it serves instead to meet the needs of First World development agents to confirm their belief in the superiority and desirability of their own consumption patterns.

2. *To create the right balance between savings and investment* it must be understood that the ideal form of taxation that incorporates fairness with encouraging savings is the consumption tax, which taxes consumption rather than income or wealth. However, this is also a tax that is impractical for many countries at present. To manage an effective consumption tax requires another change in both the developing and developed world, which involves a much greater attention to international banking standards. Measuring consumption means being able to measure changes in assets. Without banking regulations to effectively trace "dirty" money — obtained through criminal operations — as well as legitimate assets that flow through offshore poorly regulated banks in developing countries or Swiss banks, where funds are difficult to trace, this form of taxation and many kinds of criminal regulation that would protect developing economies are impossible.

3. *To strengthen the capabilities of different levels of government,* an ideal tax regime distributes the powers of taxation among governing authorities at different levels. An appropriate tax regime complements a policy of decentralization and the strengthening of development at the grassroots level.

RECOMMENDATIONS

We propose a variety of taxes in order to provide the necessary revenues for new social programs and to repay Ecuador's national debt. We estimate that they would generate revenue equal to more than 10 % of the current government budget.

Taxes with Implications for Health

<u>Specific Consumption Items</u>

<u>Tobacco</u>. A 50 % tax on tobacco would raise 15.5 billion sucres a year.

<u>Sodas</u>. A tax of 50 % would raise between 7.5 and 18.8 billion sucres annually.

<u>Alcohol</u>. A minimal increase in taxes on alcohol would generate sufficient funds for the treatment of alcoholism, for recreation centers to provide alternatives to alcohol consumption, and for the prevention and for the treatment of battered women and abused children.

<u>Salt.</u> A tax of only 20% would raise 1.47 billion sucres.

<u>Meat</u>. A tax of just 20 % would raise between 10 and 17.5 billion sucres annually. We suggest that half of these funds be earmarked for the new Ministry of Fisheries.

Taxes with Implications for National Pride and the Protection of Ecuadorian Culture

We propose a tax of 300 % on imported ties, suits, perfumes and the imported materials used to make these products domestically and an additional tax on motion pictures of 10 % (which would raise 150 million sucres annually and could be earmarked for a national film industry).

Improvements in the Collection of Taxes

We suggest that Ecuador accept the assistance offered in the past by international organizations in the training and professionalization of customs officials and in stemming the flow of illegal or untaxed items into the country. The Organization of American States is currently working in this area and we recommend that Ecuador request special assistance from the O.A.S. in its special capacity as an international organization.

New Forms of Taxes

Luxury Taxes. A tax on luxury consumer goods would reduce the consumption of items which are not essential to development and could improve income distribution since luxury goods are primarily consumed by the middle and upper classes. We conservatively estimate that a tax of 10 to 20 % on the sale of luxury consumer goods would reduce consumption of those items by 5 % and would raise between 6 and 12 billion sucres annually. An important advantage of a luxury tax on consumer goods of whatever origin is that it does not produce an incentive for substitution of these products with domestic goods. If Ecuador did wish to promote substitution for imports with internal production, it is clear that it would seek to promote substitution of goods essential for development rather than luxury goods.

Consumption Tax. In the long run, the Ecuadorian government should consider a tax on consumption in place of a tax on income. This form of taxation has the advantage of discouraging consumption of luxury items while promoting savings and capital formation.

We consider taxes in five different areas:

• taxes with implications for public health;

• taxes with implications for national pride and the protection of culture;

• improvements in tax collecting;

• changes in the administration of the tax system as a means of better coordinating taxing and spending (which fits in with our strategy of decentralization); and

• new objects and forms of taxation.

Taxes with Implications for Public Health

Tobacco. Every year Ecuador spends almost twice as much on tobacco as the entire budget of the Ministry of Health! As one of the strongest threats to public health, with severe implications for unborn infants, the families of smokers, and economic productivity, an economic incentive to reduce tobacco consumption would have a major, beneficial impact on health and development.

The national consumption of tobacco in 1986 was 21.428 billion sucres. If we use the inflation rate measured by the Banco Central of 81 % in the previous two years (less than the World Bank's figure of 133 %), the consumption of tobacco in 1988 would be 38.79 billion sucres.

We estimate that a tax of 50 % would diminish consumption by 20 % and would raise 15.5 billion sucres, yearly! This alone would increase the national budget by 4 % and provide enough revenue for the program that we propose to address the problem of population growth.

Beverages — Sodas and Alcohol. Although the dangers of drugs and alcohol are well known, the effects of soda consumption — malnutrition and resultant damage to brain function and bones — have not received much public attention. A reduction in the consumption of sodas and alcohol and their replacement with juices, milk, and water would promote health and development.

It is hard to estimate precisely the consumption of sodas and alcohol in Ecuador. The category for consumption of "beverages" in the

National Budget for 1986 amounted to 52.029 billion sucres. If we estimate an inflation rate of 81 %, the category would amount to 94.18 billion sucres in 1988. If we estimate that between 20 and 50 % of this category represents the consumption of sodas, this would be between 18.83 and 47.08 billion sucres.

With a tax of 50 % and a drop off in consumption of 20 %, the government of Ecuador would raise between 7.5 and 18.8 billion sucres, yearly.

Alcohol is slightly more difficult to tax because a rise in alcohol taxes would merely encourage home production, with all of its additional risks to public health.

In any case, *a minimal increase in taxes on alcohol would generate sufficient funds for the treatment of alcoholism, for recreation centers to provide alternatives to alcohol consumption, and for the prevention and for the treatment of battered women and abused children.*

Salt.   Less well known and more hidden than the health effects of other products are the dangers of the consumption of salt — which can lead to hypertension and premature death.   A reduction in salt consumption, like the reduction in consumption of tobacco, soda, and alcohol, would contribute significantly to health and development.

There are no current statistics available for the consumption of salt in Ecuador. The category is only an "aspiration" of the Central Bank's National Accounts office, to be measured sometime in the future. In any case, we believe that the quantity of salt consumption is roughly equal to that of sugar, for which statistics do exist.

(While we would like to impose a tax on refined sugar for reasons of health and diet — a category of consumption that is more than the entire budget of the Ministry of Health — we believe that a tax on sugar would only encourage farmers to begin their own production without changing their diets and with a net economic loss to the country as a whole.)

By comparing market prices, we found that the price of salt is 20 % that of sugar. If both categories are the same in terms of quantity, the consumption of salt in 1986 would be about 20 % of 21.428 billion sucres, or 4.285 billion sucres. If we convert this to current sucres, we can estimate the category at 7.755 billion sucres in 1988.

A tax of just 20 % and a decline in consumption of 5 %, would raise 1.47 billion sucres yearly.

Meat.   It is well known in development that one of the greatest losses in food production is the conversion of vegetable to animal protein. In most cases, the same land can support more people if it is used for cultivation of human food products instead of animal feed. At the same time, the consumption of meat and meat products (lard, for example) contributes to the incidence of health problems such as heart disease and obesity. We are not opposed to the consumption of meat as a source of protein but only to overconsumption, which has consequences for health and development.

Although it is possible that some lands in Ecuador that are currently used for cattle raising could not be productively converted to food crops, we believe that this conversion would be possible on a large part of the country's land and would also result in improved land use practices, which would prevent degradation of the land.

The amount of meat consumption in the country is difficult to estimate. In 1986, households consumed 25.558 billion sucres in the category "Animal Production" and 62.087 billion sucres worth of "Processed Meats and Fish." It is difficult to know what percentage of these categories included chicken, processed fish, rabbit, guinea pig, and other types of animal protein that are healthful and efficient to produce.

If total consumption in these two categories in 1988 is estimated to approach 158.6 billion sucres and if only between a third and half of these categories include meat sold and not consumed by the producer, this totals between 52 and 79 billion sucres.

With a tax of only 20 % in the market and a resultant decrease in consumption by 5 %, this would raise between 10 and 17.5 billion sucres yearly, which represents an increase in the annual budget of 2 to 4 %!

We recommend that half these taxes be earmarked for a new Ministry of Fisheries. Statistics clearly demonstrate the advantages of fish production. *Planting and harvesting fish from a pond that uses the same amount of land as raising cattle produces more protein with less labor.*

Taxes with Implications for National Pride and the Protection of Ecuadorian Culture

Ecuador can protect its culture and boost national pride while raising revenues for development by taxing foreign goods that do not satisfy basic needs and do have local substitutes; thereby reducing their purchase.

We found it sad when a young man in Quito, who was 16 years old and dressed in a European suit and tie, explained to us why he had decided to reject his own culture. "Its true that I would prefer to dress in Ecuadorian clothes," he told us, "[but] we feel inferior to Europe and we adopt European clothing for our formal occasions. Young people in the country can't do anything to change this."

The truth is that dependency and feelings of inferiority *can* be changed if Ecuadorians wish to do so. One way is to impose higher taxes on these items. Instead of imposing taxes on a general category, we prefer to identify specific items for special attention and higher taxes. These articles include suits and ties (and imported material for their manufacture), perfumes, movies, and non-educational foreign television programs.

Suits, Ties, and Perfumes.   From the perspective of development and efficient resource use, the production of ties, suits, and perfumes does not have a single practical function but rather exists only for ornamentation and the strengthening of distinctions between social classes. We see these expenses as large economic losses in both our economy and that of Ecuador.

For Ecuador, compared to the United States, the import of these products or materials to manufacture them makes even less sense and does more harm to society. The use of these products represents a rejection of Ecuadorian culture and is ironic, given the country's world renown in the production of textiles and unique styles. We recommend a tax of 300 % on these articles.

Movies and Noneducational Foreign Television Programs. The great majority of foreign films shown in Ecuador focus on sex, violence, materialism, and the values of Western industrialization. Probably, these films are as inappropriate to our own Western society as they are for Ecuador. While we have no objection to artistic freedom or the exchange of international works, it worries us that Ecuador lacks its own resources for expression in this medium and has to substitute foreign images. Most of these films come from the United States, where they are designed to make money by alleviating the frustrations of young Americans who are dissatisfied with their prospects for the future.

Our study of film attendance in Quito and in small cities revealed a per capita attendance rate of 1 and 2.6 times, respectively, per year. With entrance fees between 240 and 140 sucres and an urban population of 52 % of the country, we estimate that the industry grosses 1.56 billion sucres annually.

By imposing an additional tax of 10% on motion picture attendance, the Ecuadorian government would collect 150 million sucres annually. *We recommend that these funds be earmarked for a national film industry.*

The Current System and Improvements in Tax Collection

While our proposals for revenue generation aim at eliminating inefficiencies in the economy rather than redistributing wealth, we agree with all the previous studies that conclude that Ecuador has the ability to improve revenue generation simply by collecting those taxes that already exist and are written into Ecuadorian law. Ecuador is a country of huge contrasts between great fortunes and great poverty. There are enough resources internally to develop the country and to pay the debt without seeking direct financial assistance from abroad.

As one step toward self-reliance and an end to dependency on other countries, we suggest that Ecuador accept the assistance offered by international development agencies for improving the collection of taxes that are already on the books.

Ecuador should pay special attention to collecting import duties. Merchants have told us about the ease with which they transport imported goods across the border, by paying bribes instead of tariffs, and the ease of buying imported goods at prices lower than if they included import tariffs, from women identified as "wives and girlfriends of members of the Armed Forces." We cannot confirm this, but we often heard that certain members of the Armed Forces did not make their best efforts to collect import duties owed to the government.

We propose that Ecuador request the assistance of international organizations in training and professionalizing customs officials and in stemming the flow of illegal or untaxed items into the country (with the knowledge, we have heard, of certain members of the Armed Forces). The Organization of American States (OAS) is currently working in this area, and we recommend that Ecuador request special assistance from the OAS.

Decentralization and the Generation of Revenues

Although we cannot estimate the effect on revenue generation of the adoption of our recommendations for decentralization and expansion of the powers of local governments, we believe that these changes will significantly increase the amount of revenues generated.

The stimulus to development at local levels, as a result of decentralization, will increase the tax base of the country by increasing the amount of income generated. Moreover, the public ought to more easily accept taxation at local levels — including new taxes legislated with the new powers of local governments — since citizens will be able to directly see the results of their payments because there is a closer relation with their locally elected officials than with the central government. Finally, the proportion of funds administered by the central government will continue to decrease with the transfer of responsibilities to local governments.

Other Taxes and Sources of Income

We considered several other potential tax alternatives, some of which merit further study.

Oil. If there were convincing evidence to prove that the low price of petroleum was favoring the use of capital goods in industrial and agricultural production over manual labor, Ecuador would be wise to consider raising the price of domestic petroleum and petroleum products, which it sets through government regulation. However, we did not find enough evidence to make a recommendation in this area.

We believe in the need for Ecuadorian industry to compete in world markets with efficient production, and if it were possible to prevent dislocations of the labor force and unemployment during the period of transition, we would support this tax alternative. However, we believe that a hike in oil prices could negatively affect those who need transportation, especially farmers who need to travel to urban centers. The figures we reviewed from the Banco Central show that 25 % of refined petroleum consumption in the country is by households, 40 % by transportation, and the rest (one-third) by industry (Banco Central 1987).

It might be more efficient to attack the problem of overconsumption of petroleum in the productive process through more direct measures and incentives to industry.

Luxury Consumer Goods — Durables and Nondurables. Ecuador has not had much success in the past in the implementation of a system of income taxes. However, there are other means of promoting a more equitable distribution of income. A tax on luxury consumer goods would reduce the consumption of goods that are not essential to development and could improve income distribution. This is because luxury goods are primarily consumed by the middle and upper classes. The consumption of durable luxury items includes private vehicles (automobiles and recreational boats), refrigerators, televisions, and other electrical household appliances, and luxury furniture. Nondurable luxury items include agroindustrial products (processed fruits, vegetables and cereals), luxury clothes (leather jackets, ties, and suits), meals in first-class restaurants, and services in private clubs. It is difficult to estimate the value of the consumption of these luxury items in the country. The figures provide only limited information.

Imports. Imports of nondurable consumer goods (not including pharmaceuticals) were $63 million and imports of consumer durables were $60 million in 1986 (Banco Central 1986).

We were not able to obtain figures for taxes on each of these subcategories (in 1986, the total amount of taxes on imports was 36 billion sucres — 17 % of the national budget). Neither were we able to obtain figures for the past year. However, we estimate that with the drop in the sucre relative to the dollar, the import of consumer goods has dropped.

In current sucres (with the rate of exchange at 500 sucres to the dollar) current consumption would be 31.5 billion sucres (import of nondurable consumer goods) and 30 billion sucres (consumer durables.) However, it is likely that this amount has decreased. Thus, a conservative estimate would be that the two categories combined are 40 billion sucres.

Domestic Production. The amount of sales of nondurable consumer goods in the manufacturing sector was 102 billion sucres in 1986. Sales of consumer durables produced in the manufacturing sector was 36 billion sucres in the same year (Banco Central de Ecuador y el Consejo Nacional de Desarollo, March 1988). Consumption in current sucres would be 185 billion and 65 billion sucres, respectively, in the two categories.

If we estimate that 60 % of imports of consumer goods are luxury items, as are 15 % of consumer goods produced in Ecuador (imported consumer goods usually consist in large part of luxury items such as automobiles, furniture, specially processed foods, and luxury clothing, while consumer goods produced in Ecuador consist of standard items such as basic clothing, traditional furniture, and basic food stuffs), we find that the amount of sales of luxury goods is roughly 61.5 billion sucres(roughly 24 billion in imported goods and 37.5 billion in goods produced in Ecuador). With a conservative estimate, a tax of 10 to 20 % on the sale of luxury consumer goods, with a reduction in consumption of 5 % (as a result of the rise in prices of those items), the government would raise between 6 and 12 billion sucres.

An important aspect of a tax on luxury items, regardless of their origin, is that it would not result in an incentive to substitute local products for the same imported products. If Ecuador were to choose to substitute imports with domestic production, it certainly would not wish to promote substitution of luxury items but rather would stimulate those goods that are essential for development. A tax on only imported luxury items would produce economic distortions, giving an incentive to inefficient use of resources for the domestic production of luxury items.

Consumption Tax. A new form of taxation that several developed countries have been considering is a tax on personal consumption. We do not believe that Ecuador has the capacity to impose this type of tax at the present time, but we present it here as an alternative for the future.

A tax on consumption has the advantages of discouraging the consumption of luxury goods and encouraging savings and capital formation. An advantage of this tax is that it is not threatening to investors because it does not impose taxes on high earnings, but only on expenses.

The tax works simply. After measuring personal income, adding it to savings and assets at the end of the previous year and subtracting what remains at the end of the current year, the result is the amount consumed.

Government can calculate a level of basic consumption, subtract this figure, and then impose taxes on any amounts above it. What this form of taxation does is to tax expenditures on nonbasic consumption, which would include imported goods, expensive materials, and services — anything over the basic material needs for survival, which one would find available for a moderate standard of living.

The difficulty in the short run in imposing this tax is more than just the difficulty of measuring income (a current problem) but also includes the problem of measuring assets for the initial calculation — assets not held in bank accounts in Ecuador such as dollar accounts or accounts in Swiss francs overseas, real assets held outside the country, or assets in the form of jewelry and precious metals.

What is necessary in order to establish this sort of system in the future is to request the assistance of foreign governments — for reasons of the national security of Ecuador — in exchanging information regarding assets and accounts outside the country.

EXCHANGE RATE POLICY:
LINKAGE WITH THE WORLD ECONOMY

Rather than being used as litmus tests of the preconditions for growth and foreign aid, we believe that financial statistics should be viewed as measurements of symptoms of larger problems that development agencies can help to treat. We view falling exchange rates and the financial conditions associated with them as merely indicators of one aspect of a complex set of development needs and as neither the most important factor in, nor a precondition to, other assistance.

The link between deficits, inflation, and exchange policies is a clear one. Countries that are experiencing substantial deficits in their budgets print money in order to meet their obligations. This often sets off an inflationary spiral and hyperinflation, quickly causing the currency to be devalued and creating a loss of confidence. The instability and decline in the value of local currency leads to speculation rather than investment and to the flight of capital into foreign currencies.

However, rapidly deteriorating exchange rates and a lack of domestic confidence may not always indicate poor government planning. They may, instead, represent larger weaknesses that only international efforts can help cure, such as rapid looting of an economy in a time of transition, looting that at times is encouraged and abetted by a weak international system for prosecuting international crime and weakness in international financial and banking laws. In the 1990s, as the economies of the former Soviet Union face government deficits, double-digit inflation, rapid devaluations, and the flight of tens of billions of dollars of foreign capital, part of the problem can be traced to international financial institutions and foreign economies that comply in accepting and harboring assets and profiting from the looting of economies in transition. The international community participates in the process through policies of "privatization," while calling for government sacrifices but paying no attention to developing appropriate domestic or international legal regimes.

Similarly, the inability to balance government budgets and the hyperinflation that occurs in developing or transition economies is not always a sign of poor government management but may be the sign of a government that recognizes its obligations to invest in human capital — education, health, community services, and the continuing purchase of foreign essentials — to maintain political stability and keep its contract with the public. The hyperinflation that results when a government tries to keep its promises but finds that it lacks the revenues should not be interpreted (as it often is by development agencies), as the inability to trim a bloated bureaucracy and maintain order. The real need may be for technical assistance to improve tax collection, to address social needs, and stop and prosecute the looting of public assets.

Whether a government should be attracting additional foreign investment over the long term is a separate issue from that of maintaining its existing investments and an environment of internal confidence and stability. Not only can investors flee in times of inflation and exchange rate fluctuation, thus devastating a country's production, but industries can come to a standstill when hit by the shocks of rising prices of inputs purchased from abroad or declining export prices if currencies experience sudden swings.

When there is little outside support for treating the underlying causes of a country's financial problems, countries must themselves choose the right policy in the face of outside and internal political and economic constraints. In doing so, there are plenty of examples to follow. A policy to create economic stability and confidence consists of three basic features.

1. Create a balanced budget in order to reduce inflation.

2. Generate confidence by avoiding a policy of exchange rate controls.

3. Use resources efficiently, substituting local inputs for foreign loans wherever possible and promoting efficiency in export manufacturing and services in industries that compete for international sales.

The classic cases testing the approaches are those of Latin America. The governments of Argentina (1985) and Brazil (1986) tried to combat inflation with policies of control, without reducing the government budget deficit. In Argentina, the "Austral Plan" used price and wage controls (and, at first, deficit reduction) to fight a rate of inflation that had reached 1,000 % per year. At first, the rate of inflation dropped to 80 % (in 1986), but in 1987, when the government budget deficit began to rise (reaching 7 % of gross national product in 1987), the rate of inflation also began to rise, reaching 332 % per year in June 1988. In Brazil, the "Cruzado Plan" neglected to consider the effect of the state budget deficit on the rate of inflation and relied solely on price and wage controls. The government budget deficit rose from 4 % of gross national product (GNP) in 1985 to 7 % in 1987. At first, inflation decreased from 260 % to 62 %, but as in Argentina, inflation soon returned, rising to 468 % per year in May of 1988 (according to the *Economist*, July 16, 1988.) All these unsuccessful efforts to combat inflation were characterized by a lack of attention to reducing the government budget deficit.

In Bolivia, by contrast, as part of the "New Economic Policy" in 1985, government succeeded in reducing inflation from 24,000 % per year to less than 10 % in 1988, without using controls. These efforts were accompanied by a reduction in the state budget deficit from 36 % of GNP to 5 % by 1987.

Since exchange policy is one of the more complicated areas of development, this chapter utilizes a variety of hypotheses and theories of government finance in the context of a case study, using national accounts data to support a series of recommendations that place exchange policy within the larger goals of development.

RECOMMENDATIONS

In order to resolve the crisis in its exchange markets, Ecuador requires a policy of confidence, not of controls. This policy should consist of three parts.

1. *Ecuador needs a sincere effort to combat inflation, not with price controls but with a reduction in the government budget deficit.* We cannot deny that inflation moves the exchange rate upward. From the experience of the antiinflationary programs of Argentina (1985 — Plan Austral), Brazil (1986 — Plan Cruzado), and Bolivia (1985 — New Economic Policy), it appears that the first two countries failed in large part because they did not reduce the state budget deficit, while Bolivia succeeded because its policies were accompanied by a significant reduction in the state budget. The basic structural inflation in Ecuador is much less than it was in those other countries. It is likely, therefore, that a policy of combating inflation will be successful if it is accompanied by deficit reduction.

2. *The policy must support productive investment in production for export and for efficient domestic production.* The most important goal is to recover the confidence of the private sector by demonstrating that investment in Ecuador is prudent and profitable. The result will be a reduction in the flight of capital and speculation, two forces that significantly affect the rate of exchange.

3. *The policy must leave the exchange rate to the free market, as is currently the case.* If inflation returns to normal, low levels and the private sector has confidence that the probability for success is high, the pressures that force the exchange rate upward will disappear.

Whatever government does, it has to do immediately. Recently, we have seen an enormous amount of monetary speculation in Ecuador because the public does not know what the new government will do. If the government does not announce its economic programs quickly, the Ecuadorian people will lose confidence in it.

A Model Development Plan

REPORT
_____

The Ecuadorian sucre has served as a model of stability for more than a decade. Since 1982, the rate of exchange had remained at 25 sucres per $1 U.S., without significant movement. However, since 1982, all that has changed. The pressures of a public deficit that reached 7.9% of GNP and the fall in the international monetary reserves from $857 million in 1980 to $210 million in 1982 (International Monetary Fund 1986), led to the inevitable step of devaluing the sucre. The free market exchange rate rose to 36.25 sucres per $1 U.S. in February 1982, almost 50 % more than the official rate, which remained at 25 sucres per $1 U.S. It was at that moment that the fall of the sucre began, and it has now reached a level of 500 sucres per $1 U.S.

What factors have produced these movements in the rate of exchange? Inflation is the most important. According to international monetary theory, domestic prices — P — are made equal to foreign prices — P^* — by the exchange rate — E. Thus the formula is, $P = E \times P^*$. When domestic prices rise, so does the rate of exchange (assuming that foreign prices are constant and that movements in the rate are those of the free market, without state intervention). With this formula, it is possible to compare the price index and the international exchange rate to see if the relationship holds (See Table 4.1).

Between 1980 and 1985, the price indices and the rate of inflation moved together. The largest difference between the two was 14 %, but in 1986, the rate of exchange began to rise much more quickly than prices. Statistics for 1988 show that the index of consumer prises was 841.5 for the month of August but the international exchange rate index

Table 4.1. Consumer price indices (CPI) and the International Exchange Rate (IER)

	1980*	1981	1982	1983	1984	1985	1986	1987
CPI	100.0	116.4	135.3	200.8	263.6	337.3	415.0	537.5
IER	100.0	100.0	132.6	216.4	268.7	383.0	568.0	886.0
Diff. (%)	0 %	-14 %	-2 %	8 %	2 %	13 %	37 %	65 %

Source: International Monetary Fund (1986).
*Base year 1980 = 100.0

was at 2000.0 (using 1980 as the base year = 100.0, a rate of exchange of 500 sucres per $1 U.S., and a rate of inflation estimated at 4.2 % per month — or 50 % per year.) Using the model of P =E x P*, the rate of exchange should be about 250 sucres per U.S. dollar. However, when two adjustments are made — one because all the goods that Ecuador sells are not sold throughout the world — and the other because the price of noncommercial goods is less in an under-developed country — the rate of exchange should still not be more than 300 to 350 sucres per $1 U.S.

Why doesn't the model work after 1985? In 1986, government left all transactions of the private sector to the free market. Thus, it is certain that monetary speculation began and that it influenced the rise in the exchange rate.

Another factor is fear and lack of confidence in the economy. Because of their fear of the future and uncertainty about the Ecuadorian economy, Ecuadorians want their money in foreign currency as a hedge against bad times. There is little doubt that the last few years of the 1980s have been bad times for Ecuador. In 1986, the price of oil fell drastically, with severe consequences for Ecuador, and in 1987, an earthquake suspended Ecuadorian oil exports. Concurrently, inflation continued to rise. Still, although the economy grew in 1984 and 1985, the rate of real growth began to fall in 1986, and 1987 was a year of negative real growth.

Still, another factor is the 1988 presidential election, which has produced uncertainty because no one knows what the new government will bring.

In sum, these events created fear in the private sector and increased the demand for foreign currency and the decline in the sucre. The price index rose from 337.3 in 1985 to almost 1,000 at present, while the rate of exchange rose from 383.0 in 1985 to 2,000.0 at present. Using the same adjustments as previously, and assuming that the price of the U.S. dollar should be 300 to 350 sucres, the exchange rate index should be between 1,200.0 and 1,400.0, respectively. If this is the case, *between 15 % and 25 % of the fall in the sucre in recent years (1986-1988) has been produced by fears in the private sector — capital flight and speculation.*

Results of the Fall of the Sucre

When the exchange rate rises, so do the prices of imports. Thus, an important consequence of the fall of the sucre is inflation. However, inflation is also a significant factor in the fall of the sucre. Inflation produces a rise in the rate of exchange, and a rise in the rate of exchange produces a rise in inflation. The result is an inflationary spiral.

According to the theory, however, a fall in the sucre (the same as a rise in the rate of exchange) also produces an increase in productive output and employment. There are two principal reasons. The first reason for the increase is the direct incentive to exports that the drop produces. Assume the export of a good, "X." The good is worth $2 U.S. in the international market. If the rate of exchange is 100 sucres per $1 U.S., 200 sucres are earned for every unit of "X" that is exported. Thus, if the rate of exchange rises toward 200 sucres per $1 U.S., earnings reach 400 sucres for each unit of "X" that is exported (2 x 200 = 400). Thus, the rise in the rate of exchange produces a direct incentive to increase the production of exports.

The second reason is the fall in real value of salaries, which produces a drop in the sucre. There is no doubt that this is occurring. Between 1980 and 1985, the real value of the minimum wage has been falling each year; for example, in 1983 it fell 16 % in real terms (Instituto Latinamericano de Investigaciones Sociales 1986). When real salaries fall, the costs of production also fall in comparison with those of other countries. This produces an advantage for Ecuadorian exporters because they can compete better in the world market, and this advantage serves as an incentive to increase production.

According to the theory, these two factors should produce an increase in production and employment. However, in recent years, unemployment and underemployment have risen, exports have diminished, and the economy is in crisis.

Why has the fall in the value of the sucre not produced the effects that the theory predicts? First, exports have fallen in recent years, though the quantity of a number of nontraditional exports (like shrimp) has actually risen. For several products, the drop in the value of the sucre has produced incentives for increased production for export. *The principal problem has been the change from production for the domestic market of noncommercial goods to production for the world market, which purchases only commercial goods.*

In the 1970s, the income from oil production gave a large boost to the Ecuadorian economy. The majority of this growth occurred in the domestic market, in the industries of substitution for imports and noncommercial goods. (Noncommercial goods are found in sectors like construction, finance, transport, and commercial services — which produce goods that for the most part, cannot be sold outside the country.) From 1974 until 1979, import substitution industries grew at a rate of 11.5 % per year, on average. However, exports from this sector never reached more than 5 % of total exports, even though imports for the same sector reached more than half of the country's total imports. In the same period, the sectors of noncommercial goods grew rapidly. Commercial service industries grew at a rate of 8.8 % per year, construction rose by 4.3 % per year, and other services rose at 8.9 % per year. The sectors of commercial goods (with the exception of the industrial sector) grew at slower rates, while the oil sector grew at a rate of 4.2 % per year, and the agricultural sector rose at a rate of 1.1 % (World Bank 1984).

When the 1980s arrived, the growth in the domestic market stagnated and it became essential to begin increasing exports. However, a decade of industrial protectionism has produced a sector incapable of competing in the world market. A decade of unlimited loans has produced an enormous debt, the payments on which are almost half the value of exports. A decade of uneven growth has produced a paralyzed economy that cannot adjust to new needs. The industrial sector contracted by 1.4 % in 1983, 1.8 % in 1984, and 1.8 % in 1985. The construction sector has contracted by   7.6 % in 1983 and the sector of commercial services (*servicios y comerciante*) contracted by 11.8 % in the same year (Economist Intellligence Unit 1987).

To alleviate this crisis, the country needs a policy of promoting productive investment in the production of commercial goods in all parts of the economy, not only for export but also for efficient production for the internal market. *Exchange rate policies play a large role in alleviating the crisis when accompanied by policies geared toward individual sectors.*

Exchange Rate Policies and the Future

There are two options that the government can choose.

Policy of Exchange Rate Controls.

The first option consists of government intervention in exchange markets. The government could direct the purchase and sale of the U.S. dollar (and other foreign currencies) through the Central Bank, as in earlier times. It could fix the rate of exchange at a real level (around 300 to 350 sucres per $1 U.S.) and regulate all monetary transactions. Through such policy, the government could control the random fall of the sucre.

However, *the policy of exchange rate control in Ecuador is very dangerous.* Instead of promoting confidence, *a policy of control can promote fear in the private sector* because it would appear the government believes there is something wrong. Instead of promoting a rational policy, *a policy of control would produce a separate and illegal exchange market* because the rate of controlled exchange would not follow the laws of supply and demand.

The flow of international monetary reserves has already produced a current deficit in Ecuador's balance of payments. If the government fixes the rate of exchange at a level lower than that of supply and demand, it would increase demand for foreign currency. If the government does not have the dollars that are being demanded, the result will be an exchange rate crisis.

Finally, if the policy of exchange rate controls is accompanied by a continuation in the government budget deficit — which adds to inflation — the inevitable pressures produced by the deficit willproduce an enormous economic crisis.

Policy of Confidence.

The second option, and the one we prefer, is a policy of confidence. We have already estimated that 15 % to 25 % of the recent fall in the sucre is a result of the flight of capital and speculation. A policy of confidence consists of dispelling the fears of the private sector in order to invite the return of capital that has already left the country or, at least, prevent further capital flight. Such a policy also requires combatting inflation, which will be difficult. The way to success is through a sincere effort by government, in which the private sector can have confidence. It would consist of three parts.

1. *There must be a real effort to combat inflation, not with price controls but with a reduction in the government budget deficit.* We cannot deny that inflation produces pressure to raise the rate of exchange. At the same time, we cannot deny that a large part of inflation occurs when government spends more than it takes in.

Ecuador faces an inflationary situation which is not as grave as that which confronted Brazil, Argentina, or Bolivia. Inflation still has not risen above 100 % per year. Thus, structural inflation in Ecuador remains much less than in those countries. It is likely that Ecuador can combat inflation without policies of controls, merely by reducing the deficit to a responsible level and avoiding the distortions that come with policies of control.

2. *The policy must support investment in production for export and efficient domestic production that intensively uses the country's most*

abundant resource — human labor — and, more important, provides
businesses with the ability to compete in the international market.
This policy consists of .incentives such as a reduction in taxes on
businesses that invest in production for export and adequate information
to businesses on the best form of exports, as well as incentives for
investment in rural areas and secondary cities, where the use of labor is
most intensive. Most important is the need to recover the confidence of
the private sector by demonstrating that investing in Ecuador is
intelligent and lucrative — in order to reduce capital flight and
speculation, two significant forces that affect the rate of exchange.

It is very important that at the same time the rate of exchange is
set free, the government does not also control the rate of interest. In
order to insure that investment will not be capital intensive, the real
interest rate must be used, both to encourage the use of domestic
resources in production and to attract savings.

3. *The policy must leave the exchange rate to the free market.* If
inflation returns to normal low levels and if the private sector has
confidence that the probability for success is high, the pressures that
force the exchange rate upward will disappear.

REFERENCES

Banco Central del Ecuador. *Memoria Anual* Quito: 1986b.

Banco Central del Ecuador. *Cuentas Nacionales del Ecuador, 1977-1986* Quito: 1987.

Banco Central de Ecuador y El Consejo Nacional de Desarollo. *Programa de Encuestas de Coyuntura: Industria Manufacturera* no. 51 (March 1988b.)

Economist Intelligence Unit. *Country Profile: Ecuador* London: Economist Publications, 1987.

Instituto Latinoamericano de Investigacioners Sociales. *Estadísticas del Ecuador* Chile: 1986.

International Monetary Fund. *International Financial Statistics* Washington, D.C.: International Monetary Fund, 1986 (and updates).

World Bank. *Development Plan For Ecuador* Washington, DC: World Bank, 1984.

5

Macroeconomic Production Strategy: Sectorial Focus

The legacy of colonialism and the continued growth of a global economy is that many countries — both developed and developing — remain reliant on, and vulnerable to, shocks in the world economy. While many development planners tend to overlook these legacies — some critics even charge that they consciously or unwittingly perpetuate them in new forms — we believe that it is important to address this issue up front and to seek strategies that eliminate even its subtle vestiges.

For many countries, the process of colonization was one that often overdeveloped specific areas of local economies — resource extraction, the supply of specific services, production of a particular crop, or other advantageous use of an endowment of natural or human resources. Development policies often sought to exploit these advantages while creating further imbalances.

Given this history, countries often find themselves with few immediate alternatives. Without modern systems of industrial production to make use of their own raw materials, they find themselves with systems of either peasant cash crop economies — in which the individual producers are subject to the vagaries of world markets or powerful producers — or subsistence agriculture, in which families eke out existence on poor soil with basic and inadequate technologies.

Ideally, for many countries without particular advantages as intermediaries in trading and with abundant fertile lands, a strategy of sustainable growth and internal reliance is often better in the long term than an export-based economy — despite efforts to globalize the world economy and increase the dependency and reliance on neighboring countries. While the ideology of trade and internationalism, of open markets, strategic advantage and free flows of labor and capital has now replaced the previous terminology of cash crop economies, resource extraction, spheres of influence and brain drain, we believe that the current approaches are not substantively different from the policies of the past because they neglect to address the underlying assumptions that drive them. Indeed, the most perceptible difference is that while production imbalances continue to be magnified with expanded trade, cultural and national identities tend to disappear, to be replaced with identification based on the economic function that workers serve in the global economy (i.e., diamond miners, textile factory workers, computer programmers, or banana harvesters).

Over the long term, a dynamic world economy must have at its basis a number of local economies that literally cut against the grain of current trends. Sustainable long-term growth depends on strong, local economies that:

• maintain their local traditions, local pride, and innovations as a means of keeping the world economy continually competitive and vibrant, thus fostering a variety of unique "laboratories" to experiment with their own approaches to production and social and economic organization and providing the sense of ownership and esteem that is an important productive incentive. The development of trade blocs and the easing of borders threatens the establishment of concentrated production in several industries, with potentially severe, long term economic and political consequences;

• reduce overall vulnerability to international shocks in the world economy, which result whenever a single system becomes centralized, by recognizing the value of diffusion and decentralization that protect the economy from acts of nature or human-made disasters that could suddenly lead to the unavailability of, or price increases in, raw materials or intermediate goods;

• minimize the potential for dependency, increase the ability of smaller countries to increase their relative standards of living, and participate in international prosperity, while maximizing the development of local skills and talents. Smaller countries with less capital or military strength remain vulnerable to political and economic leverage from the more powerful countries in setting the terms of trade or the price of labor in an interdependent global economy and can best protect themselves and foster sustained development by increasing their self-reliance; and

• promote individual freedom, democracy, and fulfillment, which free markets promise when they disperse the holdings of productive and human capital — encouraging individuals to own their own means of production and exercise their own powers of decision — rather than concentrate them.

The unfortunate trend has been that within countries, the acceleration of globalization and the reliance on export industries continues to magnify tensions between the "modern sectors" (intermediaries for First World purchasers) and the people who live on the land where the resources lie, cultivate the land used for cash crops, or provide the cheap labor for the factories where export goods are produced. Increased globalization and international competition mean increased pressures to force people off the land or to transform traditional practices for the benefits of the modern sector.

Nevertheless, despite the ideal for long term sustainable and self-reliant development, the reality is that many countries are currently dependent on specific exports — whether exporting cheap skilled or unskilled labor by producing goods for the world market, cash crops, or the availability of a valuable raw material or resource that is extracted and sold.

In the short run, developing countries must focus on improving the management and productivity of their existing sectors — even if they are not ultimately related to sustainable growth — while looking to the long term.

We choose two sectors of many on which to focus our attention here. First is food production within the agricultural sector — the dominant economic sector for many less developed nations as well as for some First World countries — which deserves special consideration. The improvement of agricultural productivity is often linked to commercial and investment policies that would put greater resources into the hands of the small farmer, not only improving productivity but simultaneously contributing to more varied production and more sustainable development. The second is tourism — one of many export sectors — which holds a special potential for promoting cultural pride and protecting, rather than depleting, the environment.

FOOD PRODUCTION

Like many other problems in development, the difficulty in the food production sector is not primarily a result of inadequate technology or an insufficient ability of local governments or development agencies to transmit this technology. The problem is a political one, and we seek to address it by confronting the issue head-on.

In many developing nations, food producers suffer at the hands of intermediaries or find it more lucrative to use their land for the production of items with great economic value that create distortion in development — such as legal or illicit addictive substances. However, in a large number of countries, the real problem is not large agricultural buyers, since farmers can often choose to produce something other than a cash crop. Rather, the problem is government.

Government policies in developing countries have, for the most part, redistributed resources from the agricultural sector toward other sectors of the economy and favored the production of products destined for agroindustry or export. Further, lands that are potentially arable or were once arable have often been stripped of their topsoil or otherwise depleted due to short-sighted policies seeking a rapid return on investments for agrobusiness or for other uses on the same or adjoining lands, such as logging or resource extraction.

Within the agricultural sector itself, there is an obvious governmental bias in favor of large and powerful producers, which has resulted in leaving the small farmers who need credit or insurance without assistance. Often (and even more fundamentally), governments fail to provide access to sufficient landholdings for small farmers to survive, even when such redistributions have been long included as part of government policies.

RECOMMENDATIONS

If Ecuador does not change its strategy for agricultural development, the country will face a grave crisis in food production. To avoid this crisis, the government must do the following.

Redirect available resources from large farms to small producers of essential foods, where there is greater potential for increased productivity (considering the primitive levels of technology used today in the majority of small farms and the potential for improvement). The production of essential foods currently receives only a fraction of available credit for the agricultural sector.

Increase technical assistance and research for the production of foods, with a particular goal of strengthening these programs to assist small producers. The government must take strong action to stimulate improved methods of cultivation, not only to improve the distribution of superior varieties of seeds and inputs, but also to improve methods of cultivation and land preservation. Resources provided for agricultural research must be directed away from expensive programs (e.g., atomic energy laboratories) and toward those programs that are more cost effective, will identify more productive uses of particular lands, and will result in improved methods for the producers of foodstuffs.

Increase support for land conservation programs that already exist, such as reforestation and special cultivation methods, since land erosion will be one of the most serious problems that Ecuador will face in the coming years.

Research the possibility of cooperation (the formation of cooperatives) among small producers as a means of improving the capacity of those producers to ensure that government programs truly help them. It is possible that the failure of some of these programs in the past was due to mistakes in the policies on which they were based.

Overall, it is very important that the government not return to the policies of the past, which involved trying to implement a program of food price controls. Such controls produce market distortions and serve as a negative incentive to production (as the history of such programs in Ecuador has shown), whereas at this time the country needs significant increases in production to satisfy a growing demand for food.

In contrast, programs that increase productivity and production could diminish the growth in prices if the supply of basic foods grows more rapidly than the demand.

REPORT

Ecuador's agricultural sector is the most important source of employment in the country, accounting for a third of the economically active population. As a source of such a significant amount of employment and of production of most of the foods consumed by Ecuadorian households, its importance needs little explanation.

A great deal of attention has focused on the problems of this sector, particularly on problems faced by food producers. The growth in productivity has been slow, while demand has continued to grow. Theoretically, the growth in food prices should stimulate production, but prices continue to rise while production grows only slowly.

Recently, it has been suggested that the system of marketing of basic food products is responsible for the problems that confront the agricultural sector. According to the argument, the intermediaries — commodity purchasers, wholesalers, and retailers — are taking greater and greater portions of the difference between what the farmer receives and what the consumer pays, continually raising the prices. As a result, the urban consumer buys fewer essential food products and the farmer suffers under the monopoly of the industry's middlemen. If, in general, it can be assumed that agricultural production responds directly to a rise in prices, it would appear that farmers are suffering from the market power of intermediaries, since prices continues to rise while production grows slowly. However, this does not seem to be the case.

Certainly, the difference between what the consumer pays and what the producer earns (the sales margin) is significant in many food products (see Figure 5.1.). Since 1980, consumers have paid, on average, 209.43 % more than the producer of pepper has received, 148.72 % more for yuca, and 147.13 % more for tomatoes. However, there are large differences between the sales margins for different products, with the lowest margins on products that are sold in the largest volume or which keep the longest (Chiriboga 1985).

A more detailed view, which considers the difficulties that confront the production of food products, requires not only a calculation of sales margins but also an examination of the factors of production. To conclude that the distribution of sales margins is, in reality, not the root of the problem, we considered three key factors — the variation in sales margins during the 1980s; the movements in the real value which the producer received (that is, real prices); and the quantity of credit directed to food production — and determined their effects on a select group of food products — rice, corn, tomatoes, potatoes, and yuca. The results follow.

Figure 5.1. Variation in Commercialization Margins and Real Prices (Six Crops)

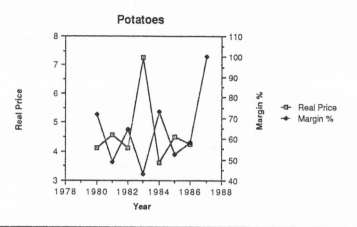

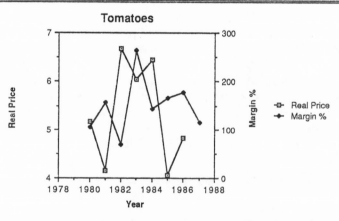

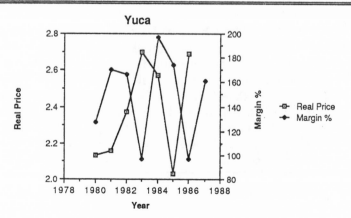

Figure 5.1. (continued)

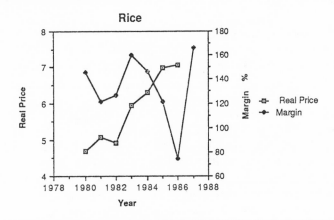

Rice

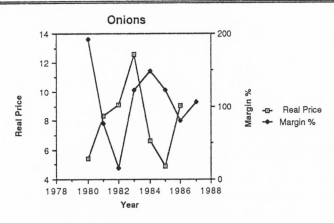

Onions

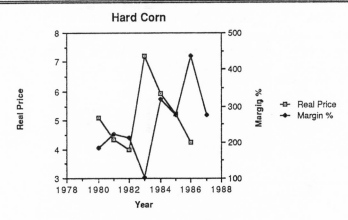

Hard Corn

187

Change in Sales Margins

A simple calculation —

[(consumer price - producer price)/producer price] x 100

— produces a margin showing the percentage of the markup on a product's price for consumers as a percentage of the producer's price. This margin reflects all the intermediate processes, but it is not a measure of either merchant or producer earnings. Despite this simplification, in considering that this margin has risen over time, the logical conclusion would be that intermediaries are receiving a larger part of the earnings and that consumers are paying the extra costs. Further, these increasing profit margins would seem to explain why the price of food products has risen so much in the last few years while the production of the same products has remained stagnant.

For each one of the products examined, the sales margins show large variations during the 1980s (see Figure 5.1). Despite this, the results of a simple regression analysis to test for trends of the sales margins over time are inconclusive. With a confidence interval of 90 %, (represented by the area enclosed by the two shadowed lines in Figure 5.2 and crossing the fitted regression line), it is impossible to say that the margins demonstrate any distinct tendency in the 1980s (see Figure 5.2). While food prices rose rapidly in 1983 as a result of crop losses produced by the El Niño storm, sales margins for dry corn, potatoes, and yuca fell substantially (see Table 5.1). This appears to contradict the argument that the recent increases in food prices are the result of exploitation of food producers and consumers by intermediaries.

An earlier study by Francisco Swett (1984) arrived at similar conclusions: *the distribution of margins allows us to draw the preliminary conclusion that while market prices of food products have been fragmented, this does not constitute exploitative, abusive, and total appropriation of the sales of producers.* Nevertheless, if farmers are receiving more for their products, why is there stagnation in production, and especially in productivity?

Figure 5.2. Distribution of Sales Margins in the 1980s (Six Crops)

Rice

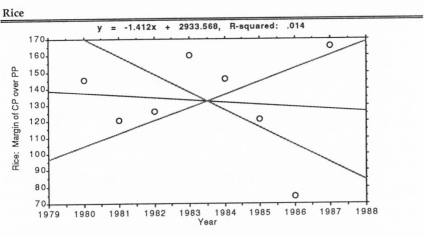

y = -1.412x + 2933.568, R-squared: .014

Onions

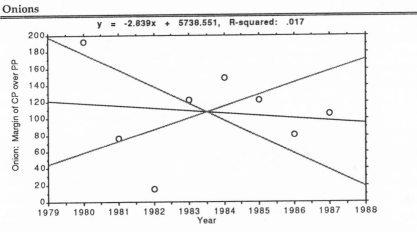

y = -2.839x + 5738.551, R-squared: .017

Dry Corn

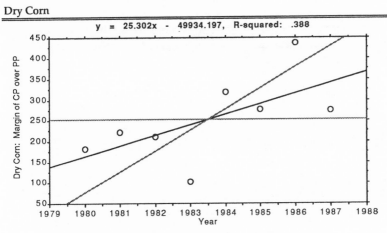

y = 25.302x - 49934.197, R-squared: .388

Figure 5.2. (continued)

Potatoes

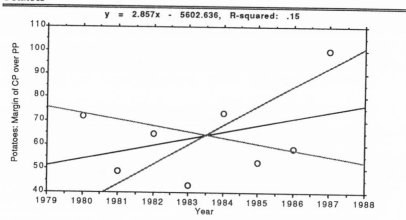

Tomatoes

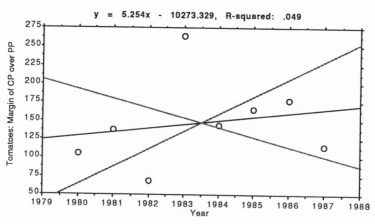

Yuca

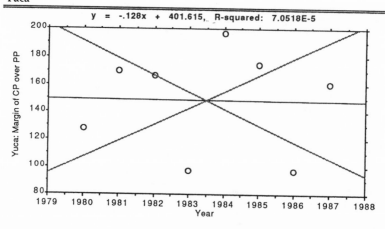

Table 5.1. Land Area of Cultivation, Production, and Yield

Product	1980	1981	1982	1983	1984	1985	1986	1987
Rice								
Cultivation	126.6	131.3	131.7	94.9	139.1	149.9	227.6	275.9
Production	380.6	434.4	384.4	273.5	437.2	397.4	575.9	780.8
Yield	3.01	3.31	2.92	2.88	3.14	2.65	2.53	2.83
Dry Corn								
Cultivation	166.7	184.7	155.4	145.3	182.8	174.3	261.3	258.9
Production	196.4	232.6	269.3	185.0	269.0	292.9	315.5	296.6
Yield	1.18	1.26	1.73	1.27	1.47	1.68	1.21	1.15
Onion								
Cultivation	3.3	4.7	4.7	4.6	5.8	6.4	8.6	7.8
Production	30.1	42.1	41.7	40.7	50.7	55.5	36.8	44.3
Yield	9.03	8.88	8.81	8.85	8.81	6.3	4.28	5.68
Tomato								
Cultivation	2.6	2.9	2.3	2.4	3.7	4.1	4.8	5.7
Production	38.1	42.3	36.8	35.0	63.0	64.7	67.6	73.2
Yield	14.88	14.75	15.90	14.86	17.12	15.63	14.06	12.85
Potatoes								
Cultivation	30.4	31.6	35.1	26.7	33.5	36.6	53.6	56.1
Production	323.2	391.6	416.4	314.0	389.6	423.2	388.7	353.9
Yield	10.64	12.39	11.86	11.74	11.63	11.57	7.25	6.31
Yuca								
Cultivation	25.2	26.0	20.0	20.1	24.0	22.2	20.0	22.4
Production	229.3	236.8	183.9	194.8	239.2	228.8	118.0	131.2
Yield	9.11	9.11	9.23	9.69	9.97	10.3	5.93	5.86

Note: Cultivated land area in thousands of hectares;
production in thousands of metric tons;
yield in metric tons per hectare.

Real Prices Received by Producers

The nominal prices that farmers received increased during the 1980s, while costs of production increased. The nominal price, as adjusted by the price index in the Sierra region (calculated by the Central Bank), reveals the real price that farmers receive for their products. (This analysis assumes that the _real_ costs of production were constant). The figures demonstrate that in 1986, the producers of potatoes, dry corn, and tomatoes were in no better position than they were in 1980, in terms of real prices. The real price of onions in 1986 was the same as in 1982. Although the real price of yuca in 1986 was as high as it was in 1983, during the previous year it was at its lowest level in the decade. The exception is the real price of rice, which shows a significant increase since 1980 (see Figure 5.1).

These figures seem to indicate that a minority of farmers, particularly those growing rice, are feeling the effects of government assistance. The results of favorable real prices for rice are shown in the figures for production and area of cultivation (see Table 5.1). In 1980, 126,608 hectares of rice were harvested. In 1987, this figure had grown by 118 %, to 275,900 acres. The level of production also increased, by 105 %, from 380,614 metric tons in 1980 to 780,776 metric tons in 1987. Rice farmers received government support when the real prices rose. _However, the majority of farmers of food products suffered no or little growth in real prices for their products._ Furthermore, the level of real prices created substantial distortions in the growth of food production, as did the policies of the farm credit system.

Financial Credit Directed to Farmers for the Production of Food

From 1979 until 1984, 44 % of all state credit directed to agricultural products (crop production) was allocated to rice production. Between 1984 and 1988, this figure increased to 46 % (see Table 5.2). After rice, the largest amount of credit was directed to the production of dry corn, with 15 % of the available total allocated to corn between 1979 and 1984, and a decrease to 13 % of the total, from 1984 to 1988. The production of potatoes received 5 % of the total agricultural credit for crops between 1979 and 1988, while the remaining products in this study (tomatoes and yuca) received less than 1 % of available credit during 1979 to 1988. Keeping in mind that these numbers reflect percentages of the total amount of credit for crops, the total is itself only 41 % of the total credit directed to the agricultural sector. The largest portion of state agricultural credit was allocated to cattle raising (primarily for milk production), which received close to 70 % of available credit, while 10 % was allocated to mechanization.

The areas that received the most governmental attention in the 1980s — dry corn, rice, cattle, and mechanization — are, in large part, the productive activities of medium and large-sized enterprises, often for export. Dry corn is produced for agroindustry while the majority of production in agroindustry comes from farms that have more than 20 hectares (Chiriboga 1985). In 1974, almost 60 % of the production of rice came from farms of more than 20 hectares (Censo Agropecuario 1974). The majority of cattle raising also occurs on large farms — farms of 100 hectares or more, which make up 46.9 % of the total area dedicated to grazing. Farms of 5 to 10 hectares account for only 24.2 % of the total area dedicated to grazing (Chiriboga 1985). *In short, credit policies during the 1980's have favored production in large enterprises which, for the most part, produce rice and raise cattle, along with products for agro-business (such as dry corn.)*

Table 5.2. State Credit Given to Agriculture

| | 1979-84 | | 1984-88 | |
Product	Nom.	% of total	Nom.	% of total
Total Food Crops	14,251.91	40.57%	54,083.91	40.82%
Grazing, Cattle	14,041.95	39.98%	49,797.89	37.59%
Livestock	10,296.25	29.31%	39,264.67	29.64%
Agr. Machinery	3,104.61	8.84%	15,402.67	11.63%
Rice	6,253.11	43.88%	24,612.82	45.51%
Dry Corn	2,150.32	15.09%	68,885.38	12.73%
Potatoes	880.61	6.18%	2,715.35	5.02%
Onion	109.32	0.77%	499.22	0.92%
Tomato	179.81	1.26%	437.87	0.81%

Source: Banco Central de Ecuador y el Consejo Nacional de
            Desarollo (January 1988).
Note: Nom. = nominal value in thousands of sucres;
            Percentage is of total credit, with the exception of
            crops, for which it is percentage of total credit
            allocated for crops.

Government Discrimination

The level of real prices and the quantity of available state credit demonstrate that food producers are not suffering at the hands of intermediaries. Rather, they are suffering at the hands of government. The case of rice demonstrates that with proper incentives, the production of food could be significantly increased. Despite this, *there is an obvious governmental bias in favor of large and powerful producers, which has resulted in leaving without assistance those small farmers, the majority of whom are in the Sierra region and who need credit.*

The producers of potatoes, tomatoes, yuca, onions, and the majority of other basic food products are small farmers. According to the agricultural census of 1974, 60 % of the potato output, 92 % of onions, 55 % of tomato, and 72 % of black beans come from farms of 20 hectares or less. These are the same farmers who receive only small amounts of government loans. Similarly, the distribution of tractors, fertilizers, and other production inputs is designed to benefit middle and high income producers (Luzuriago and Zuvekas 1982, p. 266). Although it is difficult to find statistics, the level of technical assistance provided by government appears to follow the example of the distribution of credit. While the government budget allocates money to a nuclear laboratory to experiment with methods of increasing milk production, small farmers in the Sierras are using primitive farming methods and cannot even obtain funds to buy fertilizer. In many cases, the small farmer has to count on intermediaries to obtain loans, seeds, and other inputs. It is the government that is to blame for placing small farmers at the mercy of these intermediaries.

The policies of government that have abandoned producers of essential food products have had serious consequences for Ecuador, and especially for the Sierra region, where the result has been stagnation in the growth in agricultural production. With the exception of rice, all the products in this study are from the Sierra, where the majority of food products are produced. *In the future, any increase in food production in the Sierra must come from increases in productivity because the quantity of new arable lands is small in such a populated region. Despite the need for increased productivity in all the Sierran products discussed here, not a single one has shown a significant increase in output in this decade (see Table 5.1). In fact, yields remained stagnant during the 1980s, and the majority have diminished in the past two years* (in part, as a result of recent bad weather conditions). All this comes as a direct result of government policies that have paid no attention to the problems of the Sierran small farmer. No single crop that has received government attention has been able to achieve significant increases in productivity. As a result, the prospects for future success are small. (It is interesting to note that the growth in production of rice during the last few years has resulted, for the most part, from increases in the amount of land that is cultivated.)

Price Controls

In the past, the government of Ecuador has attempted to intervene in the market to regulate the price of food products. *These policies, for the most part, have served to redistribute resources from the agricultural sector toward other sectors of the economy and have favored the production of products destined for agroindustry or export.* Under these policies, the real prices that producers received for essential food products were kept artificially low. As a result, there was a dramatic decline in cultivated lands (as well as in production) for many of these products between 1972 and 1982. For example, the land area used to cultivate black beans fell 17.9 % from 1972 to 1982, land for wheat fell 56.5 %, land for yuca fell 38.5 %, land for onions fell 16.8 % and land for potatoes fell 6.9 % (Chiriboga 1985). Since 1982, the role that government has played in the market has diminished. At present, there is no government intervention, with the exception of minimal activity in the marketing of select products (e.g., rice and milk.) As a result, the cultivated area of the majority of basic food products has been increasing.

Land Use

Of course, part of the stagnation in productivity can be explained by a change in the average yield that results when new lands and marginal lands, which are less useful, are cultivated. However, *it is undeniable that the productivity of the agricultural sector did not grow in the 1980s. If this situation does not change, Ecuador will encounter serious problems in the 1990s.* The Sierra has reached its practical limits in the expansion of cultivated land; actually, it has passed its limits in many areas, with serious consequences in land erosion. In several areas, slopes of more than 45 % are used for cultivation, causing erosion to deplete the soil. It is doubtful that the land can last under these conditions for more than a few years. With erosion impoverishing much of the land, it will be increasingly difficult in the future to achieve increases in productivity. The Ecuadorian government is thus faced with an enormous challenge. If it does not respond, the result could be an unprecedented growth in food imports, in a country already confronted with substantial balance-of-payments problems.

Meeting the Needs

Recommendations for saving the agricultural sector complement those we presented in the sections on decentralization (Chapter 2), and population (Chapter 1). *What is necessary is an increase in the flow of resources to the areas outside the metropolitan centers, and especially to rural areas.* The components of this program for the agricultural sector are the following.

Resources.

The production of essential foods receives only a fraction of the available credit granted to the agricultural sector. To solve this problem, *government must redirect available resources from large farms to small producers of essential foods, where there is great potential for increased productivity* (considering the primitive levels of technology used today in the majority of small farms and the potential for their improvement). Theoretically, *this type of program could be implemented with the use of regional development banks* — as described in the section on decentralization (Chapter 2) — which would pay more attention to the needs of local farmers than the National Development Bank currently does.

A redirection of resources to the agricultural sector would complement the strategy of directing resources to rural areas for employment there, thus increasing the positive effect the growth of rural income on reducing population growth. This program would also avoid the problem that growth in demand for basic food products would create if there were not a simultaneous increase in the supply of the same products. If the demand were to rise without an increase in production, the result would be an enormous jump in the prices of foods.

Technology.

A natural complement to a strategy of making more resources available to rural areas is to increase technical assistance and associated research for the production of foods, including increasing the abilities of these programs to assist small producers of food products. *The Ecuadorian government must take strong action to stimulate more advanced methods of cultivation, not only through improving the distribution of superior varieties of seeds and hybrids, but also by improving methods of cultivation and land preservation.* Land erosion will be one of the most serious problems that Ecuador will face in the coming years. Only by increasing support for conservation programs that already exist — (such as reforestation) can the country solve this problem. Resources provided for agricultural research must be directed away from expensive programs (e.g., atomic energy) and toward those programs that are more cost effective, identify more productive uses of particular lands, and lead to improved methods of food production.

Cooperation.

In the past, cooperation (through cooperatives) has had little success in Ecuador. Nevertheless, it is possible that the failure of these programs was a result of a mistake in the political conditions under which they operated. It is possible that *the cooperation of small producers would increase their clout, giving them greater power to demand the resources they need* so as to increase the prices they receive for their products and help them improve marketing methods.

Prices and State Intervention.

Any attempts at implementing government price controls in the future are destined to be unsuccessful. Instead of intervention, programs for increasing productivity and production will diminish the rise in prices if the supply of basic foods simply grows more rapidly than the demand for the same products. A program of price controls would produce market distortions and serve as a negative incentive to production at a time when the country needs significant increases in production to satisfy a growing demand.

TOURISM

While an economy that is heavily reliant on exports is not the ideal of sustainable development, we recognize that the reality of the world's distribution of resources and skills is such that many developing countries must derive large shares of their earnings through exports. Export sectors should not be the focus of development, but they are critical concerns in any development planning efforts not only because of their contribution to a country's earnings — and their ability to finance other development needs — but because of the risks they present: their particular vulnerability to international factors and the real impact they have on a country's peoples, environment, and social organization.

Given the integral role of exports in developing economies, less-developed countries must pay careful attention to the quality of management of the resources placed in, and earnings from, the sector. Countries must take advantage of the best technical management skills to obtain from an export the highest price for the country for the longest possible period, while considering their other long-term cultural, environmental, and economic needs at the same time.

Any country with a major export industry, particularly one that depends on natural resources, must devote its efforts to:

• protect against the negative cultural or environmental impacts of extracting and selling the resource;

• continually "renew" resources or prepare for the ultimate depletion of an "unrenewable" resource; and

• prepare against shocks in the world economy that could quickly affect demand, price, or the price or supply of intermediate goods in producing or selling the resource.

In the case of raw material exports — of oil and minerals — developing economies face potentially catastrophic shocks from the loss of a major source of earnings when those resources are depleted or prices fall. Natural resources are really assets held in deposit as a form of endowment rather than productive resources for developing economies, and their sale is not a real measure of productivity. The attention of policies in the export sector must be to continually invest: to wean an economy from reliance on its income from a nonrenewable resource by funding new industries as the resource is depleted.

Among "export" industries, one of the most vulnerable, but also most potentially advantageous, is tourism. Tourism is highly dependent on the world market, relying as it does on the existence of an international leisure class. At the same time, while it does not extract any raw materials and thus create major environmental devastation, tourism has the potential for bringing unwanted disruptions to local cultures at the price of catering to the wishes of a foreigners who have little stake in local peoples and view the areas they visit as playgrounds for their fantasies.

If properly managed, however, the tourist industry can actually be a boon to indigenous cultures and resources. Depending on a country's ability to promote its unique history, traditions, and natural features, tourism offers a potential to develop and maintain cultural patrimony, preserve much of a country's ecology, and, ironically, turn the country's cultural diversity to a commercial advantage that generates funds to protect and save it. Indeed, some regions have exceptional good fortune in their resource endowments and can combine the "export" industry of tourism with the goals of protecting their natural resources as well as much of the local culture.

The Amazon region is one such example. The area is a treasure chest of resources. From one perspective, this means oil, minerals, and hydroelectric power, but from another, it involves the world's supply of oxygen and power to cleanse the globe, bio-diversity and its potential, human diversity, and breathtaking beauty. Although concerns for extracting oil and minerals and growing cash crops compete with the potential for other uses, the chance to turn pristine natural beauty into an asset while supporting less-destructive extraction policies is part of an enlightened view of development. Some companies have begun to "harvest" collectible resources of the rainforests — such as nuts, berries and oils — while maintaining these areas and the people in them, simultaneously developing a new export industry of "ecotourism" as a means of showing off the area's treasures without exploiting them.

RECOMMENDATIONS

As foreigners working abroad, investigating development problems but also sampling the many attractions of foreign countries, we had the chance to see developing countries as tourists, as well. From these experiences, we have derived a number of suggestions for improving tourist services and increasing the profitability of the tourist industry while better protecting Ecuador's natural resources and cultural heritage. As a result of our investigations, we recommend that:

• Foreigners should be charged significantly more than Ecuadorians for museums, anthropological sites, domestic airline flights, and so forth.

• Localities should establish more museums displaying local traditions, history, and artwork.

• Ecuador should open more archaeological sites to tourism. By charging foreigners admission fees to these sites, part of the additional revenues could be allocated to preserve these sites as educational resources and sources of cultural pride.

• Reserves should be designed for high-budget, nature-conscious tourists (such as those who visit the Galápagos), which would serve the dual function of preserving the ecosystem and providing revenues through "ecotourism."

• DITURIS, the government travel agency, should publish a weekly bulletin describing local special events and listing artesanía (crafts) shops in the cities.

• DITURIS should also distribute a guide to museums, historic buildings, and churches to make them more accessible to tourists.

Ecuador is blessed not only with the remarkable beauty of its beaches, mountains, the Amazon, and the biological diversity of the Galápagos Islands, but also by the strength of a number of indigenous peoples who cling to their traditions and sometimes live in areas with historical and archaeological treasures.

With the notable exception of the Galápagos Islands, however, tourism seems to be a rather underdeveloped industry for Ecuador. The country's extreme diversity in such a small geographic area make tourism a viable but, as of yet, largely untapped source of additional revenues.

General Revenue Increases

We recommend that tourist attractions increase their prices for foreigners. In the same way that foreigners must pay more than Ecuadorians to visit the Galápagos Islands, *foreigners could pay more for museums, anthropological sights, and domestic airline flights.* At present, prices are so low that they could be raised substantially and still be very affordable for tourists.

We do think it is important, however, not to raise the prices for Ecuadorians. Museums and anthropological sights are extremely effective media for Ecuadorians to learn more about the value and diversity of their own cultures.

Local Museums

Ecuador's rich and varied cultural heritage is a potentially valuable source of revenue and could be better preserved through the establishment of local museums to display local customs, ways of life, local art, and so on. Such exhibits would not only attract many foreigners interested in learning more about Ecuador, but might also serve to remind local inhabitants of the vastness and significance of their past, thus increasing pride in their individual heritage. We were particularly impressed by museums in Salango, Guaranda, Pompeya and Manta, which boasted both archaeological and more recent historical displays. Potential applications for other regions might include the following.

We think many tourists would be willing to pay to see a museum displaying the history of the artisan industry in Otavalo. Foreigners are interested in seeing exactly how the products they are buying are made and would appreciate a "museum" that showed actual weavers at work. If Otavalans feel that such a project could be integrated into their culture without damaging their sense of pride and integrity, we think they could derive significant revenues from it.

A functioning model Shuar village could attract many foreigners whose interest in the group has been sparked by their *tsantsa* fame (the shrunken human heads that their warrior ancestors produced). Again, decisions over the appropriateness of commercializing their traditions should be made by the Shuar rather than outsiders.

Esmeraldas prides itself on rhythm and dance. Such talents could effectively be used to attract tourists to dance shows and other performances.

Archaeological Sites

Ecuador's many undeveloped archaeological sites seem to us to be a prime example of an underutilized resource. Many are unnecessarily difficult to reach and are not being well cared for. Others, such as the uniquely crafted Manabí stone *sillas* (seats), have been stripped of many of their artifacts which have been sold at ridiculously low prices and are now in museums in the United States and Europe.

To prevent further losses and deterioration of the archaeological treasures, we recommend that *Ecuador open more sites to tourism. By charging admission fees to foreigners at a level sufficient to protect and develop the sites, additional revenues would preserve these educational resources and sources of cultural pride for Ecuadorian visitors as well.*

For instance, the archaeological site Salango near Puerto López receives 15 tourists per day. If we assume that 12 of these are foreigners, a 400 sucre entrance fee for all foreigners would net 4,800 sucres every day. Subtracting 1,000 sucres per day to generously pay an attendant, the site would generate 1.330 million sucres in revenues every year (assuming it was operating 350 days per year). Additional revenues could go to local youth who could learn the history and hire themselves out as guides.

We await with great anticipation our next visit to Ecuador, when we hope to visit:

• the Sangay mounds, which appear as human figures from the air;

• the "missing link" discoveries in the Oriente which bridge the historical gap between ancient Brazilian cultures and the pre-modern Shuar;

• unexcavated mounds in Morena-Santiago, between Sucúa and Huambi;

• the full excavations of Agua Blanca and nearby coastal sites; and

• the "Lost City," a colonial Amazonía town that was destroyed in the sixteenth century by indigenous groups.

Wildlife

There is no reason why certain regions in the Oriente cannot be set up for ecotourism — as havens for biologists and naturalists — in the same way that the Galápagos have been. We understand, for example, that forests in Zamora-Chinchipe are a bird watchers' paradise and could attract wealthy tourists who would pay handsome fees for a specialized visit to the region. Others areas which are rich in wild orchids, would undoubtedly attract many nature lovers. Such *reserves would serve the dual function of preserving the ecosystem and providing revenues through tourism.*

Zoos offer another valuable mechanism for increasing revenues through the use of wildlife. Ecuador has the advantage of being able to display the animals relatively close to their natural environment (as in the zoo in Baños) which is especially attractive to tourists who normally only see these creatures in a city zoo. *By charging an entrance fee for foreigners but not Ecuadorians, these zoos could generate revenues and provide a free educational resource for Ecuador's youth.* It is particularly important, however, that animals be treated humanely and be given enough space. Cramped cages and cruel treatment, which we observed in the zoos in Baños, Vilcabamba, and Quito, can result in tourists recommending to other foreigners that they not visit the region.

Fluvial tours through the Oriente are one area in which we do see Ecuadorians already utilizing a great deal of the potential for tourism. Tours leaving from Misahuallí cost tourists 7,500 sucres per day and generate substantial revenues. Given that there are 8 passengers on a boat, gasoline and other supplies total 10,000 sucres per day, and a guide can be hired for 4,000 sucres per day, the boat owner makes 46,000 sucres per day. At 1 million sucres for a boat, such an investment would pay for itself in only three weeks. The current owners seem to have an oligopoly. One entrepreneur with whom we spoke felt there would be too much pressure preventing entrance into the business. Although it would probably be better if this oligopoly were broken so that profits could be shared among more people, and while we believe that lower prices might attract a greater volume of tourism, (ourselves included!), this illustration does indicate that at least a few Ecuadorians have realized the potentials of tourism.

Tourist Information

In the larger cities, we believe that many tourists would be interested in a weekly bulletin explaining what social events, theater performances, festivals, and other events were taking place. Such a weekly could also include an index of local *artesanía* merchants. Such brochures could be financed easily by selling ads to local stores and restaurants that already appeal to tourists. We found it difficult at times to obtain information on transportation. Guides and brochures could greatly facilitate the process of using buses, both within cities and in traveling to sites such as Ingapirca and Agua Blanca.

DITURIS offices (the government travel agency) should be stocked with guides, to be sold or distributed freely, describing a city's museums, historical buildings, churches, and other sites. These guides could also generate government revenues by selling advertising space to area merchants.

Finally, we think that a tourist's last memory of Ecuador should be a pleasant one. The current $25 exit tax is not. In order to attract future tourists through recommendations from other travelers, we recommend either lowering the country's exit tax and making up the loss through higher charges on tourist attractions within the country or simply explaining how the money is being used. We recommend distributing small momentos of Ecuador to departing tourists as well — Ecuadorian flags or pins.

REFERENCES

Banco Central de Ecuador y el Consejo Nacional de Desarollo. *Programa de Encuestas de Coyuntura: Sector Agropecuario* no. 48 (January 1988).

Chiriboga, Manuel. "El Sistema Alimentario Ecuatoriano: Situación y Perspectivas," *Ecuador Debate* no. 9 (September 1985).

Ecuador. Instituto Nacional de Estadística y Censos. *Censo Agropecuario* Quito: 1974.

Luzuriaga, Carlos, and Clarence Zuvekas, Jr. *Distribución del Ingreso y Porbreza en las Areas Rurales del Ecuador, 1950-80* Quito: Banco Central, 1982.

Swett, Francisco. *Los Precios Agrícolas en el Ecuador: Politicas, Fundamentos y Resultados, 1970-83* 1984.

6

The Appropriate Role of the Major Institutional Actors in Development

In most development plans and strategies, the key actors with the largest amounts of resources and influence are often ignored in entirety or discussed with little mention of the critical aspects of their political, economic, and social roles. Among them are the national armed forces and police, organized religious institutions (domestic and foreign based), the military and cultural agencies of foreign governments (and former colonial powers), and multinational enterprises.

In many cases, the omissions are intentional. Commenting on their role is viewed as "engaging in politics." In some cases, addressing the impact of these institutions would be politically dangerous, while for the powerful actors in development, omitting them is, more likely, politically expedient.

It is unfortunate that many development agencies view commentary on these institutional actors as "political," while judgments on the value of preserving indigenous cultures and communities, favoring foreign investment over using local resources, lauding the merits of large enterprises over entrepreneurial ownership, or maintaining policies that favor the rich over the poor or look away from corruption are described as neutral or nonpolitical.

We believe that the real issue in designing development policies is not defining what is political but rather taking a holistic view of development so as to comment on an entire social and economic system, the influences on it, the directions in which it is moving, and its ability to change. In many cases, it takes courage to confront the reality of existing power and challenge it when it stands in the way of development, particularly when the actors making the evaluation may be benefiting from inequities and inefficiencies embedded in the existing structure. Nevertheless, we believe that an appropriate development policy may require some amount of confrontation, as well as self-examination and self-criticism.

While many development organizations view military and police organizations, organized religion, and foreign political actors as existing in separate or private spheres that are outside of the realm of government or economic policies — in the same way that some market societies label corporate economic and political power as no longer within the accepted sphere of society's direct control — these institutions are not merely direct actors on the landscape of economic and political development. Their role is much deeper and more pervasive because of their ability to influence values and cultural behaviors that change the entire context of development. Further, they are also particularly important subjects for Western development planners to incorporate in their development strategies because they represent major areas in which Western influence is transmitted and because they change the development environment.

In any society, institutions for war, social control, and religion play important roles that are intricately tied to development. Warfare in traditional societies, through ritual battles or expansion into other territories for resources, has always been a means of keeping the population in check and in balance with available resources. Religious institutions have served as community repositories of savings and redistribution in times of individual or group crisis as well as centers of socialization and community organization.

During the colonial period, new and expanded forms of military organization and organized religion were often imposed by the imperial powers and served to transform the economies and cultures of the areas in which they were placed. Religions in much of the developing world were brought by outsiders through their Missions, while military hierarchies were imposed, where they did not already exist, as part of political rule and economic exploitation.

In addition to the institutions that remain to continue these legacies in developing countries, foreign influences also often continue. Armed forces and police continue to be linked with, and trained by, the West, with weaponry a major import purchase. Local churches often take their orders from religious centers in the developed world, as they welcome missionaries and their communications networks. Western culture pours into the developing world in the form of media symbols, products, and economic organization. Some of this is beneficial and fits with local goals of development, but much does not. Appropriate development planning must find a way to separate the positive influences from the negative.

Indeed, in all these institutions, whether existing in the developing countries or outside them, there are vast quantities of capital, which could be used for development, along with large demands on local labor, which divert it from more productive uses. Armed forces and religious organizations in both developing and developed countries own not only large tracts of land and buildings — important productive assets — along with the labor they command, but often factories, hospitals, cultural and artistic resources (orchestras, bands, and choirs), and stored wealth (gold, silver, artwork, and historical treasures) as well. Their role must be evaluated to determine whether they are making appropriate contributions to development and to review how they use the responsibility of their power and ability to influence a country's future.

The next three sections — on armed forces and the national police, religion, and foreign governmental actors — do not cover the full range of institutional actors on development from within and outside a country. One of the most important actors — large corporations and multinational enterprises — is considered in other sections but also deserves special attention on its own. In their decisions on investment, labor, resource use, effect on communities, and their ability to affect the political process though networks and political pressures, economic institutions are important actors whose roles must be reconsidered, along with forms of oversight that should apply to them. (See the section on governmental reform in Chapter 2.)

THE ARMED FORCES AND THE NATIONAL POLICE

International figures show that developing countries spend, on average, 16 % of their national budgets and 4 % of their gross domestic product (GDP) on military expenditures, an amount slightly more than education or community services (Stockholm International Peace Research Institute 1993, pp. 392—93).

With the end of the Cold War, the world average on military expenditures is finally starting to drop, from 5 % of GDP in 1985. However, it still averages 16 % of national budgets and amounts to almost a trillion U.S. dollars annually.

While a certain amount of spending on military and police is necessary even in the poorest of countries, the most important question to ask is whether the amount spent on military and police budgets are consistent with that threat and whether there are more efficient ways by which that threat can be reduced. If there is one principle that should be used to guide a country in allocating scarce funds to military and police, it should be the principle of oversight and accountability: the decision of the appropriate amount to be spent should be made by the citizenry in conditions that demonstrate openness and freedom from fear. Any other decision is a clear indication that the amount being spent is going toward other purposes — namely, coercion and social control for the benefit of an economic or ethnic elite — and represents an inefficiency in development.

Even in developing and developed countries that are viewed as democracies, in which elected leaders have legal authority to supervise the military and police forces, the unfortunate reality is that military and police organizations often maintain their own power bases and distort the allocation of resources due to their special clout. Not only are armed forces expenditures too often an inefficient use of resources that diverts funds from pressing needs. The fact that the existence of military and police forces are not directly accountable to public oversight and control results in other severe threats to development.

In many cases, military and police forces acting on their own or in concert with other interests serve, not to maintain order, but to prevent economic competition and to supervise or prevent investigations into corruption. In some countries, military and police forces maintain control of entire industries (and sometimes use prison labor or force and threats of force to extinguish union movements, in order to keep wage costs low), thus distorting market forces.

The ability of military forces to socialize young people from different regions and ethnic groups in a country, as part of their special power to command the labor of young people, often instills values that are counterproductive to development: attitudes about independence and creativity, as well as about gender roles and the value of community and ethnic heritage. While national pride is something that should be encouraged, often it has no meaning and is merely knee-jerk loyalty to militarism, the state, and to violence.

More than anything, the climate of fear and futility that is spread by unchecked military abuses saps the spirit of opportunity, national pride, and optimism, which are important spurs to development.

In a sense, even developed countries that have never had any fear of authoritarian rule are not immune from many of these problems. While in the case of some First World countries, there are perverse arguments that military and police spending has actually been economically efficient in the sense that it has expanded spheres of economic influence and access to resources (through conquest and subordination), served as a social control on minorities that would have opposed technological growth and rapid industrialization, and even worked as a form of population control through deaths in warfare, these are neither long-term, sustainable strategies nor desirable alternatives when measures for quality of life are added into the development equation.

The long-term results of military command systems in industrial countries such as the Soviet Union or pre-World War II Germany indicate that the advantages for long-term economic growth are short-lived. In the post-Cold War world, similar problems are already appearing in the economy of the United States, where roughly 50 % of men over age 21 have served in the armed forces. Consistently, the society appears to be one where men prefer military solutions in foreign conflicts and, in some cases, domestically, and where the spirit of competition, independence, and originality that characterized growth in the seventeenth and eighteenth centuries seems to have been replaced by a mentality of following orders.

In all the industrial states, armed forces and state security organizations maintain closed budgets and sophisticated internal security apparatuses. Combining large resources with sophisticated devices threatens to insulate state and private agencies from any attempts at controlling them, thereby completely and permanently removing them from the scrutiny and control of civilian governments and their citizens.

Any effective development policy must include provisions for *direct citizen oversight of the military and police forces*, with sufficient enforcement power to hold these agencies accountable under citizen control with no independent power base or ability of either to exert a threat on their own, and *retraining of veterans on return to civilian life* such that any specific values that are necessary for their function in these organizations — such as obedience to hierarchy, training for violence, removal from their communities, and gender segregation — do not, upon their return to civilian life, negatively influence their commitment to civic attitudes, individual initiative, community, and other attributes of development.

At the same time, *resources that do go to the military and police forces should be used in the manner most productive for development,* with these agencies not only serving the roles of law enforcement and defense but also organizing national efforts, where necessary, in emergency relief as well as in national development projects of construction and safety, in cases where they are either more effective than other agencies or can combine these functions with routine training and other activities.

RECOMMENDATIONS

Although we had hoped to study the important role of the Ecuadorian Armed Forces and the National Police in greater detail and heard throughout the country several suggestions and recommendations for reform in these areas, we are restricting our suggestions to realms in which the U.S. government and embassy can offer assistance.

We have dealt with several problems that we observed in the nation's military in other sections — on population (regarding policy in the Amazon region and with relation to Peru; see Chapter 1), migration (Chapter 1), communities (Chapters 1 and 2), and symbolism (Chapter 7).

In addition to those recommendations, we propose that the government of Ecuador request the continued assistance of the United States in the training and professionalization of the Armed Forces, the National Police and the Immigration Police, and that such training be conducted with close and constant civilian oversight from both countries with attention to issues of accountability and control. We recommend that the government of the United States and the Organization of American States provide the resources and assistance necessary in this area through the U.S. Department of Justice and development agencies, and particularly to aid in enforcing the law against those who are misappropriating national resources.

We spoke with journalists, intellectuals, government officials, peasants, and day laborers about the role of the Armed Forces and the National Police. All of them gave us the same response: "They are separate [from us]" (*"aparte"*).

We also received some "friendly" advice in our efforts to understand the role of these organizations in the economy and political system of Ecuador. One journalist told us that the government deports foreigners who try to study the Armed Forces in Ecuador, an outcome we hoped to avoid.

As U.S. citizens, we are in a special position with respect to the Armed Forces in Ecuador. On the one hand, we do not wish to intervene where we have no business. On the other hand we know that taxes we pay in the United States have been used to train the National Police of Ecuador (between 1963 and 1973, 250 Ecuadorian police attended academies established by the United States in Washington D.C. and in Panama, according to the *Handbook on Ecuador*, published by the U.S. Department of Defense [Weil et. al. 1973]) and we were also informed that our tax money is used pay the salaries of 15 employees of the U.S. embassy in Ecuador who work with the Armed Forces there. In the airport in Quito, an agent detained two members of our team for half an hour with what in the United States would be an unwarranted stop and search (without probable cause and in violation of our constitutional rights). They looked through our bags, searched us for drugs, and informed us that their bosses were agents of the U.S. Drug Enforcement Agency and were working for our embassy.

In all our contacts with the Armed Forces and the National Police, despite our having been stopped, we found that members of these forces demonstrated courtesy and respect. We offer our recommendations in the same spirit as President Borja: the Armed Forces ought to be subordinate to civilian government and, in this time of economic crisis, should be organizations that participate in development, following the recommendations of civilian government.

Expenditures on the Armed Forces

With regard to economic development, we had hoped to measure the resources that Ecuador has contributed to the Armed Forces and to compare them to the benefits for the country, but such an analysis is complex.

Table 6.1 Government and Defense Expenditures — Percent of National Budget

	1965	1972	1973	1975	1980	1982	1984
Min. of Defense	12.7	13.6	U.A.	17.5	9.8	U.A.	11.3
Min. of Government	4.0	3.5	U.A.	6.3	3.7	U.A.	4.5
Total	16.7	17.1	14.6	23.8	13.5	18.8	15.8

Source: World Bank (1973, 1984); Banco Central (1987).
Note: U.A. = unavailable.

Table 6.1 shows no observable trend in the amount of national resources directed to these two ministries.

Another method of calculation, however, suggests that the role of the Armed Forces is growing. In 1972, 1 % of the labor force served in the Armed Forces and consumed 2.33 % of the gross domestic product. These numbers rose to 1.4 % and 3.1 % in 1985, indicating that the size of the Armed Forces is 40 % larger in real terms (Weil et. al. 1973, Economist Intelligence Unit 1987).

We received advice from several economists not to trust in only a single statistic regarding the Armed Forces, particularly with respect to the national budget. One economist told us that the sources of support for the Armed Forces includes huge economic investments in the country, particularly in the shrimp industry. A professional working for CONADE (the national planning advisory board), confirmed that the Armed Forces invest in the economy but told us that CONADE had no statistics to measure this, could not get them, and was afraid to try. (We did not try, either.)

While international figures suggest that Ecuador, in comparison to other developing countries, is quite "fortunate" in that the Armed Forces drain only half as much of gross domestic product as in the average developing country (roughly 4 % in 1990), we found that of little comfort (Stockholm International Peace Research Institute 1993).

What we saw was that the Armed Forces have the best of everything in Ecuador — potable water on their bases in areas where neighboring communities do not have it, top-quality health care, musical bands, and beautifully architectured buildings. We note that the Armed Forces have their own resources and economic power, with their revenues tied to the country's oil industry, shipping, and civil aviation. Basically, this means that they receive funding from sources that are outside public control. As U.S. citizens with experience in a country with a strong military-industrial complex, we find this alarming, even though the overt political role of the Armed Forces seems to have declined in recent years.

The Militarization of the Amazon Region

Although we do not have comparative statistics for the past several years, the militarization of the Amazon provinces is obvious to all those who live in or pass through the region.

We heard several justifications for, and explanations of, the presence of the Armed Forces in such strength in the region. It is possible that we are mistaken in our conclusions due to lack of data and a more extensive study. However, we could not find any other reason to explain the large presence of the Armed Forces in the jungles of Ecuador other than the fact that there exists a (subconscious) strategy in Ecuador of reconquering lands lost in the war with Peru in 1942. While we support the use of the military to protect against the exploitation of natural resources and intrusions on the habitats of native peoples, we were not convinced that this was a major concern. It appears that the current strategy of colonization, combined with militarization, is to increase the presence of Ecuadorians in the region until there is no other alternative for Ecuador but expansion across the borders.

Several members of the Armed Forces explained the military's role in the region as that of promoting development through construction projects and assistance to the colonists. However, we saw little that would confirm this.

A high official in Lago Agrio explained that the presence of the Armed Forces in Napo was to protect against Colombian insurgents. He explained that Colombians enter Ecuadorian territories in order to steal arms not from citizens but, "from the Armed Forces." When we asked what the Armed Forces do to prevent this and whether they diminish their presence and their supply of arms, he answered, "No, they send more."

Others told us of the importance of the Armed Forces in protecting Ecuador from the "Batallón Americano," a group allegedly consisting of members of the revolutionary groups M-19 (Colombia), Eloy Alfaro Vive (Ecuador), and the Sendero Luminoso (Peru). Almost no one with whom we spoke, however, believed that this battalion exists. Some clerics told us that this battalion was imaginary and was used as an excuse for the mistreatment of indigenous peoples and poor farmers in the region. We saw nothing to either directly confirm or disprove this.

Several people told us that the presence of the Armed Forces was meant to control the entry of drugs into the country. However, despite the expressed policy of fighting drugs, we visited a community in the Sierra where it is no secret to anyone there that drugs are being produced there for export to Colombia! We saw, too, the open use of marijuana by rich youths in a restaurant in Quito, and the entrance of drugs into a prison run by public authorities.

We heard that Peru is threatening the Ecuadorian border. Although we did not visit any border areas, several people told us that no colonists on the Peruvian side of the border are developing the region with the same intensity and speed as is being done on the Ecuadorian side. Given the social problems facing Peru at this moment, it is difficult to imagine how they would have the resources and energy to support a military conflict outside their borders. Even without the presence of the Ecuadorian Armed Forces, it is difficult to imagine the risk of conflict in certain regions, given that every Ecuadorian colonist is armed with his own shotgun to protect his land.

We fear that the militarization of the Ecuadorian border with Peru will only encourage the strengthening of the Peruvian Armed Forces in response. The result, unfortunately, will be to weaken the democratic civilian government in Peru.

The New Nationalism

We believe that Ecuadorian national pride is something that should be encouraged, yet at the same time, the nationalism we saw has no meaning; it is merely loyalty to militarism. The military values of "following orders for the good of the Fatherland," completely disregard the most important incentives and behaviors needed in a country with a developing economy — initiative and self reliance. At the same time, removing most of the young men from their home communities creates a unity in the Armed Forces but also a lack of responsibility to communities where they are placed and an end to concern for their home communities. These are replaced merely by loyalty to "the Fatherland."

We do not know which organizations have created this type of military nationalism, but it is reflected in every institution. The following are but a few examples of where this can be seen.

In Primary School Borja Number 1 in Quito, children of various ancestries color pictures of white children carrying the Ecuadorian flag. In a school ceremony in Baños, all of the young boys wear military clothes and carry toy rifles. What bothered us the most about what we witnessed is that all the children already had military clothes and toy weapons in their homes. In the military model followed in all public schools, children dress in uniforms, kiss the flag at ceremonies, and recite their lessons in loud voices, echoing the teacher. Moreover, in recruitment posters, we read slogans such as: "Young Man, Enlist. Your Future is in the Fatherland."

We do not have structural solutions to change these attitudes. Our proposal is merely that half the members of the Armed Forces and the National Police be stationed in their home province. (See the section on migration in Chapter 1.) We emphasize this recommendation because of the effect that the Armed Forces has had, and may continue to have, on homogenizing Ecuadorian culture and society, to its detriment.

This sense of nationalism without meaning that we believe the Armed Forces creates is a sense of nationalism and militarism without interest in one's own community and without an understanding of the values necessary for development. With their power to change the minds of all young men in Ecuador during an impressionable age, the Armed Forces has the power to change the future of the society.

It is not true that the Armed Forces have not done anything for the benefit of the public. They open their health clinics, help in family planning, invite the public to their recreational facilities, and open their bases for parties. However, we heard that they also create other changes in the communities. We were told that their presence increases the number of mestiza and indigenous women entering prostitution and that abuses are committed against indigenous peoples by members of the National Police and the Armed Forces due to the lack of understanding of local situations. Moreover, we know that many who leave their communities for military service never return to help the communities where they were born.

It is for these reasons we believe that *increasing ties between the Armed Forces and the National Police and the communities (by requiring that 50 % of recruits be from the home province) would improve relations and benefit the communities.*

A recruit who spent 320 hours of his training exercises digging a fish pond for a peasant farmer would produce 100 kilos of fish annually for the farmer and learn the techniques and benefits of new forms of production, himself.

The Armed Forces and National Police play an important educational role and ought to fulfill this role in the manner that is most advantageous for the future of their recruits and for the development of the communities in which they serve. We believe that this is the true meaning of national security and of nationalism.

Abuses by Certain Members of the Armed Forces, the National Police, and the Immigration Police

Although we cannot confirm much of this directly, we have heard from several sources that certain members of the Armed Forces, the National Police, and the Immigration Police participate in activities in violation of the laws of the Republic. We have heard that the extent of these violations is so widespread that it requires special attention, beyond that which can be provided by these organizations themselves or by the civilian government with its own resources.

The Abuses

National Police. We directly observed that certain members of the National Police engaged in the act of extorting money from motorists, including drivers of automobiles and buses.

The Armed Forces and the Immigration Police. We cannot confirm this, but we heard several times that certain members of the Armed Forces have not exercised their best efforts in collecting taxes owed to the government. Merchants told us of the ease by which they bring imported goods across the border with the payment of bribes in place of import tariffs and the ease of purchasing imported goods at reduced prices (under the prices which would be charged if import duties had been paid) from women identified as the wives and girlfriends of members of the Armed Forces.

Some analysts believe that the total economic losses from these activities justify extreme measures. Therefore, *we recommend that the National Government ask for the assistance of organizations such as the OAS and the U.S. government in order to improve the professionalization of these forces and to enforce the law against those who are violating it and misappropriating national resources.*

RELIGION AND DEVELOPMENT

One of the most powerful, but also most hidden, actors in development has been organized religion; in particular, the institutional hierarchy of the church and its representatives, who long ago rooted themselves in developing societies. In addition to aggregating vast amounts of resources in the developing world and its visible development activities — distributing resources to the poor, and providing counseling, health care and community centers — it has also played a major role in shaping cultural attitudes. In many developing countries, the church has implanted its views on birth control, the economic and social role of women, equity and income distribution, social incentives, attitudes toward indigenous culture, and community. All these have had an important impact on development.

Historically, the church was never a hidden actor in the policies of colonization, and its role in development follows that legacy, though many individuals within and outside the church have questioned — and even challenged — this role. The organized religions of developed nations served as the intermediary for the initial contacts with native peoples, paving the way for other relationships, which were often exploitative. In the eyes of many, organized religion was the first arm of a policy of cultural genocide and assimilation, as it prepared native peoples for hierarchy and for military and economic conquest that would follow.

While development policies cannot undo history, and while Western organized religions are now so deeply rooted in the cultures of many developing countries that it is difficult to even attempt to separate or restore an indigenous culture without recognizing the important needs and beneficial roles that organized religions now fill, it is important to consider their role in any strategy of development.

We believe that a development strategy properly incorporating the role of organized religion must:

- evaluate the amount of the country's resources that are held by organized religion and consider whether they are being used effectively, particularly in light of the social role of religions as community centers and means of redistributing resources to the needy;

- consider the messages embedded in religious doctrines and how they contribute to the goals of development — for promoting the role of women, controlling population growth, encouraging pride in local traditions and culture, and fostering individual initiative and political action in a democracy, as well as equity and a sense of community;

• safeguard the political system and protect minorities against the dominance of any one religion and against the linking of church and state; and

• in the case of organized religions funded from abroad that send their missionaries into developing countries, regulate the role and influence of these actors in the context of development and their impact on culture and values.

RECOMMENDATIONS

Separating Church and State

Representatives of religious institutions should not participate in official government ceremonies and events in a role other than that of private citizen. Moreover, officials of the government should not receive or accept special honors or awards from religious institutions or their representatives.

Protecting the Integrity of Indigenous Communities

The government of Ecuador should not allow the establishment of new missions except in cities with populations of more than 25,000 persons. In order to protect the religious liberties of Ecuadorians, we define "mission" as a religious organization that has funds or people from outside the country.

REPORT

Church and State

With the goals of stimulating the sense of justice, equal treatment for all, and conformity with written constitutional laws in a manner that encourages initiative and promotes development, we recommend that *representatives of religious institutions should not participate in official government ceremonies and events in a role other than that of private citizen. Moreover, officials of the government should not receive or accept special honors or awards from religious institutions or their representatives.*

We are alarmed that in the recent inauguration of President Borja, in a country that professes a separation of church and state, a Catholic archbishop was seated on the podium in the place reserved for leaders of state. Although religious figures play a large role in the life of many Ecuadorians, the concept of separation of church and state has signified the belief that religion and politics play different roles and should not be intertwined. The presence of the archbishop on the dais during the inauguration clearly presents a message that the Ecuadorian government considers the church on a par with leaders of state.

Further, the appearance of a Catholic representative serves as a signal of official support of Catholicism and automatically alarms all Ecuadorians who are not Catholic. We have seen conflicts between Catholic and Protestant groups in several communities and believe that these conflicts result in an inefficient use of development resources. Such sentiments cause much unnecessary divisiveness at a time when all Ecuadorians need to work together to resolve their common problems.

Missions

In investigating the role of missions in Ecuadorian development, we find it difficult to generalize about their effect in the communities where they are situated. We realize that many missions make positive contributions to the development of small communities, but in other cases they only worsen conditions in the region.

To start, it is important to recognize the positive contributions that many missionaries have made in urban areas. In cities, they have dedicated themselves more to the improvement of physical conditions and less to religious conversion. By extending on these activities, they can make great contributions to development. We have seen many examples of these types of help.

Several missionaries in the Comité del Pueblo in Quito have collaborated with the Fundación Investigación-Acción para el Desarollo in a project that uses an area census for convincing the local government to provide potable drinking water to various communities. The same mission offers information on family planning to all members of the community.

A missionary in Tena told us that his family has provided enough capital to a local family to enable them to purchase their own newsstand. The recipient family earned enough from its business to quickly pay back the loan. Several missionaries have organized community stores in order to help their communities purchase basic necessities at low prices. Other missionaries organize villagers as an active political force, educating them about their constitutional rights.

Unfortunately, these successes are accompanied by many failures. It seems to us that in the majority of cases where a mission has done more harm than good, it has been in rural and isolated areas. Frequently in these situations, the missions have radically changed the life-styles of indigenous peoples without helping them. The lack of knowledge of some missionaries about the problems that they cause to many of the people whom they seek to help amazes us. At the same time, the absence of respect for indigenous cultures alarms us.

One prominent missionary who has worked for years with various tribes of the Amazon, told us that "the twentieth century has arrived and [his mission] wants to make the transition for indigenous peoples as smooth as possible." He does not realize that *the twentieth century for the Shuar does not have to be the same as the twentieth century for residents of Quito.* The same missionary explained later that the purpose of the mission was to "uproot the culture" through the construction of a landing strip for planes, a house, and a garden for the missionary. When we asked him, "What are the advantages of your work for the indigenous people?" he paused and then told us, "I don't know." We were amazed that someone who spent so many years working with indigenous peoples did not know how or whether he was helping them.

Missionaries say that they are invited in order to teach Spanish, which actually has no function in these isolated villages other than prestige. In the majority of these distant villages, the missionaries are the only people who speak that language. One missionary told us with pride that he saw a pair of indigenous people struggling to speak Spanish, though they could speak in their own language quite easily. Using Spanish helps them to communicate with another type of people, but does not help to improve their conditions either materially or spiritually.

In the process of converting indigenous peoples to Protestantism or Catholicism, several missionaries have turned one village against another and have also divided people of the same village. As a result, many indigenous peoples have replaced their common culture with conflict. This makes it more difficult for them to organize in order to oppose the conditions and prejudices that affect all indigenous peoples, whatever religion they may adopt.

We conclude that frequently missionaries enter rural areas and cause more problems than they solve. Although it cannot be said that all missionaries in rural areas are alike, we think that the establishment of additional missions presents more threats than advantages to the community.

Therefore, we recommend the following: *the government of Ecuador should not allow the establishment of new missions except in cities with populations of more than 25,000 persons. In order to protect the religious liberties of Ecuadorians, we define "mission" as a religious organization that has funds or people from outside the country.*

We hope that this restriction can eliminate the unnecessary destruction of cultures that still have few contacts with Western civilization. At the same time, we believe that there are so many development needs in urban areas that a mission with a sincere interest in helping in those areas should be able to do so.

THE ROLE OF THE UNITED STATES IN ECUADOR

One of the hardest things for development agents to do is to turn their lenses away from the needs and problems of developing countries and engage in self-reflection and self-criticism. Not only are many development agencies the conduits for transporting unresolved problems within their own "developed" countries to poorer nations, but the presence of foreign agencies in developing countries has become part of the social structure of those countries and needs to be reexamined.

Many of the critical development concerns of the Third World are not unique, but rather reflect back on problems within developing countries. Where inequities, inconsistencies, and inefficiencies exist in developed countries — inadequate protection of minority cultures, unequal access to education and other forms of human capital or productive resources, inequitable access to political or legal resources, inadequate public oversight of government and large economic and social institutions, and so on — it becomes even much harder for these outside agents to promote appropriate development strategies or have credibility in implementing those policies.

In this sense, development policies in wealthy and poor nations are linked. Promoting economic efficiency, political democracy, and the enhancement of communities and ethnic pride in the Third World depends on the ability to address similar political, economic, and cultural problems within developed countries. Indeed, to apply the general to the specific, in submitting this report as American citizens, it is ironic that the governmental and economic institutions that we would most hope to influence with our ideas seem beyond our control and unresponsive to our concerns as citizens. (Nevertheless, we present our concerns as part of this analysis in the hope that we are wrong.)

While there are many foreign agencies and actors in any country — reflecting its history, orientation, and the spheres of political and economic influences that shape it — what applies to the actors of one First World country is analogous to others, as well as to multilateral actors. As U.S. citizens, we chose to focus this section on our own agents: the various arms of the U.S. government.

Among the many arms of the U.S. government acting in developing countries are the U.S. military, the U.S. Agency for International Development, the Peace Corps, and the U.S. Information Agency. If there are any overall guidelines that should be uniformly applied to them, they are as follows:

These agencies should be held to legal and professional standards. They must be accountable to their own policies; to their missions, as legally and historically defined; U.S. law, and international law and agreements, including those with international organizations.

They must be accountable to their own citizens in developed countries through much fuller information, greater access and oversight, and openness to all citizens and backgrounds rather than those of special privilege. One of the key reasons for failed development policies seems to be the insular nature of the agencies, which are sheltered from American citizens as well as from the majority of host country citizens. This lack of openness has fostered policies in which contacts with developing countries most often strengthen relations between elites in the United States and Western-leaning elites in developing countries. The long-term result of contacts is one in which military, corporate, and political heads in developing countries earn U.S. university degrees and develop special contacts with elites in the United States while becoming further removed from their own people. At the same time, much of the information transferred to developing countries by U.S. agencies is out of touch with the reality in the United States and the need to recognize that country's problems and to seek solutions. There is little transfer of information about the problems of the American model or guidelines as to how developing countries can surmount these problems.

They must be held to moral standards. Too often, with no ethical guidelines to follow, the policies that are chosen are part of the politics of convenience and reflect little ability to see the world through the eyes of citizens in the developing country. While it is difficult to establish a set of guidelines of morality, the means toward more ethical policy involve greater oversight by a wide range of American citizens as well as greater communication with citizens in the developing country. Too often, slogans of morality — such as "noninterference in the sovereignty of foreign nations" — have been used to create the appearance of ethics. A policy of noninterference in the sovereignty of a foreign country is too often an excuse for inaction in the face of exploitation and the acceptance of previous foreign actions (creating and supporting a military regime or tolerating exploitative policies of multinationals) rather than a protection of popular movements. The test is really one of inclusiveness, of not hiding behind the shield of slogans.

They must seek greater participation and inclusiveness of the full range of a developing country's citizens in the formation and implementation of assistance projects. Development agencies should be more incorporative and should uphold their missions of sustainable development by recognizing their constituencies, not as host governments, but as the citizens of developing countries. For example, policies of "promoting democracy" are not limited to bolstering elections but require full participation and an extension of equal rights of citizenship (e.g., education, access to lawyers, jury systems, and shared prosecution) while helping the poorest of the poor and the smallest of minorities. To do so is to set professional standards of inclusivity.

While these guidelines apply to governmental agencies, they must ultimately be applied to other First World institutional actors that also exert political and economic power. The next step is for First World governments to lead the calls for openness, oversight, and accountability of foreign-based multinationals operating in developing countries. Since the problems of institutional oversight exist in both wealthy and poor nations, this would be a major step forward, not only for developing countries, but also for the economies of the developed world.

Some preliminary steps — such as the voluntary "Sullivan Principles" for foreign corporations in South Africa, which promoted the transition away from Apartheid — have already been taken but need to be taken farther. Principles of, and enforceable mandates for, corporate oversight for enterprises operating abroad are essential as a means of creating greater trust and efficiency, preventing abuses of power, and serving as a model for corporate oversight of domestic enterprises within developing countries.

RECOMMENDATIONS

The Governmental organizations of the United States in Ecuador should assist Ecuador in meeting its most pressing needs and widen its focus to include assistance in the following areas:

U.S. Agency for International Development (USAID)

We recommend that USAID focus its resources on assisting the government of Ecuador in:

• transferring responsibilities and powers to local governments, and providing the necessary training at those levels;

• meeting the needs of the "poorest of the poor" through systems of rural credit (see the section on migration in Chapter 1), infrastructure, and assistance to children so that they have the resources to attend school; and

• improving the civil service system at all levels of government. (See the section on decentralization and governmental reform in Chapter 2.)

The Peace Corps

We believe that the Corps ought to:

• work with USAID and the Ministry of Education in the training of Ecuadorian teachers in order to develop methods of instruction which encourage initiative and self reliance. (See the section on education in Chapter 3);

• increase the number of volunteers working in small rural communities identifying needs for integrated rural development, and see that these volunteers coordinate their work with those working with government ministries in provincial capitals; and

• develop and provide funds for a new technical assistance organization staffed by U.S. citizens who are of Ecuadorian descent.

The Cultural Section of the Embassy and the U.S. Information Service

We urge USIS and the cultural section of the U.S. Embassy to make better efforts to inform Ecuadorians about the realities of life in the United States.

The U.S. Armed Forces

The U.S. Armed Forces hould offer assistance in the training and professionalization of the Ecuadorian Armed Forces, the National Police, and the Immigration Police in order to stem the violation of laws by certain members of these organizations. (See also the section on the Armed Forces in Chapter 6.)

REPORT

As citizens of the United States, we feel a special obligation to comment on the role of our government in Ecuador. It troubles us that many of the actions of our government are hidden from us and from the Ecuadorians, but there are areas where we can contribute several recommendations.

This is a special time for reaffirming the friendship between our countries and for suggesting some changes in relations between them on account of the change in government in Ecuador. We know that the view of the United States that Ecuadorians hold is mixed and, in many ways, filled with misconceptions. This is something that we hope to improve. There are various reasons for these misconceptions. The representatives and symbols of our country in Ecuador present enormous contradictions — movies like *Rambo* and *American Ninja*, evangelists, oil workers, tourists, Peace Corps volunteers, government bureaucrats, and members of the National Guard. All these represent distinct parts of American society. Some reflect the best of our ideals and aspirations, and others, the worst.

We have, for example, enormous pride in the energy, spirit, and ability of our Peace Corps volunteers. They represent the implementation of the best of our 200-year-old traditions, and we commend the individuals who serve us and Ecuador in this capacity. At the same time, it troubles us to visit an office of the Agency for International Development which is helping Ecuador to improve nutrition, and to note that in the same building there is a representative of the Department of Commerce promoting the sale of imitation-cheese chip junk food for Ecuadorian children.

Moreover, although we are sure that there are historic reasons for this, we find it sad that our Embassy has to appear to Ecuadorians like a fortress. Indeed, it is a place where we did not always feel comfortable or welcome — a building that does not really represent us.

Finally, as representatives of our country, we had a great deal of difficulty explaining some of the policies of the U.S. government in Ecuador. For example, we did not understand why our National Guard was sent to Ecuador. It seems strange to us that our government would send troops whose purpose is not to serve outside of the country, who have no reason to train in jungle climates since there is no similar climate to that of Ecuador's in the continental United States, and who don't even have the skills to build roads, to Ecuador with the task of building roads. (They didn't succeed.) We don't understand why the government failed to send the Army Corps of Engineers, which does have the know-how to build roads in the jungle. We can understand why some Ecuadorians might be upset about this and why they might think that the National Guard was really here training for a war in Central America.

Given that there are things we can neither explain nor change, we can, nonetheless, offer suggestions in a few categories, in addition to those we have offered elsewhere in this volume.

The U.S. Agency for International Development

The Foreign Assistance Act of the United States is clear. The law exists to "satisfy . . . the basic needs of the poor through equitable growth." It continues:

> Best efforts should be made in the administration of this part to stimulate the participation of the people in the process of development through the encouragement of democratic participation in private activities and local governments, and the development of institutions appropriate to the needs of the recipient countries. (U.S. Code 22 § 2151 and following.)

We take pride in several aspects of the policies of the U.S. Agency for International Development in Ecuador — such as help with cooperatives and agrarian reform in the 1960s and 1970s and current programs to transfer rural technology and train indigenous peoples in developing their artisanal industries (e.g., the conference which was scheduled to take place in New Mexico and to include several weavers from the Sierra). At the same time, we believe that in the past few years, as a general rule, the U.S. government has strayed from the intention — and clear meaning — of the law.

Apparently a policy of "productivity and growth" with a focus on the private sector has replaced efforts for integrated rural development, decentralization, the formation of cooperatives that would benefit peasants who wish to compete in the private sector, and the construction of infrastructure in rural areas.

It seems a shame, for example, that USAID has abandoned a policy that many peasants remember well, which was designed to help the poorest of the poor — the provision of clothing and school materials for children without resources so that they could attend school.

It troubles us, too, that in the area of nutrition, USAID places its emphasis on education. Most of the people with whom we spoke already knew about nutrition but what they need are better roads so that they can receive a wider selection of fruits and vegetables from other areas of the country where they are grown, at a price they can afford, as well as credit, training, and technical assistance so that they themselves can grow what they need. The decision to place less emphasis on infrastructure and credit is inappropriate.

USAID already has the experience, capability, and mandate to provide assistance in all of these areas. In decentralization, for example, USAID has had great success in training provincial governments in the Philippines through the Provincial Development Assistance Program (PDAP). Therefore, we recommend that USAID provide assistance that more directly responds to the needs of Ecuador and at the same time more clearly fulfills its legislative mandate. USAID should:

• *Assist the Government of Ecuador in transferring responsibilities and powers to local governments, and in providing the necessary training at those levels.*

• *Pay attention to the needs of the "poorest of the poor" through systems of rural credit (see the section on migration in Chapter 1), infrastructure, and assistance to children so that they have the resources to attend school.*

• *Aid in improving the civil service at all levels of government (see also "Decentralization" in Chapter 2).*

The Peace Corps

We have the greatest respect and admiration for Peace Corps volunteers in Ecuador. Therefore, we direct our recommendations here more to the structure of the organization.

It seems strange to us, for example, that after 25 years in Ecuador, with the goal of creating self-reliance and independence in several capacities, with the exception of the "year in rural areas" program for medical school students, the one thing the Peace Corps has not been able to transfer to Ecuador is the idea of volunteerism itself. We consider it a failure that the Peace Corps has not transferred or replicated the idea in the form of a group of skilled Ecuadorian volunteers from the upper classes and urban areas who would spend a year or two in rural areas in order to contribute to economic development in their own country. We think that the Peace Corps needs to spend some time in reflection and self examination in this area.

It seems strange to us, too, that where the needs are greatest — in small communities, for example, where some sort of integrated development is needed beyond assistance in seeking resources from government (due to indigenous peoples' inability to speak Spanish and lack of understanding of modern culture and the political system) — there are no Peace Corps volunteers. Volunteers are concentrated in cities (provincial capitals) working with the ministries. We understand that through affiliation with the ministries, volunteers can (and do) help many communities at once. However, we believe it would be best to place volunteers in both settings — in the field, to identify community needs (and the needs of neighboring small communities as well), and in the ministries, where they can assist in providing services to communities where other volunteers have identified needs. We believe that this type of cooperative working in tandem — identifying needs and providing them — would make the Peace Corps more effective.

Therefore, *we believe the corps ought to increase the number of volunteers working in small rural communities, identify needs for integrated rural development, and see that these volunteers there coordinate their work with the volunteers who are working with government ministries in provincial capitals.*

We have another suggestion that perhaps fits within the current mandate of the Peace Corps but perhaps should exist outside it — in parallel. *The corps ought to develop and provide funds for a new technical assistance organization staffed by U.S. citizens who are of Ecuadorian descent.* The goal of this proposal is to compensate Ecuador for the loss of human resources of the country due to migration to the industrial centers of the world (brain drain) and to provide Ecuadorian-Americans with a better sense of, and pride in, their cultural heritage. Thus, we propose to set up a second Peace Corps for Ecuador, consisting of Ecuadorian-Americans. (We also recommend this for other groups in the United States who have migrated from lesser developed countries.)

Finally, *we recommend that the Peace Corps work with USAID and the Ministry of Education to train Ecuadorian teachers in order to develop methods of instruction that encourage initiative and self-reliance* (see also "Education" in Chapter 3).

The Cultural Section of the Embassy and the U.S. Information Service

We believe that *the cultural section of the U.S. Embassy and the U.S. Information Service (USIS) ought to make better efforts to inform Ecuadorians about the realities of life in the United States.*

We love our country and are proud to be Americans. However, we must recognize, at the same time, that our country is facing serious problems — homelessness, high unemployment and underemployment (which are not well recorded by government statistics), a lack of community spirit, industrial decline, problems of drug addiction, racism, child abuse, alcoholism, violence, and a government that is not adequately accountable, among others. The United States is not a model that we suggest for Ecuador, nor for other countries faced with very different circumstances.

Given this, it troubles us that many Ecuadorians seem to want to imitate the Americans and replace their traditions with ours. It pains us to see Ecuadorians smoking American cigarettes, drinking American softdrinks, dressing in ties and suits, and building fast food restaurants.

It is natural for us to want to present our best qualities to others, but before they choose to adopt our culture, and its problems along with it, or to migrate to the United States rather than stay in Ecuador and contribute to their countries, Ecuadorians should be aware of both sides. Thus, *we recommend that these sections of the U.S. Embassy and USIS make better efforts to present a more complete picture of the United States.*

REFERENCES

Banco Central del Ecuador. *Cuentas Nacionales del Ecuador, 1977-1986* Quito: 1987.

Economist Intelligence Unit. *Country Profile: Ecuador* London: Economist Publications, 1987.

Stockholm International Peace Research Institute (SIPRI). "World Armaments and Disarmaments" In *SIPRI Yearbook* Oxford University Press, 1993

Weil, Thomas E., et. al. *Area Handbook for Ecuador* Washington, D.C.: U.S. Government Printing Office, 1973.

World Bank. *Development Plan For Ecuador* Washington, D.C.: World Bank, 1973.

World Bank. *Development Plan For Ecuador* Washington, D.C.: World Bank, 1984.

7

Changing State of Mind

A strategy of development involves more than just choosing the right policies and making the appropriate institutional and structural changes. It also involves changing ways of thinking: changing the way in which individuals see themselves, their neighbors, their communities, their countries, and their place in the world.

Many of the policies we have recommended in previous chapters involve this kind of national and personal transformation — taking pride in one's ethnicity and community; directing attention toward health, education, and self-improvement and fulfillment; valuing human life and tolerance over militarism and conflict; raising the status and image of women; and nurturing feelings of competence and independence. To do so requires special attention to the images that nations, peoples, and individuals hold about themselves, as part of efforts to change their state of mind and reinforce other efforts.

Even when presented with the greatest of resources and opportunities, efforts to improve conditions can fail, either because of outside forces or because of the inability of people to grasp their reality and circumstances and overcome difficulties of the past.

Developing societies face the future, not only with tangible material problems, but also with the need to heal and overcome deep-seated, psychological harms suffered by survivors of civil wars, genocide, and colonial rule. The attitudes of victimization, defeatism, and fatalism can be self-perpetuating and self-defeating, even when the conditions that caused them have been removed. Often on an individual level, people become their own abusers by choosing self-destructive behaviors, even after actual abuse is removed. On a national level, former colonial regimes often recreate their histories of colonialism within their own borders, colonizing their own peoples, while victims of authoritarian regimes often recreate their own tyrannies. Indeed, the history of many groups coming into contact with outsiders for the first time was that they died, not from military force or even from new diseases, but from their own psychological vulnerability — their loss of will, their inability to adapt, and the collapse of their social systems.

Critical to development is the ability of people, as individuals and together to feel a sense of control over their environments and destinies, which is characterized by feelings of self-esteem and competence.

While it is difficult to prescribe the remedy to cure the emotional legacies of history — to develop a set of national therapeutic and healing prescriptions — in order to lead to a psychological shift, it is possible to identify certain ways of redefining a nation or group's sense of self as independent and capable through declarations of aspirations and ways in which it seeks to measure its own progress and change. At the same time, it is possible to remake one's environment to change its symbols and references and models in order to mark those aspirations.

DEPENDENCY

The legacy of colonization in many countries of the developing world has been a difficult one to erase, in part because many of the mechanisms of colonial policies continue, although in more subtle forms. What began as an exploitation of labor and resources following military conquest continues less through the actual threat of force than through created dependencies and the perception of weakness.

The reality is that many developing countries are dependent — on outside aid, military protection, international private capital, changes of their neighbors to the global environment, their neighbor's populations and control of diseases, and, no less, the goodwill of more powerful neighbors which prevents them from imposing policies by force. However, much of that dependency is also created by, or partly to blame on, developing countries themselves: through the import of foreign consumer goods, inappropriate technology, and addictive, nonessential products, and in seeking the assistance of international development banks and the implications this creates for a new form of dependency — debt.

While much of the ability of developing nations to be self-reliant is still in the hands of their more powerful neighbors — to regulate the activities of first world and international institutions, from missionaries and militaries to multinationals and media, and open them to greater scrutiny — developing countries must take responsibility in cases where they do have control and the opportunity to empower themselves and their peoples.

While the strategies recommended in the previous chapters — for cultural autonomy, decentralization, the development of community, and economic self-reliance — all incorporate the goals of independence, there are several steps within these broad recommendations that are "self-activating" and empowering on individual and local levels.

Among some of the steps that developing countries ought to highlight as means of changing their cultures and mind-sets from the grass roots upward are the following.

The Utilization of Appropriate Technology

Thinking small and applying technology in entrepreneurial ways using existing resources is a direct means of encouraging independence.

Local Control of Bank Credit

Giving citizens themselves the direct power, not only in raising their own sources of funds — through rotating credit pools and other methods of community savings — but in overseeing loans and national borrowing policies, is a means of teaching them financial responsibility and encouraging a more efficient and self-reliant uses of funds.

Local Control of Environmental and Natural Resources

Like control over bank credit, expanded citizen participation and responsibility in managing resources puts one of the basic tenets of capitalism into practice: when people have some control over their own resources — their own capital — and live with the consequences of their own decisions on how it is used, they are more likely to use it wisely.

Redirection of Local Education to Regional Needs

Basing education in communities and allowing citizens to shape institutions to their needs is both efficient and empowering.

Coordination and Education of National and International Development Agencies

Rather than serve as passive players in development, one of the means of overturning deeply rooted attitudes of dependence in relations with First World countries and the central governments in developing countries that deal with them is to create new mechanisms at the local level for giving citizens a role in shaping the activities of outside development agents working in their communities.

RECOMMENDATIONS

The Ecuadorian government should encourage the formation and strengthening of popular organizations which empower citizens. We recommend the following measures. In general, and as part of our overall strategy to be reiterated and echoed in all aspects of planning:

- Government decentralization, and

- Cultural autonomy.

In new structural changes:

- Coordination and education of national and international development agencies.

In specific application:

- The utilization of appropriate technology,

- Local control of bank credit,

- Local control of environmental and natural resources, and

- Redirection of local education to regional needs.

In a sense, Ecuador has already taken the first step toward coming to terms with its colonial past and seeking to strengthen itself for the future. Its constitution declares the following in its preamble (Article 4): "The Ecuadorian State condemns all forms of colonialism, neocolonialism, and racial discrimination or segregation. It recognizes the right of peoples to liberate themselves from these oppressive systems." However, translating declarations into actions is a much harder task, particularly when many actions are subconscious and when mechanisms of discrimination and subordination are often subtle.

Ecuador should be more concerned with its external relations and how these relations have affected the internal structure of the country. Internal traditions of dependency now impede the ability of the people to solve their problems without interference from institutions that are dominant in the world economy. Gifts taken by Ecuadorian authorities on behalf of the nation have solidified a social structure that promotes oppression internally.

We stress the importance of supporting grassroots citizen organizations. A strategy of bottom-up development will help Ecuador overcome a cycle in which domestic elites merely replace a foreign external elite.

Development Agencies and Their Role in Appropriate Development

Development agency staff are foreigners coming to Ecuador to suggest what they think Ecuadorians need and do not necessarily promote what Ecuadorians themselves identify as their needs. Indeed, the best-intentioned development organizations can sometimes make things worse through their actions.

For this reason, we suggest, not only that the Ecuadorian government be cautious of outside assistance, but that there should be additional mechanisms for evaluating and monitoring the activities of development agencies to determine their impact on particular communities and their ability to promote equitable growth and the full participation of Ecuadorian citizens.

At the same time, we have heard from several members of national and international development agencies that their activities could be more effective if they were better coordinated with other groups. Such communication and coordination would not only enable communities to directly communicate their needs and desires, thus improving cultural

sensitivity and promoting cultural considerations, but would also help
to coordinate outside assistance.

Office of Development Agency Coordination

The Ecuadorian government ought to establish an office of
coordination and produce a development newsletter. We recommend
that the organization be funded through a tax of .25 % of the annual
budget of each agency operating in Ecuador.

All the agencies with a budget of more than $10,000 U.S. should
have an annual meeting to discuss problems, progress, success, and
failures and to share data, propose projects, and consider the
significance and validity of their role in the communities where they
work. Members of communities in which development officials work
should also be invited to attend in order to bring some of the concerns of
the people to the development agencies, directly, at a high level.
These meetings should be forums of development and should be
attended by representatives of national and international
organizations, both private and public, large and small.

Local Meetings

The office of coordination should also set up provincial-level
offices and arrange for regular monthly meetings. In a typical province,
these meetings could include a volunteer from the Peace Corps, a
member of a women's artisanal cooperative, a missionary working with
small businesses, and an employee of the Ministry of Agriculture and
Animal Husbandry (Ministerio de Agropecuaría y Ganadería). Such
variety is certain to generate a number of themes for discussion and
ideas to share. Currently, many problems and confusions remain
unaddressed due to the lack of a system of information exchange and
interorganizational coordination, particularly at the local levels. The
creation of this office would help centralize information resources to
make them more readily available to communities seeking assistance,
as well as to organizations wishing to provide help.

Local Inclusion

In addition to monthly meetings, the government of Ecuador should
work with development organizations in establishing regulations and
guidelines for the work of development organizations. Such guidelines
can include demands that the organizations:

- Seek the ideas of Ecuadorian citizens — particularly members of indigenous groups that have long been tied to specific geographic areas — not only in ideas for possible projects, but also in formulating solutions. The communities themselves may have the best understanding of their environments and the feasibility of different proposals but lack the resources to carry them out.

- Be sensitive to local and national attitudes and customs. Often, the lack of local knowledge by foreigners insults their hosts and impedes collaboration.

- Withhold financial resources from joint projects until it is determined that the community is unable to contribute its own resources or it is clear that providing aid will lead to other long-term benefits.

- Support the use of appropriate technology and the goal of self sufficiency. Organizations should evaluate whether the aid they offer meets local needs (for example, if expensive fertilizers are going to benefit poor peasants who do not have the capital to purchase them when the project or assistance terminate). Organizations must continually question whether their presence is contributing to making the communities in which they are operating more self-sufficient.

- Support projects for women. Women represent the most productive sector in rural areas but are often ignored by assistance programs because the husband is the head of the household. To deny women the direct benefits of working with foreign organizations is to lose the potential for helping the hardest-working and least-recognized group.

The Special Role of Religious Organizations

Among the activities of religious organizations in Ecuador are those that empower Ecuador's poor by educating them about their rights and motivating them to participate in government. Among several representatives of the Catholic Church in Ecuador whose projects and churches we visited, we were particularly impressed by those clergy who practice the tenets of liberation theology and espouse its goals. They have been able to unify religious teachings and positive development activities that promote equitable development by assisting Ecuadorians in their efforts to achieve self-sufficiency. (See also "Religion and Development" in Chapter 6.)

SYMBOLISM

An often-neglected aspect of economic development, but one with an integral role, is the use of symbols. It is through symbols and role models that the values of a country are taught to the next generation and can raise aspirations, encourage pride and self-confidence, shape attitudes toward diet and health, and promote economic initiative, tolerance, and full participation in community life.

In many cases, the messages embedded in the environments of developing countries are holdovers from the past and difficult to change; these are found in lavish governmental palaces and religious buildings, historical monuments, and artworks. In other cases, current expenditures on symbols — statues, monuments, paintings, placards, billboards, advertisements, exhibits, and other forms of media — represent a continuing misallocation of current resources which, in themselves, could be better spent on other aspects of development, as well as a transmission of messages that are completely opposite to those that should be sent in order to foster development.

Since the presentation of symbols can be costly — requiring either a large investment of private capital or an expenditure of public funds — the majority of symbols in developing countries are created both by the state and by those who have the financial resources to influence attitudes in the country with the approval of the state.   Unless the state takes an active role in shaping public spaces and the symbols in them and in regulating private spaces and symbols that influence the public for the benefits of development, the attitudes they reflect may be those that reinforce existing authority and ideologies that may be counterproductive.

Overall, a dynamic environment that reflects a value for the sanctity of each individual, through equality, independence, and the ability of each to fulfill his or her potential fulfills the goals of development by reinforcing the following messages:

Respect and Pride in Local Cultures and Communities

In many former colonial regimes, it is not uncommon to still find statues in public squares of the conquering peoples, with depictions of the natives as savage, or of nonindigenous religious figures in hierarchical relationships with each other and natives, over whom they have special powers. Such symbols send messages, not only that the conquerors and their descendants are more powerful, but that they and their life-styles are more worthy than those of the people they conquered or assimilated. Such messages about the inferiority of native peoples work to perpetuate discrimination and reinforce feelings of victimization and powerlessness, which can only stall development. Symbols of indigenous leaders and peoples, by contrast, create a sense of pride.

Respect for Tolerance and Peace Rather than Glorification of War and Hierarchy

At the same time that many historical symbols show natives as being conquered by outsiders or dependent on them for kindnesses, such depictions glorify militarization, conquest, and hierarchy which stand in the way of development. Symbols of tolerance and equality, and of role models who had such qualities, are more positive and conducive to sustained development.

A View of Women as Equals of Men Who Can Make Important Contributions with Their Minds

In developing countries as in many developed countries, it is not unusual to find depictions of women only as mothers or objects of sexual desire. To encourage greater respect for women and their potential economic roles, it is important to show symbols of woman in a greater variety of roles, as well as to show men in roles as parents and equal partners.

A Focus on This World and Life and on Making Them Better Rather than on an Afterlife or Beforelife

It is common in many developing and developed countries to find vast amounts of religious symbolism, much of which is disempowering. Religious symbols often promote a "second-chance philosophy" involving a belief in the afterlife rather than this one, along with views of people as inherently sinful and lacking power in themselves. These messages are discouraging and disempowering. Messages to promote development could better depict community and individual action, as well as a respect for natural resources and the sanctity of human differences.

A Demonstration of the Importance of the Acts of Individual Citizens Rather than the Omnipotence of Political Leaders

Monuments, statues, photographs, and other glorification of political leaders are also disempowering. Reinforcing the traditions of strong men and charismatic leaders rather than rights and laws, as well as of centralization and the dependence of individuals on privileges bestowed by the mighty, interfere with development. Greater emphasis on the heroics of common people and their communities and less emphasis on leaders would encourage even greater individual efforts.

Protection of Citizens through Controls on Advertising Messages That May be Harmful to health or Distort Other Development Needs

Among the greatest influx of new symbols that pattern a variety of behaviors — diets, health practices, consumption, family and interpersonal relationships, and other aspects of life-styles — are those created by outsiders, by advertisers of multinational products as well as foreign media. Many of these symbols and images catch an unwary public that is unskilled in sorting truth from manipulation or screening out subconscious messages. Developing countries need to exert careful controls over foreign and domestic advertising and media symbols as a means of correcting unequal bargaining power and knowledge between those who create and transmit these symbols and those who receive them.

Mirrors

In addition to creating competing symbols or changing and regulating those that are already in or entering developed countries, an important means of countering feelings of dependency and powerlessness is to simply place mirrors (figuratively, in the form of museums and artwork reflecting the lives and traditions of the people in the community, and literally, in the form of actual mirrors in schools and public buildings for people to see themselves rather than those who have power over them) in impoverished regions — to reflect back the strength of individuals and cultures whose own histories are disappearing while encouraging individual and cultural pride. Seeing oneself and one's strengths is in itself an important step raising self-esteem, confidence, and activity.

RECOMMENDATIONS

Removing Old Symbols

The Ecuadorian government ought to announce an immediate moratorium on signs that attribute the construction of public works to a particular public official and should reduce the number of signs that announce the construction of public works to a minimum.

Promoting New Symbols as Sources of Pride

We recommend that the government make a special effort to recognize the achievements of women, as well as of indigenous communities and their leaders, in the construction of monuments and murals and the naming of new governmental districts and streets.

Regulating the Effects of Advertising

The Ecuadorian government ought to impose a tax on all commercial advertisements of tobacco, soft drinks, products containing sugar, and other products that threaten public health, in the amount of 1.5 times the cost of the advertisement. These funds should be earmarked directly for the Ministry of Health for the creation of advertisements of equal size and distribution in order to inform the public of the risks of, and possible substitutes for, these products.

REPORT

In the form of street and town names, monuments, signs, and commercial advertisements, we saw the reflections of various aspects of Ecuadorian culture. Some of these symbols reflected cultural pride, community spirit, initiative, and artistic expression, while others reflected foreign ideas fostering attitudes of dependency, promoted poor health habits, and represented a misallocation of the country's resources.

A Few Examples

"Otra Obra de León" (*"Another Work of President Leon Febres Cordero"*). The simple and sad fact is that *for each well known sign in Ecuador with the words, "Otra Obra de León," another poor child had to go without potable water* because of the diversion of public monies to presidential symbolism and away from the needs of development.

We calculate the cost of each sign denoting a public works project of the national government at 9,160 sucres. We estimate the following for each sign of four square meters:

Cost of metal, 4 square meters	6,160 s
(4,620 s per 3 square meters or 1,540 s per square meter);	
Cost of paint in order to cover 4 square meters	1,200 s
(6,000 s per gallon; each gallon covers 20 square meters)	
Cost of two beams of 4 meters in length	1,000 s
(125 s per meter)	
Cost of labor to paint, and erect the sign,, including transport;	
(Minimum wage for one day)	800 s

Total:	9,160 s

Source: Data compiled through phone calls and visits to randomly selected stores in Quito.

In comparison, bringing potable water to one person costs less than the cost of a sign.

Cost of a system of potable water for 200 families   8 million s

---

Cost per family/ household   40,000 s

Average number of people per household   5

Cost of potable water per person: 8,000 s

Source: PLAN Internacional, Guaranda, Bolivar;
Ecuador (1983).

We did not count the number of these signs in the country, and indeed, the number itself is not important. Nor is this an assignation of blame. We do not know, nor do we consider it important, whether this represents the work of one political party or person in Ecuador or if it represents a historical tradition in the country.

What is important is not only to recognize this use of public funds but to understand the message that the public receives from these signs and its impact on economic development.

Although communities have to ask repeatedly and wait a great deal of time in order to receive potable water from the central government, and while many people organize themselves in *mingas* (community labor teams) to dig trenches for the pipes, the signs only mention the funds that come from above, from the central government, and the power that the state exercises as a *patron*. The message is clear. It reinforces dependency — the belief that the people cannot do anything with their own resources and that the state has an interest in glorifying itself in place of simply fulfilling its role of serving the citizens.

The Monument to the Indian Guarango. We were greatly impressed by the new monument and cultural center in the city of Guaranda. We felt a spirit of community pride, energy, and optimism in the province of Bolivar, something that we saw reflected in and inspired by the monument to the historical leader of the indigenous peoples of the region.

For the Guarandans, this monument is a symbol of strength, community, and history. More than just a monument, it serves also as a place of reflection, contemplation, and unity. In the museum underneath the monument there are exhibits of works by artists from the community, photographs, historical objects, and explanations of the history and economy of the region. The building itself is a recreational center where films are shown. This was a symbol that showed us feelings of joy and pride in being Ecuadorian, Bolivaran, and Guarandan.

Other Monuments and Signs. There are numerous monuments, street names, names of regions and cities, buildings, religious statues and paintings, and plaques that represent the history of Ecuador, the values of the country, and the distinct cultures that make up the country. While none of these in themselves threaten or could stall economic development in the country, together, these representations can be disadvantageous in the future.

We did not gather specific data regarding monuments, but it was not difficult to note that:

• almost all the statues of human figures are of men;

• the majority of the statues of men and street names are not of indigenous nor mestizo descent but of Spanish origin (representing a minority of Ecuadorians and not representative of the citizens of Ecuador) and show only a small group of families;

• many of these statues have a military significance, glorifying the legacy of war, which runs counter to the country's claims that it wishes to develop a tradition of democracy and peace; and

• of the statues of women, the majority show women doing nothing more than carrying children in their arms. None depict women in the nonmaternal (and indispensible) roles that women fulfill in Ecuador.

The consequence of this bias for development is subtle but severe. The message that these symbols present in regard to the social position of indigenous peoples and women is one that stifles their aspirations to take initiative and participate as active members in Ecuadorian society. Although this might be convenient for a few groups in Ecuador, what it suggests about Ecuador and the potential for conflicts in the future, is obvious.

We already see the result of the representation of Ecuadorian women as nothing more than mothers. More than the loss of important human resources by the exclusion of women as equal participants in society, we foresee a population explosion that threatens to destroy the country. This explosion will be almost impossible to stop.

Along with the crisis that will arrive in 10 to 40 years if drastic measures are not taken immediately to slow population growth, the resentment of certain groups who will be actually, as well as symbolically, excluded in Ecuador is likely to erupt in violence.

For us, the effect of these symbols was reflected in one provincial capital in a province with sharp divisions between rich and poor — between certain well known families and indigenous peoples. In the highly ornate and austere office of the governor, who is a member of one of the wealthy families, hangs a series of portraits of all the past governors of the province. Peasant farmers will no doubt wait nervously in the office of the governor when undergoing the fixed stares of these men of Spanish origin, who share a lack of interest in representing them.

Commercial Advertisements

As much as the use of public capital for symbols, which are officially approved by the government for public display, reflect contradictory values and discourage economic development in the country, so, too, do commercial advertisements.

We heard representatives of the Ministry of Health and doctors in almost every province that suffers from problems of public health and nutrition, speak about the difficulty of educating the people — or even just reaching people — with radio or television announcements or billboards due to the lack of funds. Thus, we were shocked to see the extent of already existing messages that run contrary to these public health objectives.

Although the country cannot locate sufficient funds for campaigns of nutrition or public health, it is saturated with billboards for "Líder" and other tobacco products, for "Coca-Cola," "Fruit," "Inca-Cola" and other sugared sodas, as well as alcoholic beverages and other sugared products.

Instead of condemning a few brands and interfering in the right of the public to choose products that they either might or might not know can harm them (we recognize the danger of determining for others their preferences in all their decisions), we would like to call attention only to the role and special obligation of government in a free market economy. That role is to provide the public with sufficient information that citizens can use to make informed decisions in an environment without pressures and manipulation by powerful groups using sophisticated techniques. In the area of public health, the government has a well-recognized and well-established right to intervene in favor of the public. This right is strong in a country like Ecuador, where traditional diets, which were nutritionally balanced by habit, have been interrupted by rapid social and economic change.

Finally, coming from the United States, we were quite surprised to enter restaurants and stores and see there calendars made in Ecuador with photographs, not of Ecuadorians, but of blonde North Americans or Europeans. Not only were the subjects not working or engaging in activities in which we are accustomed to see them in our country, they were either nude or seminude. Besides what this says about the view that the Ecuadorian people must have about us and other foreigners, and besides what it means for relations between our countries, we are worried about what this says about the Ecuadorian self-image and what it signifies for the future of the country.

REFERENCE

Ecuador. Instituto Nacional de Estadística y Censos. *Censo de Vivienda, 1982* Quito: 1983.

Bibliography and Other Sources

INTERNATIONAL DEVELOPMENT LITERATURE

GENERAL

Cardoso, Fernando Henrique, and Enzo Faletto. *Dependency and Development in Latin America* Berkeley: University of California Press, 1979.

Janvry, Alain de. *The Agrarian Question and Reformism in Latin America* Baltimore: Johns Hopkins University Press, 1981.

Kim, Kwan S., and David F. Ruccio. *Debt and Development in Latin America* Notre Dame, Ind.: University of Notre Dame Press, 1985.

Lang, James. *Inside Development in Latin America* Durham, N.C.: University of North Carolina Press, 1988.

Meier, Gerald M. *Leading Issues in Economic Development* Oxford, U.K.: Oxford University Press, 1984.

Naipaul, V. S. *The Middle Passage* New York: Vintage Books, 1962.

National Bi-Partisan Commission on Central America. *The Report of the President's National Bipartisan Commission on Central America* New York: Macmillan Publishing Company, 1983.

Octavio Paz. *The Labyrinth of Solitude* Transl. Lysander Kemp 1961. Reprint. Grove Press, 1985.

Picon-Salas, Mariano. *A Cultural History of Spanish America: From Conquest to Independence* Berkeley, CA: University of California Press, 1966.

Sheahan, John. *Patterns of Development in Latin America* Princeton, N.J.: Princeton University Press, 1987.

Stockholm International Peace Research Institute (SIPRI). "World
    Armaments and Disarmaments" In *SIPRI Yearbook* Oxford
    University Press, 1993

INTERNATIONAL FINANCIAL STATISTICS

Cline, William R. "Economic Stabilization in Developing Countaries:
    Theory and Stylized Facts" In William R. Cline and Sidney
    Weintraub, eds., *Economic Stabilization in Developing Countries*
    Washington, D.C.: Brookings Institution, 1981.
International Monetary Fund. *International Financial Statistics*
    Washington, D.C.: International Monetary Fund, 1984 (and
    updates).
International Monetary Fund. *International Financial Statistics*
    Washington, D.C.: International Monetary Fund, 1986 (and
    updates).
Mitchell, Craig. "Ecuador — 1982: Case Study on the Effects of
    Devaluation" Unpublished m.s., May 1988.
Stern, Joseph J., Richard D. Mallon, and Thomas L. Hutcheson. *Foreign
    Exchange Regimes and Industrial Growth* Harvard Institute for
    International Development Discussion Paper no. 222 Cambridge,
    Mass.: Harvard University, March 1986.

INTERNATIONAL RELATIONS

Kries, William L. *Ecuadorian—Peruvian Rivalry in the Upper Amazon*
    Prepared for U.S. Department of State Unpublished m.s., 1978.
"Latin Reagonomics: Will It Work?" Special report. *Miami Herald*,
    April 21, 1986.
Riding, Alan. "Colombian Drugs: A Problem at Home" *International
    Herald Tribune*, August 22, 1986.

ECUADOR

GENERAL

Crowther, Geoff. *South America on a Shoestring* Australia: Lonely Planet Publications, 1983.

Enock, C. Reginald. *Ecuador* London: T. Fisher Unwin Ltd., 1914.

Ecuador. Instituto Nacional de Estadística y Censos. *División Político—Administrativa de la Republica del Ecuador* 1983.

Instituto Latinoamericano de Investigaciones Sociales. *Los Gobiernos Seccionales del Ecuador* Quito, 1986.

Rachowiecki, Rob. *Ecuador and the Galapagos Islands: A Travel Survival Kit* Australia: Lonely Planet Publications, 1986.

Salgado, Hernan. *Instituciones Políticas y Constitución del Ecuador* Quito: Instituto Latinoamericano de Investigaciones Sociales, 1984.

South American Handbook New York: Random House, 1988.

Weil, Thomas E., et. al. *Area Handbook for Ecuador* Washington, D.C.: U.S. Government Printing Office, 1973.

PLANNING

Consejo Nacional de Desarollo (CONADE). *Planificación*, no. 24 (October 1986).

Consejo Nacional de Desarollo (CONADE). *Planificación*, no. 25 (December 1987).

Ecuador. Gobierno de Ecuador. *Plan Nacional de Desarrollo 1985 - 1988* Registro Civil, October 25, 1985.

International Bank for Reconstruction and Development. *Current Economic Position and Prospects of Ecuador* Washington, D.C.: 1973.

International Bank for Reconstruction and Development. *Ecuador: An Agenda for Recovery and Sustained Growth* Washington, D.C.: 1984.

United States Agency for International Development. *Country Development Strategy Statement: Ecuador: FY 1986* January 1984.

World Bank. *Development Plan For Ecuador* Washington, DC: World Bank, 1973.

World Bank. *Development Plan For Ecuador* Washington, DC: World Bank, 1984.

DEVELOPMENT ISSUES AND STATISTICS

Banco Central del Ecuador (Quito). *Boletín-Anuario* no. 9 (1986a).
Banco Central del Ecuador. *Memoria Anual* Quito: 1986b.
Banco Central del Ecuador. *Memoria Anual* Quito: 1988.
Banco Central del Ecuador. *Cuentas Nacionales del Ecuador, 1977-1986* Quito: 1987.
Centro Andino de Acción Popular (Quito). *Ecuador Debate: Empleo y Reproducción Social* no. 11 (June 1986).
Centro Andino de Estudios Economicos y Sociales. *Estudio de Factibilidad de la Provincia Nororiental de Cuyabeno-Putumayo* Lago Agrio, Ecuador: January 29, 1986.
"La Cuestion Alimentaria" *Ecuador Debate* September 1985.
Economist Intelligence Unit. *Country Profile: Ecuador* London: Economist Publications, 1987.
Economist Intelligence Unit. *Ecuador: Economic Structure* London: Economist Publications, 1988(I).
Ecuador. Instituto Nacional de Estadística y Censos. *Censo de Población 1982* Quito: 1983.
Ecuador. Instituto Nacional de Estadística y Censos. *Censo de Vivienda, 1982* Quito: 1983.
Ecuador. Instituto Nacional de Estadística y Censos. *Anuario de Estadísticas Vitales, 1986* Quito: 1987.
"Ecuadoran Sucre" *World Currency Yearbook* 1986.
Instituto de Investigaciones Economicas. *Economía* (Universidad Central de Ecuador, Facultad de Ciencias Economicas), no. 85 (January 1988). Special issue on marginals and the informal urban sector.
Instituto Latinoamericano de Investigacioners Sociales. *Estadísticas del Ecuador* Chile: 1986.
International Labour Office. *Yearbook of Labour Statistics, 1987* Geneva: International Labour Office, 1987.
Jaramillo, Marco. *Diagnostico Socio-Economico de la Provincia de Esmereldas*, Coleccion Pendoneros. Otavalo: Instituto Antropologico de Otavalo, 1981.
Lopez Silva, Luis. *Las Categorias Fundamentales del Proceso de Desarollo Económico y Social* Quito, 1982.
"Migración" *Ecuador Debate* March 1985.
Navarro Jimenez, Guillermo. *La Concentración de Capitales en el Ecuador* 1976.

Health

Centro de Estudia de Población y Paternidad Responsible. *Population Reports* Quito: 1984.

Greene, Lawrence S. *Malnutrition, Behavior, and Social Organization* New York: Academic Press, 1977.

Mangelsdorf, Karen Ruffing. "A Development Administration Approach to Primary Health Care in Rural Ecuador" Dissertation, University of New Mexico, 1986.

Sociedad Ecuatoriana de Salud Publica. *Ecuador Trás una Política de Población*. Conference, 1986, December 2-4, Quito.

Suarez-Torres, Jose. "Health Needs Assessment in Specific Population Groups in the Cayambe Region, Rinchincha Province, Ecuador: An Epidemiologic Study of the Impact of Agriultural Development on Health Status" Dissertation, University of Michigan, 1984.

United States Agency for International Development. *Primary Health Care Workers in Ecuador: a PVO's Experience* Imprenta Landes.

Agrarian Reform and Agriculture

Banco Central de Ecuador y el Consejo Nacional de Desarollo. *Programa de Encuestas de Coyuntura: Sector Agropecuario* no. 48 (January 1988).

Blankstein, Charles S., and Clarence Zukevas, Jr. "Agrarian Reform in Ecuador: An Evaluation of Past Efforts and the Development of a New Approach" In *Economic Development and Cultural Change*.

Chiriboga, Manuel. "El Sistema Alimentario Ecuatoriano: Situación y Perspectivas," *Ecuador Debate* no. 9 (September 1985).

Chiriboga, Manuel. *El Problema Agrario en el Ecuador* Quito: Instituto Latinoamericano de Investigaciones Sociales, 1988.

Glover, David James. "Contract Farming and the Transnationals" Dissertation, University of Toronto, 1983.

Griffin, Keith. "Systems of Labour Control and Rural Poverty in Ecuador" In *Land Concentration and Rural Poverty* 1976.

Luzuriaga, Carlos, and Clarence Zuvekas, Jr. *Distribución del Ingreso y Porbreza en las Areas Rurales del Ecuador, 1950-80* Quito: Banco Central, 1982.

Miño, Wilson. *La Comercialización Agropecuaria en el Ecuador* Quito: Facultad Latinoamerica de Ciencias Sociales, 1986.

Phillips, Lynne Patricia. "Gender, Class and Cultural Politics: A Case Study of Rural Provinces, Ecuador" Dissertation, University of Toronto, 1985.

Pomeroy, Cheryl Susan. "Environment, Economics, and Family Farm Systems: Farm Expansion and Adaptation on the Western Slopes of Andean Ecuador" Dissertation, University of Illinois, 1986.

Redclift, Michael R. "The Influence of the Agency for International Development on Ecuador's Agrarian Development Policy" *Journal of Latin American Studies*, 11: 1 (1979): 185.

Swett, Francisco. *Los Precios Agrícolas en el Ecuador: Politicas, Fundamentos y Resultados, 1970-83.*

Waters, William Fairbank. "Access to Land and the Form of Production in the Central Ecuadorian Highlands," Dissertation, Cornell University 1985.

Land Use

Collins, Jane L. "Small Holder Settlement of Tropical South America: The Social Causes of Ecological Destruction" *Human Organization*, 45 (Spring 1986): 1-10.

Pomeroy, Cheryl. "Agro-Pastoral Zones and Farm Production Organization in the North Andes" Paper presented at American Anthropological Association conference, 1984.

Pomeroy, Cheryl. "Deforestation and Desertification in the Ecuatorial Andes" Paper presented at American Anthropological Association conference, 1984.

Industry

Banco Central de Ecuador y El Consejo Nacional de Desarollo. *Programa de Encuestas de Coyuntura: Industria de la Construccion* no. 51 (March 1988a).

Banco Central de Ecuador y El Consejo Nacional de Desarollo. *Programa de Encuestas de Coyuntura: Industria Manufacturera* no. 51 (March 1988b.)

Berry, Albert. "Employment and the Role of Intermediate Cities in Ecuador During the Coming Years" ms., 1984.

Consejo Nacional de Desarrollo. *Estadísticas Industriales (1980 - 1986)* Vol II. Quito: January 1988.

Nell, Philippe Gerard. "Exports of Manufactures under Market Imperfections: Case Studies of Venezuela and Ecuador" Dissertation, University of Denver, 1985.

Paredews, Eduardo A. *La Oligarchía y la Crisis* Centro de Estudios y Difusión Social, 1985.

Zuvekas, Clarence, Jr., and Carlos C. Luzuriaga. "Ecuador: A
    Macroeconomic Assessment of Trends in 1982 and Projections for
    1983-87"   Quito: United States Agency for International
    Development (USAID), 1982.

Oil Industry

Matthews, Robert O. "Political Economy of Oil Exploration in the
    Amazon Basin" *Ecological Imperative* (Anthropology Resource
    Center), (1976).
"Quake Halts Ecuador Oil" *New York Times*, March 7, 1987.
United States. Federal Energy Administration Office of International
    Energy Affairs. *Relations of Oil Companies and Foreign
    Governments* 1976.

Politics

Centro de Estudios y Difusion Social. *Los Grupos Monopólicos* Quito:
    1986.
Conaghan, Catherine Mary. "Industrialists and the Reformist
    Interrregnum: Dominant Class Behavior and Ideology in Ecuador,
    1972-79" Dissertation, Yale University, 1983.
Ecuador. Tribunal Supremo Electoral *Principios Ideologicos y Planes de
    Gobierno* August 1981.
"Exclusivo: Borja y Sixto, Cara a Cara" *La Otra* (Quito) no. 42 (January
    14, 1988).
Hidrobo Estrada, Jorge Alfronso.   "Industrialists, State and
    Industrialization in Ecuador" Dissertation, University of Texas at
    Austin, 1986.
Hurtado, Osvaldo. *El Poder Político en el Ecuador* Quito: Letra Viva
    de Editorial Planeta, 1988.
"A Luchar por un Gobierno de Izquierda Revolucionaria" *En Marcha*,
    January 4, 1988.
Menendez-Carrion, Ampara. "The 1952-79 Presidential Elections and
    Guayaquil's Suburbio: A Micro-Analysis of Voting Behavior in a
    Context of Social Control"   Dissertation, John's Hopkins
    University, 1985.
Pyne, Peter. "The Politics of Instability in Ecuador" *Journal of Latin
    American Studies* 7: 1 (May 1975): 10.
Zevalos, Jose Vicente. "Oil, Power and Rural Change in Ecuador: 1972-
    79" Dissertation, University of Wisconsin at Madison, 1985.

Human Rights

Amnesty International. "Ecuador" *Amnesty International Report 1986*
Amnesty International. *External Bulletins.*
La Liebre Ilustrada, May 18, 1986.

Indigenous Peoples and Regional Issues

Tribes include Auchuar, Auca (Waorani), Canelos-Quichua, Cayapas,
  Coaiquer, Cofán, Colorados (Tsatchela), Huambisa, Jivaro/Shuar,
  Napo/Quijos ("Yumbo"), Orejones, Secoya (Siona-Secoya), and
  Zaparos.
Benitez, Lilyan, and Alicia Garces. *Culturas Ecuatorianas: Ayer y Hoy*
  Quito: Abya-yala, 1987.
Pontífica Universidad Católica del Ecuador, Departamento de
  Antropologia. *Antropología: Cuadernos de Investigación* (Quito),
  no. 4 (1987).

Pre-Inca

Murra, John. "The Historic Tribes of Ecuador" In *Handbook of South*
  American Indians vol. 2, p. 785.

Spanish Epoch

Murra, John. "The Tribes of Ecuador" In *South American Indian*
  Handbook vol. 2, pp. 813-820.

Riobamba (Provincia de Chimborazo)

Casagrande, Joseph B. "Religious Conversion and Social Change in an
  Indian Community of Highland Ecuador" *Amerikanitische Studen*
  (Estudios Americanistas), (1978).
Ecuadorian Institute of Agrarian Reform and Colonization and Cornell
  University. *Indians in Misery.* 1973.
Muratorio, Blanca. "Protestantism, Ethnicity, and Class in
  Chimborazo" In Norman E. Whitten, Jr., ed. *Cultural*
  Transformations and Ethnicity in Modern Ecuador. Chicago:
  University of Illinois Press, 1981.
Schroder, Barbara Clare. "Haciendas, Indians, and Economic Change in
  Chimborazo, Ecuador" Dissertation, Rutgers University, 1984.

Secoyas and Cofan

"Confeniae Denounces Agribusiness in Ecuador — An Open Letter" *Cultural Survival Quarterly* 10, no. 1, (1986): 33.

"Ecuador: Land Demarcation" *Cultural Survival Quarterly* (Fall 1981): 10.

Emerson, M. R. and R. H. Johnson. "A Secoya Tribe in the Oriente of Ecuador" *Man*, 61 (1961): 201.

Steward, John. "Tribes of Peruvian and Ecuadorian Montana" *South American Indian Handbook* vol. 3 p. 651.

Vickers, William T. "Ideation as Adaptation: Traditional Belief and Modern Intervention in Siona-Secoya Religion" In Norman E. Whitten, Jr., ed. *Cultural Transformations and Ethnicity in Modern Ecuador*. Chicago: University of Illinois Press, 1981.

Vickers, William T. "The Jesuits and the SIL: External Policies for Ecuador's Tucanoans through Three Centuries" In ed. Soren Hvalhot and Peter Aaby, *Is God an American?* Denmark: ISGIA, 1983.

Auca, Shuar, and Jivaro

Blomberg, Rolf. *The Naked Aucas: An Account of the Indians of Ecuador* 1957.

Cotlow, Lewis. *Amazon Head Hunters* Signet, 1953.

Descola, Philippe. "From Scattered to Nucleated Settlement: A Process of Socioeconomic Change Among the Achuar" In Norman E. Whitten, Jr., ed. *Cultural Transformations and Ethnicity in Modern Ecuador*. Chicago: University of Illinois Press, 1981.

Harner, Michael J. *The Jivaro: Sacred People of the Waterfalls* Anchor Books, 1973.

"El Hombre de 'El Dorado,'" *El Comercio*, Sunday August 22, 1986.

Salazar, Ernesto. "The Federacion Shuar and the Colonization Frontier" In Norman E. Whitten, Jr., ed. *Cultural Transformations and Ethnicity in Modern Ecuador*. Chicago: University of Illinois Press, 1981.

"The Shuar," *Cultural Survival* (Summer 1980): p. 11.

Steward, John. "Tribes of Peruvian and Ecuadorian Montana" *South American Indian Handbook*, vol. 3 1949, p. 617.

Taylor, Anne-Christine. "God-Wealth: The Achuar and the Missions" In Norman E. Whitten, Jr., ed. *Cultural Transformations and Ethnicity in Modern Ecuador*. Chicago: University of Illinois Press, 1981.

Yost, James A. "Twenty Years of Contact: The Mechanisms of Change in Wao (Auca) Culture" In Norman E. Whitten, Jr., ed. *Cultural Transformations and Ethnicity in Modern Ecuador*. Chicago: University of Illinois Press, 1981.

Amazon Region (General)

Chiriboga, Manuel. "El Analisis de las Formas Tradicionales en Ecuador" *Anuario Indigenista*, December 1983, pp. 83-99.

Costales S., Alfredo. "Misiones Catolicas y Protestantes Entre los Aborigenes del Oriente Ecuatoriano" *America Indígena*, 21 (1961): 269.

Ecuador. El Consejo Supremo de Gobierno. *Ley de Colonización de la Region Amazonica.*

Metraux, Alfred. "Jesuit Missions" In Julian H. Steward, ed., *Handbook of South American Indians* vol. 5. Washington, D. C.: U.S. Government Printing Office, 1949, p. 646.

Press, Robert M. "Amazon Indians Mobilize to Defend Land" *Christian Science Monitor* January 2, 1987, p. 5.

Robinson, Scott S. "Fulfilling the Mission: North American Evangelicals in Ecuador" In Soren Hvalhof and Peter Aaby, eds., *Is God an American?* Denmark: ISGIA, 1983.

Swanson, Jeffrey Wallace. "The Moral Career of the Missionary" Dissertation, Yale University, 1985.

Vickers, William T. "Indian Policy in Amazonian Ecuador" In Marianne Schmink and Charles H. Wood, eds., *Frontier Expansion in Amazonia* University of Florida Press, 1984.

Whitten, Norman E., Jr. *Amazonian Ecuador: An Ethnic Interface in Ecological, Social, and Ideological Perspectives, International Work Group for Indigenous Affairs* Document 34 Copenhagen, Denmark: 1978.

Whitten, Norman E., Jr. "Etnocidio y Etnogenesis Indigena" *America Indigena* 39, no. 3 (July 1979) p. 540.

Whitten, Norman E., Jr. "Amazonia Today at the Base of the Andes: An Ethnic Interface in Ecological, Social and Ideological Perspectives," in ed. Whitten, *Cultural Transformations and Ethnicity in Modern Ecuador*, University of Illinois Press, Chicago, 1981.

Inca, Quechua, and Sierra

Incas
Kubler, George. "The Quechua in the Colonial World" In *South American Indian Handbook*, Vol. 2, p. 331.
Rowe, John. "Inca Culture" *South American Indian Handbook*, Vol. 2, p. 210.
Von Hagen, Victor. *Realm of the Incas* New York: Mentor Books, 1957.

Modern:
Alberti Amalia Margherita. "Gender, Ethnicity, and Resource Control in the Andean Highlands of Ecuador" Disseration, Stanford University, 1986.
Bromley, Ray. "Market Center and Market Place in Highland Ecuador: A Study of Organization, Regulation, and Ethnic Discrimination" In Norman E. Whitten, Jr., ed. *Cultural Transformations and Ethnicity in Modern Ecuador*. Chicago: University of Illinois Press, 1981.
Harris, Marvin. *Culture, Man and Nature.*
Mishkin, Bernard. "Contemporary Quechua" In *South American Indian Handbook*, vol. 2, p. 445.
Stutzman, Ronald. "An All Inclusive Ideology of Exclusion" In Norman E. Whitten, Jr., ed. *Cultural Transformations and Ethnicity in Modern Ecuador*. Chicago: University of Illinois Press, 1981.
Weiss, Wendy Arlene. "Es El Que Manda: Sexual Inequality and its Relation to Economic Development in the Ecuadorian Sierra" Dissertation, Bryn Mawr, 1985.

Cuenca, Loja, and Saraguro
Belote , Jim and Linda Belote. "The Limitation of Obligation in Saraguro Kinship," *Andean Kinship and Marriage* Ralph Bolton and Enrique Mayer, eds., American Anthropological Association no. 7 1977.
Belote, Jim. "Changing Adaptive Strategies Among the Saragurans of Southern Ecuador" Dissertation, 1987.
Belote, Linda Smith, and Jim Belote. "Development in Spite of Itself: The Saraguro Case" In Norman E. Whitten, Jr., ed. *Cultural Transformations and Ethnicity in Modern Ecuador*. Chicago: University of Illinois Press, 1981.
Ekstrom, J. Peter. In Norman E. Whitten, Jr., ed. *Cultural Transformations and Ethnicity in Modern Ecuador*. Chicago: University of Illinois Press, 1981.

Finerman, Ruthbeth Dana. "Health Care Decisions in an Andean Indian Community: Getting the Best of Both Worlds" Dissertation, University of California at Los Angeles, 1985.

Nayon
Beals, Ralph L. "Social Change in an Ecuadorean Village" In Sol Tax, ed., *Acculturation in the Americas* Chicago: University of Chicago Press, 1952.

Otavalo
Buitrón, Aníbal, and John Collier, Jr. *El Valle del Amanecer* Otavalo: Instituto Otavaleño de Antropología, 1971.
Casagrande, Joseph B. "Strategies for Survival: The Indians of Highland Ecuador" In Norman E. Whitten, Jr., ed. *Cultural Transformations and Ethnicity in Modern Ecuador*. Chicago: University of Illinois Press, 1981.
Meier, Peter C. "Los Artesanos Textiles de la Región de Otavalo" *Sarance*, no. 10 (July 1985): 127-47.
Salomon, Frank. "Weavers of Otavalo" In Norman E. Whitten, Jr., ed. *Cultural Transformations and Ethnicity in Modern Ecuador*. Chicago: University of Illinois Press, 1981.
Villavicencio Rivadeneira, Gladys. *Relaciones Interétnicas en Otavalo: Una Nacionalidad India en Formación* Mexico: Instituto Indigenista Interamericano: 1973.
Walter, Lynn. "Otavaleno Development, Ethnicity, and National Integration, *America Indigena* 61, no. 2 (April-June 1981) 319.

Colta
Muratorio, Blanco. "Protestantism and Capitalism Revisited in the Rural Highlands of Ecuador" *Journal of Peasant Studies* 8, no. 1 (1980): 37.

Coaiquer
Hernandez de Alba, Gregorio. "Highland Tribes," *South American Indian Handbook* vol. 2, p. 927.

Napo, Runa, Quijo, and Orejones

Irvine, Nickie, and Ellen Speiser. "New Road Brings Multi-Nationals to Runa Land" *South and Central American Indian Information Center* vol. 3, no. 1, (Fall 1986): 12.
Macdonald, Theodore Jr. "Indigenous Response to an Expanding Frontier: Junge Quichua Economic Conversion to Cattle Ranching"

In Norman E. Whitten, Jr., ed. *Cultural Transformations and Ethnicity in Modern Ecuador*. Chicago: University of Illinois Press, 1981.

Steward, John. "Tribes of Peruvian and Ecuadorian Montana" In *South American Indian Handbook* vol. 3, p. 652.

Steward, John. "Western Tucanoan Tribes" *South American Indian Handbook*, vol. 3 1949, p. 737.

Cayapa and Colorado

Murra, John. "The Cayapa and Colorado" In *South American Indian Handbook*, vol. 4, p. 277.

Zaporan

Steward, John. "Tribes of the Peruvian and Ecuadorian Montana" In *South American Indian Handbook* vol. 3, pp. 521, 637-651, 629-31.

San Lorenzo and Morenos

Schubert, Grace. "To Be Black is Offensive: Racist Attitudes in San Lorenzo" In Norman E. Whitten, Jr., ed. *Cultural Transformations and Ethnicity in Modern Ecuador*. Chicago: University of Illinois Press, 1981.

Whitten, Norman E., Jr. *Class, Kinship, and Power in an Ecuadorian Town* Stanford, CA: Stanford University Press, 1965.

Urban Areas — Marginals, Migration, and Family

Middleton, Dwight R. "Ecuadorian Transformations: An Urban View" In Norman E. Whitten, Jr., ed. *Cultural Transformations and Ethnicity in Modern Ecuador*. Chicago: University of Illinois Press, 1981.

Manta

Brooks, Rhoda, and Earle Brooks. *The Barrios of Manta* New York: Signet Books, 1965.

Middleton, Dwight R. "Migration and Urbanization in Ecuador" *Urban Anthropology*, 8, nos. 3-4, (1979).

Naranjo, Marcelo F. "Political Dependency, Ethnicity, and Cultural Transformations in Manta" In Norman E. Whitten, Jr., ed. *Cultural Transformations and Ethnicity in Modern Ecuador*. Chicago: University of Illinois Press, 1981.

Loja and El Oro

Brownrigg, Leslie A. "Economic and Ecological Strategies of Lojano Migrants to El Oro" In Norman E. Whitten, Jr., ed. *Cultural Transformations and Ethnicity in Modern Ecuador.* Chicago: University of Illinois Press, 1981.

Guayaquil

Moser, Caroline O. N. "Squatter Housing Strategies in Guayaquil" In Alan Gilbert and J. E. Hardor, and R. Ramirez, eds., *Urbanization in Contemporary Latin America* New York: John Wiley and Sons, 1982.

Scrimshaw, Susan C.M. "Adaptation and Family Size from Rural Ecuador to Guayaquil" In Norman E. Whitten, Jr., ed. *Cultural Transformations and Ethnicity in Modern Ecuador.* Chicago: University of Illinois Press, 1981.

Quito

Farrell, Gilda. *Los Trabajadores Autonomos de Quito* Quito: IIE-PUCE, June 1983.

Salomon, Frank. "Killing the Yumbo" In Norman E. Whitten, Jr., ed. *Cultural Transformations and Ethnicity in Modern Ecuador.* Chicago: University of Illinois Press, 1981.

Witcher, Bethann Sandlin. "Internal Migration and the Nutritional Status of School-Aged Children in Cotocollao Alto, Quito, Ecuador" Dissertation, Michigan State University, 1985.

FICTION

Murra, John V. "Jose Maria Arguedas — Introduction to a Quechua Poet," *Cultural Survival Quarterly*, 10, no. 3 : 8-10.

"La Poesia Feminina Peruana" *Cambio*, January 1986, p. 12.

Rodriguez, Marco Antonio. *Historia de un Intruso* Quito: Oswaldo Guayasamin Press.

Rodriguez, Marco Antonio. *Plegaría al Tío Sam* Quito: Editorial Rafael Perugachi Ecuador, 1982.

OTHER ECUADORIAN SOURCES

Newspapers

El Comercio
Hoy
El Mercurio
El Universo

Magazines

Comentarios de Pancho Jaime
La Otra
Vistazo

Organizations and Individuals (Selected)

Ecuadorian Organizations and Their Representatives

Centro Andino de Estudios Económicos, Sociales y Tecnológicos —
 especially the rector, Dr. Luis Lopez Silva.
Manuel Chiriboga, Centro Andino de Acción Popular.
Confederación de Nacionales Indígenas del Ecuador (CONIAE).
Fundación Nuestros Jovenes — Silvia B. DeLaufer.
Hernan Mendez, Mascarilla Cooperativa, Valle de Chota.
Pedro F. Porras Garcés, Director, Centro de Investigaciones
 Archeológicas, Universidad Católica.
Marco Antonio Rodriguez, Director, Casa de Cultura.
Carlos Tapuy, Director FOCIN, Tena.

Ecuadorian Government and Civic Organizations

Centro de Reconversión Economica del Azuay, Cañar y Morena
 Santiago, Macas, and especially Doctor Mancheno.
Centro San Jose, Comunidad Shuar.
Colegio Mixto de Misahuallí.
Corte Suprema, Esmeraldas: Ministros.
Oswaldo Flores, Alcalde, Coca.
Diputado Gonzalez, Lago Agrio.
Leonardo Mackliff, Comisión de Energía Atómica.

Ministerio de Agricultura: Victoria de Rodriguez, Subsecretaria de la
    Amazona and Inginiero Garcez.
Municipalidad, Prefectora y Gobernanción de Macas.
Professor Enrique Suarez Pimentel, Oficina del Consejo Provincial,
    Esmeraldas.
Gobernador Tamariz, Pastaza.
Tribunal de Menores — Juan Mora Moscoso, Presidente.
Zapallo Grande, inhabitants of.

Religious Organizations and Missions

Los Carmelitos.
Combañanos.
Misión Evangelica, Macas — especially Mike.
HCJB.
Lloyd Rogers, Mission Aviation Fellowship
Salesianos.
Visión Mundial.

Ecuadorian Citizens Providing Specialized Information

Samuel Padilla Caento, Huarani Bar Owner, Quito.
Economista Castro, Esmeraldas.
Dr. Wilson Cellerí, Esmeraldas.
Jose Parker Estrauss, Coca.
Elsie Monge.
Gilbert Nobilio, Chemist, Tena.
Hilda Ruiz.
Rafael Vega, Parque Industrial, Cuenca.
"William" — Merchant, Ipiales Market, Quito.

U.S. Government Organizations and Employees

U.S. Agency for International Development: Patricio Maldonado,
    Program Officer; David Alberion, Agriculture; Kate Jones Patron,
    Health.
U.S. Department of Commerce: Eric Weaver, Peter Aloise.
U.S. Embassy: Linda Pfeifle, Political Section; Gordon Jones, Economic
    Section; David Langford, Administration.
U.S. Peace Corps Volunteers at their sites: Kevin Barnard; Sue Diaz;
    John MacKinney; Clarice Olson; María Ornes; Tony Pinder; Brian
    Riley; Julie Schwantes; Andy Smith; Joe Vieira; Joseph and
    Sandra Winkelmaier.

Other Embassies

Israeli Embassy: Meir Mishan
Посолство Советского Союза: Николай В. Андрианов.

International Businesses

Standard Fruit Company, Guayaquil.
Texaco, Lago Agrio y Quito.

U.S. Citizens in Ecuador Providing Specific Information

Richard Boroto, Director, Instituto Abraham Lincoln, Cuenca.
Carole Kohl and family, Tena.
Rupert Smith, U.S. citizen imprisoned in Guayaquil.
Norman Whitten, Anthropologist.
Steve Yanger, Professor of Economics, Williams College—Fulbright
    Scholar.

General Index

Advertising, 246-48; and economic efficiency, 152-53; and health, 143-44, 248. *See also* Corporations; Media; Symbols
Agrarian reform. *See* Land use
Agriculture, 179-81, 182; agro-industry, 73
Argentina: Austral plan, 169, 171, 176
Armed Forces. *See* Military

Banking Industries: credit policy, 157, 168, 182, 240. *See also* Investment; World Bank
Birth Control. *See* Women: family planning
Bolivia: New Economic Policy, 169, 171, 176
Brain Drain, 73, 135, 234. *See also* Communities; Human resources
Brazil, 240; Cruzado Plan, 169, 171, 176
Budget, 151-57; and inflation, 154, 168-70. *See also* Deficit reduction; National accounts

Catholic Church, 220-21. *See also* Religion
Colombia, 216-17
Colonialism, legacy of, centralization, 97, 107, 117, 119-20, 156, 179, 207-9,

237-40, 246-7. *See also* Catholic Church; Culture; Decentralization; Dependency; Military
Community Development, 73-77, 89-98, 115-6, 133, 181, 226, 237, 239; and investment, 153; and military, 212. *See also* Decentralization
Competitive Markets, 152, 181, 211. *See also* Corruption; Economic Competition; Ownership
Consumption, 156-57; *See also* Culture; Dependency; Savings
Consumption Tax, 157
Corporations: accountability of, 91, 95-96, 152-53, 207-9; and health, 144; and labor, 135. *See also* Industry; Multinationals
Corruption, 89-91, 152-53, 168-69, 207; and Swiss banks, 157. *See also* Government Reform; Politics
Credit Policy. *See* Banking industries.
Crime, 76. *See also* Corruption; Unemployment
Cultural Diversity, 115-16. *See also* Indigenous Peoples; Social Indicators
Culture, 237-240, 246-49; and development, 115-16, 143;

Special Index (Ecuador)

About the Authors

DAVID H. LEMPERT is an anthropologist, attorney, and consultant with degrees from the University of California, Berkeley, Stanford, and Yale. He has worked as a contractor for the United States Agency for International Development in the Philippines, as a consultant on projects for legal and political reforms in Russia and Ukraine, for the political section of the U.S. Embassy in Costa Rica, for the economic section of the Organization of American States in Washington, D.C., and on business education reform in Vietnam. He is presently Adjunct Associate Professor at George Washington University.

KIM McCARTY has worked as coordinator for the Neighborhood Revitalization Program in Minneapolis, overseeing experimental programs for revitalizing the economic and social health of the inner city.

CRAIG MITCHELL is presently in a Ph.D. program at the University of California, Los Angeles, as the Alfred P. Sloan Foundation Doctoral Dissertation Fellow, in international economics.

ISBN 0-275-95068-9

90000>

EAN

9 780275 950682

HARDCOVER BAR CODE